Foreign-owned Firms

Foreign-owned Firms

Are They Different?

Edited by

Rolf Jungnickel

First published 2002 by
PALGRAVE MACMILLAN
Houndmills, Basingstoke, Hampshire RG21 6XS and
175 Fifth Avenue, New York, N. Y. 10010
Companies and representatives throughout the world.

PALGRAVE MACMILLAN is the new global academic imprint of
the Palgrave Macmillan division of St. Martin's Press, LLC and of
Palgrave Macmillan Ltd. Macmillan® is a registered trademark in
the United States, United Kingdom and other countries. Palgrave is
a registered trademark in the European Union and other countries.

ISBN 0–333–96626–0

This book is printed on paper suitable for recycling and made
from fully managed and sustained forest sources.

A catalogue record for this book is available from the British Library.

Library of Congress Cataloging-in-Publication Data
Foreign-owned firms: are they different?/edited by Rolf
Jungnickel.
        p. cm.
    'Papers presented at a HWWA workshop on "Foreign-owned
firms—are they different?" in late 2000'—Foreword.
    Includes bibliographical references and index.
    ISBN 0–333–96626–0
    1. International business enterprises–Congresses.
2. Corporations, Foreign–Congresses. 3. Investment, Foreign–
Congresses. 4. Investment, Foreign, and employment–Congresses.
5. International business enterprises–Europe–Congresses.
6. Corporations, Foreign–Europe–Congresses. 7. Investments,
Foreign–Europe–Congresses. 8. Investments, Foreign, and
employment–Europe–Congresses. I. Jungnickel, Rolf.
HD2755.5 .F66 2002
338.8′8–dc21   2002025338

10 9 8 7 6 5 4 3 2 1
11 10 09 08 07 06 05 04 03 02

Printed and bound in Great Britain by
Antony Rowe Ltd, Chippenham and Eastbourne

Contents

Foreword

This volume is part of the activities in the Hamburg Institute of International Economics (HWWA) research programme, International Mobility of Firms and Labour, which is one of the institute's six research programmes. It contains (most of) the papers presented at an HWWA workshop on 'Foreign-owned firms – are they different?' in late 2000. The workshop was not only a self-contained product: it also served as an input to an HWWA research project on the role of foreign-owned firms in the labour market undertaken on behalf of the Federal Ministry of Economics and Technology. It was partly funded by the HWWA guest researcher programme. I am grateful to both sources of financial support.

During the organization of the workshop and editing of the contributions I have become indebted to a number of people both from inside and outside HWWA. My colleagues in the research programme, Christine Borrmann and Dietmar Keller, participated in the organization of the workshop and helped to make it a success. Katri Aarnio, Mali Gondesen and Sabina Ramonat were engaged with the often troublesome job of making a coherent book out of the individual studies. The authors are, however, responsible for any remaining deficiencies and errors.

ROLF JUNGNICKEL

Notes on the Contributors

Christian Bellak is Assistant Professor at the Department of Economics, University of Economics, Vienna, Austria. His main research interests are industrial policy, small countries, foreign direct investment and multinational enterprises.

Lutz Bellmann is head of the section 'Research on Company Labour Demand and Innovation' at the Institute for Employment Research (IAB), Nuremberg. His main research interests are in the analysis of labour market effect of operational and technological developments, innovation research, analysis of establishments and company determinants of employment. He is in charge of the IAB establishment panel.

Henrik Braconier is head of the research division of the National Institute of Economic Research in Stockholm. He has done research on economic growth and foreign direct investment.

Karolina Ekholm is associate professor at the Stockholm School of Economics, specializing in international trade and investment.

(Both Henrik Braconier and Karolina Ekholm have been engaged in doing empirical research on multinational firms while holding positions at the Research Institute of Industrial Economics (IUI) in Stockholm.)

Florence Hubert is a member of staff at the Bank of England. She was formerly a Research Officer at the National Institute of Economic and Social Research (NIESR) where her research interests included the impact of foreign direct investment, the location of multinational production and European economic integration.

Rolf Jungnickel is head of the research program 'International Mobility of Firms and Labour' at the Hamburg Institute of International Economics (HWWA). Main research interests: foreign direct investment and multinational enterprises, industrial policy, European integration.

Rémi Lallement is a chargé de mission at the department for technological and industrial development of the Commissariat général du Plan (CGP) in Paris. He has published on foreign direct investment, competitiveness, the German economy and Franco-German relations.

Nigel Pain is a Senior Research Fellow at the National Institute of Economic and Social Research (NIESR). Prior to joining NIESR he worked at HM Treasury. He has published widely on the determinants of location choice by multinational corporations, and on their impact on the growth prospects and industrial structure of host and home economies.

Michael Pfaffermayr is Professor of Economics at the University of Innsbruck. His main research interests are foreign trade and multinational corporations, industrial economics and panel econometrics. He has published widely on these issues.

List of Abbreviations

CEPII	Centre d'Etudes Prospectives et d'Information
CES	Constant elasticity of substitution
CGP	Commissariat Général du Plan
DOF	domestically-owned firms
DTI	Department of Trade and Industry
EEA	European Economic Area
FDI	foreign direct investment
FO	foreign ownership
FOF	foreign-owned firms
FSAs	firm-specific assets
GDP	gross domestic product
HP	Hewlett-Packard
HPLG	Hewlett-Packard Labs Grenoble
HWWA	Hamburg Institute of International Economics
IAB	Institute for Employment Research (Nuremberg)
ICT	information and communication technology
IMF	International Monetary Fund
INSEE	Statistical Office (France)
IUI	Research Institute of Industrial Economics (Stockholm)
LAD	Least absolute deviation
M&A	mergers and acquisitions
MNE	multinational enterprise
NBER	National Bureau of Economic Research
NIESR	National Institute of Economic and Social Research
NIS	national innovation system
OLS	ordinary least squares
OMC	Organisation Mondiale du Commerce
OST	Observatoire des Sciences et Techniques
P	Probability
PC	personal computer
R&D	research and development
RCA	revealed comparative advantage
SESSI	Statistical Department, Ministry of Industry (France)
SME	small and medium-sized enterprise
TFP	total factor productivity

UBO   ultimate beneficial owner
UNCTAD   United Nations Conference on Trade and Development
USPTO   United States Patent and Trademark Office

1
Introduction

Rolf Jungnickel

There are two reasons for this volume and for the workshop it is based upon: (1) the rapid increase in the globalization of business has led to a large proportion of economies being controlled from abroad, and (2) this process is not evenly spread over all countries. Both aspects are of interest for economic policy in (potential) host countries since the appearance of foreign investors and the change of ownership of productive assets may have implications for income and employment in the economies concerned. Implications could result from various mechanisms, such as the direct transfer of income and jobs across borders and the rather indirect effects of knowledge transfer and strategic changes imposed on the foreign affiliates. Foreign-owned firms (FOFs) could behave differently, undertake activities that would not have been undertaken by indigenous firms or phase out the activities of formerly indigenous firms. It has been shown that the most important implications of internationalization can be assumed to come about via transfer of ownership rather than via the transfer of capital (Lipsey, 2000). Therefore, the question of whether, and in what respect, FOFs are different from indigenous firms deserves the attention of economic research. Its relevance depends, among other factors, on the volume of inward foreign direct investment (FDI).

Globalization of firms and of economies has progressed rapidly in terms of sales, production, sourcing, finance and investment in the past decade. This process is amply documented albeit, often on an uncertain database.[1] Despite such uncertainties, it is obvious that FDI has been the driving force behind the globalization process (United Nations Conference on Trade and Development, or UNCTAD, 2000). Border-crossing mergers and acquisitions (M&A) reached all-time highs in the late 1990s. An ever increasing number of firms changed ownership and became foreign-owned. The worldwide FDI stock was estimated at roughly US$6,300 billion at the end of 2000, more than three times the value as at the end of 1990 (UNCTAD, 2001). To some extent, this increase was due to a rise in the price of firm acquisitions mirrored by a development of stock indices parallel to the M&A values (Wortmann, 2000). In addition to price increases, however, the internationalization of production had a real basis. Both sales and gross product of foreign affiliates, which are not influenced by stock prices, still increased over 50 per cent faster than the world's gross domestic product (GDP) and also faster than foreign trade. Sales of foreign affiliates were estimated at more than US$15,000 billion in 2000, more than twice the value of foreign trade in goods and services. Internationalization of production has outpaced foreign trade. The number of people employed at foreign affiliates has doubled during the 1990s. It is now estimated at almost 46 million worldwide.

Western Europe came into the spotlight for multinational investors in the late 1980s when the companies (both European and from overseas) prepared for the internal market. Its share in worldwide inward FDI jumped from about 30 per cent in the early 1980s to over 40 per cent towards the end of the decade, and then stayed at that level. UNCTAD (2001) estimates are 40 per cent for the year 2000. The Western European FDI position is, however, not lopsided. Outward FDI by Western European firms increased even more strongly and it clearly surpasses the inward value. Over half of the worldwide FDI stock is of Western European origin and over half of that went to locations in other Western European countries. Intra-EU direct investments (which, in the case of M&A instead of greenfield ventures, do not necessarily go along with real investment) gained momentum later than intra-EU trade, but it can be considered a main feature of European integration now.

The surge of both inward and outward FDI in Western Europe was not evenly spread among the countries. German locations apparently did not fully participate. Even in the latest upwards-revised data, Germany's share in FDI (between 15 and 18 per cent) is lower than one could have expected given the size and purchasing power of the domestic market, its central location in Europe and the ample financial assistance available, particularly in Eastern Germany. These factors should 'normally' have led to an above-average volume of inward FDI in Germany. UNCTAD (2001) puts the 1999 inward FDI to GDP ratio at 13.7 per cent, about half the ratio for the UK and slightly less than in France. Therefore the question for Germany, as well as for Italy in the context of inward FDI, is: does the number of FOFs, which is lower than expected, entail losses of jobs and income for the country or does foreign ownership not matter? In Reich's (1990 and 1991) terminology the question would be: is there a difference between 'us' and 'them'?

Unequal participation in the globalization process and the significance of FOFs can be made more visible by using employment data which are not subject to valuation problems which can be easily compared with national employment data. Employment shares of FOFs are shown in Table 1.1 for the manufacturing sector in a number of countries.[2] Obviously, Germany was not lagging behind the other countries in 1985. However, in contrast to the development in most other Western European countries (Italy is an exception), the share of FOFs did not increase over the following 13 years, but rather stagnated. Thus far, the employment data confirm the picture of the inward FDI data.

Two obvious questions arise from the differing degree of participation in the globalization process: do countries with a low level of inward FDI sustain losses in income and employment, and do countries which are in the focus of foreign investors profit in terms of income and jobs?

Table 1.1 Share of foreign-owned firms in the manufacturing sector of selected countries[a]

Host country	1985		1990		1998	
	Sales	No. employed	Sales	No. employed	Sales	No. employed
Germany	26	16	26	17	25	16
France	27	21	28	24	36[b]	30[b]
UK[b]	19	15	25	16	33	19[c]
Italy[b]	17	14	14	10	12[c]	9[c]
Belgium					35[d]	27[d]
The Netherlands	39	15	33	19	47[e]	19[e]
USA		7	15	11	15	14
Japan[b]	4.6	1.6	2.4	1.1	1.2[c]	0.8[c]

[a] Sales and employment in per cent of the respective values for total manufacturing
[b] Majority holdings only
[c] 1996
[d] 1994
[e] 1997
Sources: OECD (1999); UNCTAD (1999); SESSI (1998); Lallement (Chapter 5 of this volume); Zhang and van den Bulcke (2000); Deutsche Bundesbank; Statistisches Bundesamt; author's calculation.

If that were the case, the FOFs would be expected to exhibit structural or performance differences compared with indigenous firms. The question of whether foreign ownership matters has often been discussed (Woodward and Nigh, 1999).

Prevailing FDI theories seem to give a straightforward answer. Those theories rest, among others, upon the existence of company-specific competitive advantages. FDI is considered a way to make use of these advantages on a broader scale.[3] This could imply a flow of resources to the foreign affiliates, be it real capital, human capital or technology. As a result, it can be assumed that FOFs have a strong competitive position and a superior performance compared with indigenous firms. According to this view, the answer to the question in the title of this volume, 'Foreign-owned firms – are they different?' is 'Yes'. There exists a difference between indigenous and foreign-owned firms or, in Reich´s (1990 and 1991) terminology, between 'us' and 'them'. Foreign ownership does matter. It could increase the competitiveness of a host economy given that FOFs do not simply displace domestic resources or have detrimental implications for competition.

In reality, however, the consequences of FOFs are less clear cut. Recent trends in the internationalization strategies could lead to a different assessment. If there is a change from traditional market orientation towards asset-seeking strategies, as Dunning (1998) argues, there could emerge a reverse flow of resources from the affiliates to the foreign parent company. The relevance of such change was shown in several empirical investigations (Barrell and Pain, 1999; Borrmann *et al.*, 2001). A similar change in the assessment of FDI could be brought about by the dominance of M&A instead of greenfield ventures, especially if foreign investors follow 'picking the winner' strategies. In that case, we would observe a difference between FOFs and domestically owned firms (DOFs), but this difference could not be attributed to foreign ownership. If an acquisition is not undertaken for efficiency reasons but as an element of 'empire building' (Bartelsman and Doms, 2000, p. 587), or if it does not meet the efficiency goals (which can be supposed in at least half of the cases), performance differences in favour of FOFs cannot be expected.

More generally, one can argue that there is reason to assume that foreign affiliates are more competitive than exclusively domestic firms but not more competitive than parent companies since companies investing abroad are among the most competitive in their respective sector and since ownership advantage is supposed to be the basis of FDI. Domestic multinationals would have to be considered at least as competitive. The competitive advantage of FOFs, therefore, should exist only over non-multinational firms in the host countries. Such superior performance of the FOFs would have to be considered a result of the integration into an international business network and not as one of foreign ownership *per se*. The more multinationalized a host country's firms are, the less there should be a difference in the performance and structure of FOFs and DOFs. This argument could be of particular relevance in the case of Western Europe since outward FDI from this region is even larger than inward FDI. The leading hosts of FOFs are at the same time among the leading outward investors, with the UK, France and Germany in the top positions in absolute terms, and Belgium and the Netherlands ranking highest when if FDI is based on GDP (UNCTAD, 2000 and 2001).

The answer to our question regarding differences between FOFs and DOFs and the effects of foreign ownership is, therefore, less straightforward than might have been assumed before. Essentially it is an empirical question about to what extent there are differences between these groups of firms. There will be different answers in different countries and in different conditions, and therefore, it seems to be meaningful to discuss the issue at hand in an international comparison, although our point of departure was the falling behind of Germany. The following chapters focus on the position of FOFs in some Western European countries which can be assumed to compete for internationally mobile investments. With France, Germany and Austria, three countries are considered which are only rarely included in empirical analyses of inward FDI.

The authors approach the general topic from different perspectives. They demonstrate the usefulness of micro data and put a focus on the thesis that foreign ownership matters, but the real difference is between multinationals and nationally oriented firms. Sources of competitive advantages and the various modes by which FOFs exert an influence on a host economy are discussed in detail.

In the second chapter, Pfaffermayr and Bellak set a conceptual framework for the analysis of FOFs and present empirical evidence for Austria. They are concerned with performance differences between FOFs and DOFs in several respects: financial performance; input of skilled labour; growth and productivity gaps; post-M&A performance. On the basis of the currently dominant theory, the authors seek to provide arguments for the superior position of FOFs over DOFs. A detailed literature survey largely supports this view. Theoretical assumptions and empirical evidence from former studies are then confronted with evidence available from a WIFO investment survey of manufacturing firms in Austria. In line with earlier findings the results suggest that the positive effects of participating in a foreign multinational´s network can mainly be found in a productivity and a profitability advantage. A further distinction between purely national firms and multinational enterprises (MNEs) reveals that both these gaps derive from gains resulting from MNE networks rather than from foreign ownership *per se*. Regardless of ownership, MNEs (parent companies and foreign subsidiaries) are more similar than MNEs and purely national firms. There is no evidence of an additional performance bonus resulting from the closer cultural proximity of German firms.

In a chapter about FOFs in Germany (Chapter 3), Bellmann and Jungnickel investigate the thesis that FOFs are more productive than indigenous firms and that the advantage is less pronounced or even non-existent in comparison to German internationally-oriented firms (as defined by their export quota). This issue is of relevance for the assessment of a German backlog of inward FDI versus Western European countries. The sectoral analysis lends support to the hypothesis. On the basis of detailed establishment data taken from a representative panel, it can be shown that the productivity advantage is brought about not only by a concentration of foreign-owned firms in high productivity sectors but also by a larger input of human capital and its integration into the international (and intra-group) division of labour. Foreign ownership *per se* seems to exert a positive influence, too. There is even an advantage over German multinationals. The larger size of FOFs does not plays a role. In line with prior expectations, the FOFs´ advantage is bigger in East Germany than in the West.

Braconier and Ekholm's contribution in Chapter 4 serves as a complement to the other chapters since it does not deal with foreign affiliates from a host country perspective. Instead it compares the characteristics of (Swedish) affiliates in different countries and identifies the role of intra-European labour cost differentials as a determinant of location decisions. The chapter uses a unique data set on the foreign activities by Swedish manufacturing firms in order to examine the performance of German affiliates, compared with affiliates in other high- and low-income regions. It is found that German affiliates, on average, have higher labour productivity, research and development (R&D) expenditure per employee and skill-intensity. This could mean that the (relatively) low FDI volume in Germany is the price paid for the high quality of such an investment. There is also evidence suggesting that German affiliates are more oriented towards selling on the local market than affiliates in other European countries. In the second part of Chapter 4, the effect of labour costs in the Swedish multinationals' decision to locate in Germany is analysed. The authors find that the location decision is sensitive to the level of wage costs in Germany and in other potential locations in high-income Europe *in which the firm does not already have affiliates*. Finally, some evidence is produced of substitutability between labour employed in German affiliates and labour employed in other high-income locations in Europe.

In Chapter 5, Pain and Hubert go beyond the characterisation of FOFs in a particular country. They assess their impact on the UK economy, which has been relatively successful in attracting inward investment over the past 40 years. FDI in knowledge-intensive sectors has grown more rapidly than in other activities. The authors find that FOFs have a clear advantage over indigenous firms in productivity and capital expenditure, and that they employ a higher proportion of skilled labour. Even after accounting for industrial structure and scale, there remains an ownership-specific advantage. Pain and Hubert then, on the basis of a CES (constant elasticity of substitution) production function, seek to assess intra-industry and inter-industry spillovers of the FOFs´ superior technology. They find that FOFs have helped to raise the level of national income and have had beneficial supply-side effects on the performance of UK-owned companies. Approximately two-thirds of the aggregate rise in the share of skilled labour in total employment are 'accounted' for by FOFs. However, the externalities available from inward investment do not always appear to have been distributed equally amongst industries or regions, and there appears to be little evidence that the average productivity gap between foreign and UK firms has been closed over time. The authors find more significant inter-industry spillovers than were found in former studies. This has implications for industrial policy which should put more emphasis on facilitating spillovers to other parts of the economy.

The final contribution, Chapter 6, written by Lallement, deals with FOFs in France, and serves as an example of a country that has been quite successful in attracting FDI during the past two decades. The author gives an overview of FOFs in France and their implications for foreign trade and the innovative capacity. In these two fields, FOFs differ substantially from French-owned firms. Survey data show that they are more active in the export and especially in the import business than domestic-owned firms, even if it is controlled for industry and firm size. They tend to be highly involved in intra-firm trade. While the manufacturing affiliates show an export surplus, the main function of wholesale affiliates consists of intra-firm imports of final products destined to be sold in France as they are. These results are consistent with studies based on FDI data showing that the global contribution to the trade balance is 'negative' on the part of inward FDI, while it is 'positive' on the part of outward FDI. This suggests that an excess of outward FDI over inward FDI indicates the strong competitiveness of the respective industry, if not of the whole economy. A breakdown of inward FDI by sectors and by home countries supports the view that FDI globally reflects the competitive strength of the the home country's firms and the competitive weakness of the French-owned firms.

The focus on innovation activities allows us to examine to what extent foreign affiliates help to generate new competitive advantages. It is shown that FOFs are concentrated in high-tech industries and are larger in size. Their turnover displays an above-average use of technology, as measured by the importance of new products. However, the R&D intensity generally appears to be much lower in foreign-owned firms than in the other domestic firms. FOFs extensively use technology imported from their parent companies or from other foreign sources. Accordingly, their average propensity to innovate is lower. National ownership still plays a major role for the innovation performance. The analysis of patents registered shows that the density of the foreign presence can be better explained by the technological leadership of an investor than by the attractiveness of the host country, France. Therefore, foreign affiliates seem to have only a moderate tendency to repatriate technology developed in the French innovation system, apart from a few important exceptions (notably on the part of US-owned firms).

The results cannot be compared quantitatively since there are distinct differences in the aims and research approaches in the various chapters, not least because of the differing quality of the databases. Nevertheless, they generally support the theses that (1) FOFs are superior to average national firms in terms of input of human capital, wages, and productivity, and (2) the difference is much smaller when size and sector distribution are controlled for and when FOFs are compared with multinationals of the respective host country. What is considered the effect of foreign ownership should often really be seen as the effect of integration into an international business network. Differences exist between multinational and non-multinational companies rather than between domestic and foreign-owned ones. This view is reinforced by the fact that the companies involved in international M&A had often been multinationals before. Then, the acquired firm is foreign-owned being an outward investor at the same time and it becomes impossible to develop a clear-cut distinction between domestic and foreign-owned firms and domestic and foreign multinationals. Belgium is a good example of this problem. Based on the Belga-First data set, Zhang and van den Bulcke (2000) show that many multinationals from foreign countries use Belgium as a platform for their FDI in Europe and beyond. This platform FDI exploits Belgium´s comparative advantages. As many as 18 per cent of the foreign subsidiaries of all Belgian-based investors are held by foreign-owned outward investors. They achieve a better performance than the indigenous multinationals.

From the trend towards M&A it could be concluded that our question regarding differences between foreign-owned and domestic firms has become irrelevant. However, in view of the results of the following chapters in this volume and of the evidence from other studies (Lipsey, 2000) such a conclusion seems premature. Foreign ownership obviously still matters. However, there remain some open questions in the interpretation of the empirical results and a clear need for further research, as set out below.

1 Most empirical analyses are restricted to the manufacturing sector. An extension to services which form the overwhelming part of FDI seems promising, not least in order to take account of the (possibly) 'new' mobility of services.
2 The question of causality needs further clarification, especially in view of prevailing M&A and 'picking-the-winner' strategies. Data from FOFs and DOFs over a sufficient period of time is needed, especially in order to perform pre- and post-merger analyses.

Another important aspect worthy of research is the implications of the degree and type of ownership. The results of empirical studies are hard to interpret and to compare since there is no uniform concept of FOFs employed in the respective national databases, although the International Monetary Fund (IMF) and OECD have recommended guidelines for the collection of FDI and foreign affiliates data.[4] In some countries higher thresholds of foreign ownership than the 10 per cent recommended are applied (e.g., Ireland and Italy), and in firm panels 'foreign ownership' is often even defined by majority holding. If the transfer of knowledge is the essence of the internationalization of firms, it can be assumed that there will be fewer such transfers by a 10 per cent share holder compared with a majority, or even 100 per cent, owner who has control over the use of the knowledge supplied. Similarly, national statistics often use a narrower concept of FDI since reinvested earnings and intra-company loans are not (fully) included as 'old' FDI can be underestimated while 'new' FDI with more knowledge transfer is overestimated.

However, especially in view of the increasing weight of institutional investors, it can be questioned whether there is a given relation of ownership percentage and performance. While institutional investors can hardly supply and organize a flow of knowledge to foreign affiliates, they can put pressure on the management to improve efficiency and thus lead to improved performance. In the assessment of Gaston and Nelson (2001, p. 25) 'the importance of different types of ownership is still very much uncharted territory for both "new" trade and labour economists'. Along with other authors, such as Lipsey (2000), they consider the ownership issue more important than the location question. On the basis of a Swedish data set, Dahlquist and Robertsson (2001) similarly suggest that most features that are associated with 'foreign ownership' result from the fact that foreign investors are typically institutional investors. It seems, therefore, that the relevance of ownership needs to be discussed in a broader context beyond the 'us' and 'them' issue.

Notes

1 The uncertainty of FDI data becomes obvious against the background of substantial revisions of the statistics as they are compiled from national data and presented by UNCTAD (2000 and 2001). Revisions in the order of magnitude of over 20 per cent within one year are no exception. In this way, inward FDI stocks in Belgium, France and Germany 'increased' substantially recently, while the figures for the Netherlands and the UK were revised downwards.
2 Although the focus on manufacturing is largely due to a better database, this also seems to be meaningful since one can presume a greater international mobility of industrial production compared with services. Due to different sources, the data presented in the table do not always fully correspond with the respective data given in the following chapters.
3 In Dunning´s (1980) terminology this advantage is called the ownership factor, while Markusen (1998) calls it knowledge capital.
4 They determine the elements of FDI (equity, reinvested earnings, intra-company loans) and set a threshold of 10 per cent foreign ownership of the voting stock for an investment to qualify as FDI. For details see IMF, *Balance of Payments Manual* (5th edn); OECD, *Benchmark Definition of Foreign Direct Investment* (3rd edn). Overviews of the statistical concepts employed in individual countries are found in Falzoni (2000) and UNCTAD (1999).

References

Barrell, Ray and Nigel Pain (1999), 'Domestic Institutions, Agglomerations and Foreign Direct Investment in Europe', *European Economic Review*, Vol. 43, 925–34.

Bartelsman, Eric J. and Mark Doms (2000), 'Understanding Productivity: Lessons from Longitudinal Microdata', *Journal of Economic Literature*, Vol. XXXVIII (September), 569—594.

Borrmann, Christine *et al.* (2001), *Standort Deutschland im internationalen Verbund*, Baden-Baden, Nomos.

Borrmann Christine, Rolf Jungnickel and Dietmar Keller (2001), 'Auslandskontrollierte Unternehmen auf dem Arbeitsmarkt', study commissioned by the The Federal Ministry of Economics and Technology, Hambug.

Dahlquist, Magnus and Göran Robertsson (2001), 'Direct Foreign Ownership, Institutional Investors, and Firm Characteristics', *Journal of Financial Economics*, Vol. 59, 3 (March), 413–40.

Dunning, John H. (1980), 'Toward an Eclectic Theory of International Production: Some Empirical Tests', *Journal of International Business Studies*, Vol. 11, 9.

Dunning, John H. (1998), 'Location and the Multinational Enterprise: A Neglected Factor?', *Journal of International Business Studies*, Vol. 29, 45–66.

Falzoni, Anna M. (2000), 'Statistics on Foreign Direct Investment and Multinational Corporations: A Survey', University of Bergamo, mimeo.

Gaston, N. and D. Nelson (2001), *Integration, FDI and Labour Markets: Microeconomic Perspectives*, Leverhulme Centre, Research Paper No. 31, Nottingham.

Lipsey, Robert E. (2000), *Interpreting Developed Countries´ Foreign Direct Investment*, NBER Working Paper No. 7810, Cambridge, MA (http://www.nber.org/papers/w7810)

Markusen, James R. (1998), 'Multinational Enterprises and the Theories of Trade and Location', in P. Braunerhjelm and K. Ekholm (eds), *The Geography of Multinational Firms*, Boston, MA, Kluwer, 9–32.

Mason, Mark and Dennis Encarnation (1994), *Does Ownership Matter? Japanese Multinationals in Europe*, Oxford, Clarendon Press.

OECD (1999), *Measuring Globalization. The Role of Multinationals in OECD Economies*, Paris.

Reich, Robert B. (1990), 'Who Is Us?', *Harvard Business Review*, Vol. 68 (January–February), 53–68.

Reich, Robert B. (1991), 'Who Do We Think They Are?', *Harvard Business Review*, Vol. 69 (March–April), 77–88.

SESSI (1998), *Industrie française et mondialisation*, Chiffres Clés, Paris.

UNCTAD (1999), *World Investment Report. Foreign Direct Investment and the Challenge of Development*, Geneva and New York.

UNCTAD (2000), *World Investment Report. Cross-border Mergers and Acquisitiooins and Development*, Geneva and New York.

UNCTAD (2001), *World Investment Report. Promoting Linkages*, Geneva and New York.

Woodward, Douglas and Douglas Nigh (eds) (1999), *Foreign Ownership and the Consequences of Direct Investment in the United States*, Westport, and London, Quorum Books.

Wortmann, Michael (2000), 'What is New about "Global" Corporations? Interpreting statistical data on corporate internationalization', WZB discussion paper, FS 100–102, Berlin, December.

Zhang, Haiyan and Daniel van den Bulcke (2000), 'The Ownership Structure of Belgian Companies: Some Evidence about a Small Open Economy in the Globalization Process', University of Antwerp, mimeo.

2
Why Foreign-owned Firms are Different: A Conceptual Framework and Empirical Evidence for Austria[*]

Michael Pfaffermayr and Christian Bellak

1 Introduction

Empirical studies continuously reveal differences in the performance of foreign-owned firms (FOFs) and domestically-owned firms (DOFs) across countries, industries, over time and also at the plant level. Empirical evidence, however, is not conclusive. In some studies, FOFs perform better than domestic ones and vice versa. Despite this ambiguity, there is considerable agreement that these differences can be referred to a limited number of explanatory factors, depending on the performance measure chosen (e.g., productivity, profitability, growth, skill or wage).

This chapter is concerned with differences between FOFs and DOFs in four related respects: first, it seeks to provide arguments from economic theory for a superior performance of one over the other group of firms. Second, it discusses pitfalls in the comparison and the methodological problems related to measurement and data. Third, empirical results of earlier studies are reviewed and compared. Fourth, based on a sample of 524 Austrian manufacturing firms, we analyse whether and why differences between FOFs and DOFs exist, and regression analysis is carried out in search of the determinants of performance gaps. Additionally, the possibility of a performance gap between German affiliates and those of other countries is explored, pursuing the argument that – especially for German firms – the transfer of FSAs (firm-specific assets) within the firms should be easier given the similarity in business culture between Austria and Germany. Therefore, overhead costs and other factors influencing

* We are grateful to the participants of the HWWA workshop 'Foreign-owned Firms – are they different?' in October 2000 for their comments.

performance (such as market experience) accrue at the headquarters in Germany, while affiliates from other parent countries have to bear a higher amount of such costs. This could be an important source of performance differences of German affiliates not only *vis-à-vis* Austrian firms, but also *vis-à-vis* affiliates from other parent countries.

A number of empirical studies have been produced which examine various performance gaps. All studies focus on the manufacturing sector, due to data availability, except Oulton (1998b), who studies the services sector. The empirical studies can be grouped into five groups: the first comprises financial performance measures; the second includes variables related to labour (skill, wage and labour relations); the third group refers to studies on post-M&A performance (see section on 'measurement problems'); the fourth group concerns growth and productivity gaps between firms; and the fifth group covers the rest. Only a few studies reveal superior performance of DOFs and only some report substantial gaps between DOFs and FOFs related to ownership. Almost all studies reveal performance gaps between firms in different parent countries and those studies that examine domestically and foreign-owned multinational enterprises (MNEs) report negligible differences.

Several studies on the *profitability gap* (e.g., Mataloni, 2000 and his review of earlier literature; Kumar, 1984; Kumar, 1990; Dickerson, Gibson and Tsakalotos , 1997 with regard to acquisitions; and Ylä-Antilla and Ali-Yrkkö, 1997) have found substantial differences between FOFs and DOFs.

Several studies include labour-related variables. Howenstine and Zeile (1992), Blonigen and Slaughter (1999) and Doms and Jensen (1998) reveal a *skill* gap between FOFs and DOFs in the USA. Of course, this is clearly related to capital-intensity and thus is a determinant of the productivity gaps discussed in section 4 below. Here, one has to control for the difference in shares of production to non-production workers[1] in FOFs and DOFs in order to take into account the skill-mix of activities across industries. Howenstine and Zeile (1992) find that foreign affiliates in the USA are concentrated in manufacturing industries that require a higher level of employment skill. They examine whether these characteristics differ significantly between FOFs and DOFs in the same industries and find that for half of the industries, payroll per employee (as a broad measure for employee skill level) in FOFs exceeds that of DOFs by more than 10 per cent. Foreign ownership is, however, not related to a factor that might explain such difference, namely average scale of plant operations. Blonigen and Slaughter (1999) find that inward foreign direct investment (FDI) does not contribute to skill upgrading within manufacturing industries. On the contrary, distinguishing by type of investment, they show that Japanese greenfield FDI has a lower demand for skilled labour.

The *wage gap* is analysed, *inter alia*, by Blanchflower (1984); Globerman, Ries and Vertinsky (1994); Feliciano and Lipsey (1999); and Oulton (1998a). The wage gap is a possible sign of a skill gap, as relative wages for more skilled workers have been rising in general. Globerman, Ries and Vertinsky (1994) find that the wage gap vanishes once they control for factors such as size or capital-intensity. Feliciano and Lipsey (1999) find qualitatively identical results for US manufacturing, with wage gaps related to industry composition. For other sectors, however, a gap of 8–9 per cent remains even after controlling for size, industry and US state. A paper by Oulton (1998a) found that foreign-owned establishments in the UK are more human capital-intensive than domestically-owned establishments, even within the same industry. Overall, the studies related to wage and skill gaps suggest that the factor demand of DOFs and FOFs – even within the same industry – varies considerably, but only a small part of the gap is attributed to foreignness; instead, size is an important factor. *Labour relations* in domestic and FOFs are studied particularly in Canada (Creigh and Makeham, 1978; Greer and Shearer, 1981; Cousineau, Lacroix and Vachon, 1989; Carmichael, 1992).

Among the miscellaneous indicators are mostly *R&D-related gaps* (see, e.g., Howenstine and Zeile, 1992; Moden, 1998; Allan and Frances, 1999) or the use of technology (e.g., Doms and Jensen, 1998). It goes without saying that these factors are closely related to productivity gaps.

The main findings for our sample of manufacturing firms in Austria can be summarized as follows: marked differences exist between DOFs which are non-multinationals and FOFs, while foreign and domestic multinationals differ only marginally. Controlling for the most important determinants we find evidence that the productivity gap and the profitability gap are not explained by foreign ownership *per se*, but that belonging to or operating an MNE network in order to optimally exploit the FSAs is an important factor behind the gaps. There are no direct effects with regard to firm growth or investment propensity. In line with many studies there remain indirect effects originating from different firm characteristics. Contrary to expectations, German-owned firms largely exhibit the same characteristics as the other FOFs.

The remainder of the chapter is organized as follows: section 2 provides theoretical arguments; section 3 defines the requirements for a proper comparison and the unit of analysis; section 4 discusses and compares the results of earlier studies; and section 5 provides new estimates on performance differences. There is also a short concluding section.

2 Theoretical arguments

The reasons for performance differences between FOFs and domestic ones are nicely summarized by the OECD: in general, they are 'due to the technological and organisational advantages of firms, which have the resources to operate internationally, the advanced industries in which they operate, and their larger average size' (OECD, 1996). These arguments are analysed in more detail below and are grouped in four parts.

First, *firm-specific assets* and their transfer to and from affiliates seem to be an important source of difference. Caves (1996) argues that FSAs (such as special know-how on production processes, reputation for high quality or simply being a well-known brand) are intangible and have public good characteristics within the firm (see Box 2.1 for an illustration). This has two consequences: first, FSAs are exploited within the firm (internalization) since arm's-length trade via markets is inefficient (licensing is not attractive). Second, they can be transferred at low (zero) additional cost to foreign affiliates. *Ceteris paribus*, this would lead to superior performance of foreign owned affiliates *vis-à-vis* DOFs, if the latter do not have access to FSAs of comparable value. Conceptually, FSAs induce spillovers between parent and affiliates (Fors, 1997) or multi-plant economies of scale (Scherer *et al.*, 1975; Markusen, 1984 and 1995). Additionally, if the potential for exports is limited by rising marginal costs of production, transportation or market access, MNEs have an incentive to invest more in FSAs because of the multi-plant economies of scale (Pfaffermayr, 1999). Note that this resembles the endogenous sunk cost mechanism of Sutton (1991). Empirically, it implies the hypothesis of additional benefits if a firm participates in a MNE network.

Box 2.1   Wienerberger Bricks Company

An illustration of firm-specific advantages and the benefits of common governance within a MNE concerns an Austrian brick manufacturer (Bellak, 2000). The company is 180 years old and has been continuously in the same business since it was founded in 1819. Being a purely domestic firm in 1985, it started an internationalization process which made it the world's largest brick manufacturer by 1996.

Brick production is a highly standardized process. Standardization in this context refers to the fact that when an innovatory shift occurs in production technology, it can be introduced in new plants anywhere around the world and the product is highly standardized, too. This leads to two types of firm-specific advantage.

First, substantial economies of scope are derived from the standardized process technology. The latest development was submitted for patent protection in 1996. In the past, a multi-layered drying and burning process was used, while the new technology introduces a drying and burning process on a brick-by-brick basis. This implies a significant reduction in the number of operations to be handled and easier control of the process. It resulted not only in an improved quality of the product but also in a reduction of operating costs by 20 per cent. The cost reduction stems from a reduction in production time of up to 80 per cent compared to the former technology, from lower energy consumption, lower maintenance costs and lower personnel expenses. The development of the new technology was only partly a response to the market (high quality standards), but was also a response to tighter environmental standards.

Second, the standardization of the brick production yields an additional firm-specific advantage, as it enables each of the plants to benefit from substantial advantages of common governance. These are enjoyed by each of the more than one hundred affiliates around the globe and derive from the experience gained in acquiring, setting up and maintaining efficient brick producing plants. A modern brick production plant – as a rule of thumb – costs Austrian Schilling (ATS) 6–11 million plus an annual replacement investment. Break-even is reached after seven to eight years on large sites (with an average service life of 20–25 years) and after only three to four years in smaller plants. The criteria for efficiency are well known and therefore each plant, more or less independent of its location, is able to take measures when deviations from the benchmark become too large. The precondition and crucial success factor is a very tight controlling process, which is carried out by the headquarters.

Both types of firm-specific advantage apply in many other industries as well. Most literature focuses on the former, whereas little is known about the latter, which might be due to measurement problems. (One very common type of firm-specific advantage arising with horizontal integration, namely brand names, does not play an important role. Instead, acquired plants keep their local brand names.)

In the international business literature, the view is very similar. Competitive advantage is defined as a concept which can be 'usefully separated into those growing out of location (or nations) and those independent of location and arising from the firm's overall global network of activities' (Porter, 1990, p. 60). The latter component brings significant performance benefits to organizations '... such as the ability to leverage scale economies, the potential to take advantage of arbitrage opportunities in factor cost differentials across multiple locations and the ability to hasten new product development and introduction' (Gomes and Ramaswamy, 1999, p. 174). It is quite conceivable 'that the benefits of the initial stages of internationalization will exceed the concomitant costs because of the advantages associated with market familiarity, leveraging home-based skills and competencies, and utilizing home base managerial and administrative resources more efficiently' (Gomes and Ramaswamy, 1999, p. 174). This suggests that the advantages for an affiliate of being part of a MNE network are high, if the affiliate is young and geographically or culturally close to the parent company. They may vary over time and a two-way relationship may develop later on. Such considerations are important, for example, with regard to German affiliates in Austria. It also implies that age and experience effects (Mataloni, 2000) are important.

Large MNEs are also more suited to fragment production stages internationally according to the location advantages of the host countries inducing further gains from specialization of affiliates *vis-à-vis* smaller, non-fragmented firms. The specialization of a foreign-owned firm in a more narrow spectrum of activities which is more suited to it could be another source of performance differences (see Egger, Pfaffermayr and Wolfmayr-Schnitzer, 2000).

A third group of arguments refers to path dependency. Affiliates of FOFs have access to newer and superior technology, whereas domestic non-MNEs may operate older, less efficient plants. Also, in an MNE, additional possibilities for learning may arise from the operation of affiliates in various economic environments in different nations.

These arguments suggest that it is not ownership *per se* which matters, but 'benefits of participation in a multinational network'. Globerman, Ries and Vertinsky (1994, p. 154) make this differentiation. Note that this has important implications for empirical research, especially for classifying firms according to foreign ownership.

Fourth, there are various accounting arguments: for example, that investments in FSAs are counted as headquarters expenses, whereas affiliates participate at zero cost, thus raising their profitability. This is usually termed 'auxiliary services' and comprises R&D, administration and so on. DOFs, although they operate affiliates themselves, have to bear those costs. So comparing a foreign affiliate with domestic headquarters (or an integrated firm) may create an artificial gap (see section 3).

A fifth issue is whether different corporate governance systems lead to performance differences. The source of a superior performance of one group over the other derives from better control. Since corporate governance structures are largely national (Buckley, 2000, p. 289), it is quite conceivable that they are an important cause of performance gaps not only between FOFs and DOFs, but also between foreign affiliates by parent countries. Performance gaps between affiliates of different parent countries are reported in many empirical studies (see section 4 below). Zeckhauser and Pound (1990), among others, argue that the existence of a strong shareholder (that is, a strategic investor) who is able to monitor the management more efficiently than a dispersed group of shareholders, is a marker for higher performance. This argument also applies in our case here. Foreign-owned affiliates under the control of headquarters form a prime example since direct investing firms usually hold a large share of the assets of their affiliates and must be viewed as strategic investors.

Summarizing the main theoretical arguments, we expect in our empirical analysis that foreign ownership – in the sense of an affiliate being part of and having access to the FSAs of the MNE network – induces a productivity and profitability gap between FOFs and DOFs, and maybe also growth differentials in firm size and productivity. The argument that it is not foreign ownership *per se* which matters should become clear when comparing FOFs with domestically-based MNEs. We are not able to test for differences in the skills composition of employment and wages due to a lack of data.

3 Methodological considerations: measurement and data problems

Concerning the methodology of comparing DOFs and FOFs we concentrate on three issues: first, we ask what is the best way to make a proper comparison; second, which is the proper unit of measurement;

and third, how best to single out endogeneity problems and idiosyncratic short-run differences.

In a proper comparison 'like is only like' if it is possible to control for those firm characteristics which are important determinants of performance (aside from ownership and control). Since not all performance differences can be attributed to ownership (see, e.g., Globerman, Ries and Vertinsky, 1994, p. 144), a simple comparison between the two groups of firms will certainly not do the job. Therefore most published descriptive statistics may actually be misleading. One has to use an econometric set-up with the estimated specifications depending on the measure of performance (such as firm growth, productivity, profitability). These should include the most important control variables suggested by theory in order to isolate the specific ownership effect. However, given the limited number of control variables available not all performance measures are well suited to comparisons based on econometric estimates. For example, labour productivity as a performance measure requires an estimate of the real stock of capital (or an appropriate proxy thereof), which is rarely available in samples of firms.

Second, the choice of the unit of comparison is essential. The usual comparison is between DOFs (including MNE headquarters and exporting firms) and local affiliates of foreign parents, which is not satisfying for a number of reasons. Basically, *three* types of comparisons are possible: affiliates as against DOFs which could be national, exporters or a domestic MNE with a multi-layer organization. Although the econometric exercise below controls for this to some extent by including indicators such as size, export orientation or market share as explanatory variables, the correct choice of the unit of measurement remains essential. Ideally, one would want to compare performance at a very disaggregated (enterprise) level to avoid the problem of dealing with fixed investment costs in FSAs, headquarters services or more general economies of scale at the firm level. For example, comparing foreign-owned plants, which pursue only marginal corporate governance and control functions (management, controlling and accounting), and do not invest in R&D and reputation (R&D, marketing), with DOFs which perform all these tasks would be misleading. For this reason we analyse the data at the corporate level where it can be assumed that both types of firms perform a similar set of activities besides production. This suggests excluding domestic corporate headquarters, and including the firms they control instead. However, a sharp distinction is not always possible as this depends on the degree of consolidation of the firm and its reporting behaviour.

Additionally, the group of DOFs is quite heterogeneous and, in order to distinguish between the pure ownership effect and that of MNE-network membership, it is necessary to differentiate also between domestically-owned MNEs and non-MNEs (Doms and Jensen, 1998).

Third, one has to look at systematic differences which persist in the long run and sort out idiosyncratic developments in particular periods. Empirically, this suggests looking at average performance over a period of time, rather than comparing a cross-section of firms at a particular point in time. To avoid endogeneity problems – for example, successful firms may be attractive for take-over by, or mergers with, FOFs – the comparison seems to be more robust when analysing *ex post* performance in the period after the status of ownership has been measured.

Nevertheless, difficulties in the 'proper comparison' remain which cannot be singled out easily: differences in age between an established firm and a new establishment (choice of location, state of the art technology and so on) cannot easily be controlled for.[2] Accounting standards and practice may lead to artificial distortions in some of the performance measures. Additionally, transfer pricing may distort performance measures of foreign affiliates if they are based on nominal figures.

Given all the problems of comparison the proposed approach leads to a second-best comparison and there are alternatives. One alternative is to use event analysis and compare a domestic firm prior to and after a take-over by a foreign MNE (cf. Moden, 1998; McGuckin and Nguyen, 1995, for the effects of ownership changes in general) or to compare internal and external growth (e.g., Dickerson, Gibson and Tsakalotos, 1997). Here it is essential to have observations before and after the take-over for a sufficiently long period since consolidation afterwards and the integration into a MNE's network usually take several years.

Yet another alternative would be to compare purely DOFs before and after they have become a MNE. However, this is a very rare case and other things have to be held constant.

Summing up, the short literature survey below and our empirical exercise based on Austrian manufacturing firms concerning performance gaps among firms originating from ownership effects is organized around the following questions. As will become clear, it deals with comparisons of firms in general, but it is also an issue of the comparison between purely domestic and multinational firms.

1   Is the gap an artefact?
2a Is the existence of a gap related to ownership or to an 'industry composition effect'?
2b How is the gap explained? And why does a gap remain between DOFs and FOFs even after controlling for industry and firm characteristics?
3   What is the appropriate level of analysis: firm, establishment, plant or enterprise level?
4   Is the gap correlated by parent country? (mostly USA vs non-USA)

4   A review of empirical results

This subsection discusses in more detail studies examining a productivity gap, a growth gap, an investment gap or a profitability gap between DOFs and FOFs (see Annex table A 2.1). It also draws on the scarce evidence for Austria (see Table 2.1 for a summary).[1] The theoretical part discussed several arguments related to a *productivity gap*. Also, empirically, this has gained the most attention (e.g., Davies and Lyons, 1991; Howenstine and Zeile, 1992; McGuckin and Nguyen, 1995; Maliranta, 1997; Ylä-Anttila and Ali-Yrkkö, 1997; Doms and Jensen, 1998; Moden, 1998; Oulton, 1998a and 1998b).

Davies and Lyons (1991) find a productivity gap of 20 per cent, which is separated into a 'structural' and an 'ownership' effect. The gap is persistent on different levels of aggregation: that is, on two-digit and three-digit level industries, the weight of both effects remains mainly unchanged. Therefore, within two-digit level industries, contrary to expectations, FOFs do not cluster in the high-productivity three-digit industries. The gap therefore is more a firm- or plant-specific phenomenon, where ownership becomes particularly important. Oulton (1998a and 1989b) studies productivity gaps in the UK: in manufacturing (1998a), labour productivity is 38 per cent higher in FOFs, which is mainly determined by their higher capital-intensity (physical and human). In service industries (1998b), where Oulton examined over 49,000 companies, a productivity gap of one-third over DOFs' productivity remained after controlling for various structural differences (size, age, parent country). Again, a more skilled labour force and a higher capital-intensity in FOFs explains most of the variation.

Table 2.1 The effects of ownership: some descriptive evidence for Austrian manufacturing firms

Median	(A) Domestic Non-MNE	(B) Domestic MNE	(C) Foreign Non-G[b]	(D) Foreign G[b]	Overall	Kruskal–Wallis Test[a]			
						(A), (B) vs (C), (D)	(A), (B) vs (D)	(B) vs (C), (D)	Overall
Employment	88.8	274.8	196.2	391.8	173.0	**	**	–	**
Sales in ATS millions	129.4	527.3	411.6	801.9	327.9	**	**	–	**
Log labour productivity	7.3	7.5	7.6	7.6	7.5	**	**	**	**
Investment/sales ratio in %	4.2	4.7	4.6	4.9	4.5	–	–	–	–
Investment/employment ratio in ATS 1,000	70.6	83.5	85.1	82.7	80.8	*	**	–	–
Exports to the EU in % of sales	22.5	35.0	35.0	37.5	30.0	**	**	–	**
Exports to countries outside of the EU in % of sales	5.0	15.0	15.0	15.0	10.0	**	**	–	**
Market share in the EU (subjective estimate by firms)	0.5	1.5	1.5	2.5	1.5	**	**	–	**
Average growth in employment in % p.a.	0.0	0.2	0.0	0.1	0.0	–	–	–	–
Average growth in sales in % p.a.	1.5	3.0	2.0	2.3	2.1	–	–	–	–
Average growth in labour productivity in % p.a.	2.3	2.2	3.1	3.0	2.4	–	–	–	–

[a] Based on difference in rank sum, $Chi^2(1)$

[b] G = German

* significant at 5%

** significant at 10%

– insignificant

Source: WIFO Investment Surveys, Austrian Institute of Economic Research, Vienna, mimeo.

A paper on US establishments by Doms and Jensen (1998) examines the role of multinationality for productivity. They compare DOFs that are multinational to FOFs (which are by definition multinational), and domestic DOFs. The multinational DOFs and FOFs perform better than domestic DOFs, suggesting that foreign ownership is of less importance.

Observed differences are considerably reduced by control variables (e.g., from 50 to 20 per cent for labour productivity). Although their analysis is at the plant level, they include auxiliary plants, thus reducing the problem of undercounting non-production workers at the establishment level. This has implications for labour productivity and skill/wage levels.

Evidence from Howenstine and Zeile (1992) shows the tendency of FDI establishments to operate in industries characterized by higher capital intensity. While this evidence is only descriptive, it gives an indication of higher labour productivity (depending on the type of underlying production function). Maliranta's (1997) study on more than 5,000 Finnish plants reveals a weak foreign ownership effect. Using a large number of control variables, *inter alia* multi-plant versus single-plant firms, it is one of rare studies on total factor productivity (inputs are: labour, machinery, electricity, rents per hour). Maliranta also points to time effects (i.e., in the implementation of technology in a newly acquired plant).

A similar question related to productivity gaps is raised in the literature on acquisitions: namely, are high-productivity properties more likely to be taken over, and how do they perform after acquisition? McGuckin and Nguyen (1995) show that high-productivity plants (in the US food industry) are indeed more likely to be taken over and that their growth performance tends to be better compared to plants without ownership change. A clear drawback of this study is that it does not differentiate between domestic and foreign acquisitions.

In addition, Moden (1998) studies post-acquisition productivity focusing on foreign acquisitions in Sweden. He finds that while foreign acquisitions have increased labour productivity, the development of total factor productivity is more uncertain, which he attributes to time effects. Such studies give some support to the 'restricted matching hypothesis', namely that FOFs pick the *ex-post* better-performing firms, yet this seems to depend on firm size and on the initial productivity level.

Growth and *size* gaps are explicitly studied by Kumar (1984), Blonigen and Tomlin (1999) and Oulton (1998a). Howenstine and Zeile (1992) provide descriptive evidence on a plant-scale gap, maintaining that foreign-owned establishments tend to be larger, on average, than US-owned establishments. This scale effect may be responsible for a large portion of the above-described skill- and capital-intensity of foreign-owned establishments compared to US establishments. From a sample of 1,752 establishments which survived over 1973–93, Oulton (1998a) concludes that the gap of the annual average growth rate of US-owned establishments in the UK was 1.82 percentage points compared to UK-owned establishments during 1973–93. Also, value added and capital per employee showed higher growth rates. Oulton reports considerable differences between US-owned and other foreign establishments in the UK.

An explicit study on plant growth is by Blonigen and Tomlin (1999), who compare size and growth of Japanese plants in the USA. They search for evidence on Gibrat's Law and ask whether the size and growth of foreign-owned and domestically-owned establishments in the USA are similar. Since firm growth is related to firm age, they control (in addition to other variables) for age. Furthermore, since the type of entry of Japanese firms into the US market may affect growth rates of the affiliate via learning, they distinguish between acquisitions and greenfield FDI. They clearly reject Gibrat's Law, since smaller plants grow faster than larger ones. Their findings also reveal substantial learning effects and the effects of earlier investments on the likelihood of future investments.

Turning to profitability gaps, it should be emphasized that profitability is one plant-level characteristic where FOFs usually perform worse than DOFs (the reasons are provided below). Using company-level data, Mataloni (2000) finds that only a small portion of the gap can be explained by an industry effect (12 per cent), while market share and age effects (i.e., market power and newness) are significantly correlated with the profitability gap. A paper by Kumar (1990) examines the determinants of profit margins of affiliates of MNEs and local firms in 43 Indian manufacturing industries. Here, FOFs have higher profit margins than DOFs, which is explained by greater protection from entry-barriers of MNEs and a persistent knowledge advantage of MNEs (as a basis for FSAs). Contrary to these results, comparing purely domestic UK firms and UK firms with FDI, Kumar (1984) shows that the degree of overseas operations has no strong influence on profitability or growth. Providing evidence on post-acquisition performance from a large panel of UK firms, Dickerson, Gibson and Tsakalotos (1997) report that acquisitions have a detrimental effect on company performance (pre-tax profits). Internal growth yields a higher rate of return than external growth.[2]

Empirical evidence on Austria is still limited (Glatz and Moser, 1989; Hahn *et al.*, 1996; Gugler, 1998). The evidence is largely descriptive and is suggestive of a residual 'ownership' effect on variables such as profitability (Gugler, 1998), productivity and value-added. The empirical part below aims at adding to this evidence on a firm-level basis.

By way of a summary, the questions posed at the end of the last subsection can now be answered as follows:

Is the gap an artefact?

Here, a caveat is in order: the possibility of a spurious relationship exists 'between foreign-ownership levels and productivity levels ... Observations of higher average productivity levels among foreign affiliates may simply reflect the fact that foreign affiliates are clustered in industries enjoying above-average productivity levels for reasons unrelated to Foreign Direct Investment' (Globerman, Ries and Vertinsky, 1994, p. 144; Howenstine and Zeile, 1992, p. 53). In many cases, controlling for firm-specific variables substantially reduces the weight of an ownership variable, putting into question some of the gaps revealed by descriptive statistics.

How are the gaps explained? And why does a gap remain between DOFs and FOFs even after controlling for various other variables?

Generally, the empirical evidence supports two arguments: first, when performance gaps 'disappear' after controlling for firm and industry characteristics, they – but not foreign ownership – account for most of the variation. When gaps do not exist at the industry level, but at the plant level, the intra-industry variation is larger than the inter-industry variation. This has been referred to as the *structural effect* or *industry composition effect* as isolated, for example, in Davies and Lyons (1991).

Second, when gaps are persistent even after controlling for firm and industry characteristics, the multinationality of the firms (i.e., the international multi-plant firm) and their FSAs are more important than foreign ownership (see, e.g., Kumar, 1984; Doms and Jensen, 1998, p. 251). In this case, DOFs and FOFs which are multinational show a similar performance and this performance is superior to that of purely domestic DOFs. This suggests the possibility of intra-firm spillovers between plants as well as inter-firm spillovers between FOFs and DOFs, and has been termed the *ownership effect*.

Productivity gap

Globerman, Ries and Vertinsky (1994) address two sources to explain a productivity gap. The first source is differentials in the mix of activities undertaken by FOFs and DOFs. 'Strategic demands frequently require that individual units be assigned differentiated roles' (Gomes and Ramaswamy, 1999, p. 177), which give rise to performance gaps within foreign affiliates themselves and thus creates a problem for comparisons as discussed in section 3. If FOFs undertake a set of activities different from that pursued by domestic plants, they might perform better (in the case of a high degree of specialization, say, in research units, which employ highly trained staff; or in highly-automated production facilities, which require highly-qualified blue-collar workers and have above average productivity levels). The foreign-owned affiliates may also perform worse than domestically-owned plants (e.g., in the case of screw-driver factories, which employ low-skilled workers and pay below average wage levels). The lower skill-intensity of Japanese greenfield investments in the USA, as reported for example by Blonigen and Slaughter (1999), is a recent example of the latter case.

The second source of productivity gaps relates to differences in FSAs. Here, ownership matters, but it is not the mere existence of FSAs that gives rise to superior productivity, but the multinationality of the firms. These results are derived from comparisons of DO and FO multinationals, instead of FOFs as against all DOFs. This aspect is stressed by Doms and Jensen (1998), who find only very few performance gaps between US DO and FO multinationals in the USA (this might also be an indication for the well-known fact that FSAs across countries on the industry level are more similar than across firms in different industries in one country). Globerman, Ries and Vertinsky (1994, p. 154) provide two types of advantages of being part of a global network within the MNEs: (1) FO affiliates enjoy better access to foreign markets through intra-firm trade and network economies, such that they can operate more profitably on a larger scale (size and scale effects have been revealed in various studies); (2) FO affiliates can draw on their parent's managerial expertise to manage the complexity of larger scale. In addition, the importance of spillovers between plants within a multi-plant firm should not be underestimated.

Also, as a third source, failure of domestic producers to adopt 'best practice technology' or 'frontier technology' (Maliranta, 1997, p. 2; Oulton, 1998a, p. 50) may explain productivity gaps. Inferior access to technology by DOFs may have several explanations: their geographical space of operation may be smaller; they may be absent from certain markets completely, lacking the opportunity to tap into the local knowledge base or not profiting from regional agglomerations; the feedback from their affiliates may be less efficient; or the activities of the affiliates might not allow technology sourcing; they might not have the necessary information; or they may lack the capability to make efficient use of acquired technology (i.e., the absorptive capacity) which is related to learning processes and path dependence. Since most of these factors are related to multinationality, it remains an empirical question whether FOFs or DOFs show better performance. Such issues have been termed 'best practice model' versus 'random model' by Davies and Lyons (1991). The latter suggests that FSAs may be randomly distributed (i.e., they are not systematically related to industry factors).

The fourth source of productivity gaps is simply a higher input intensity per worker, which is related to capital or technology. Yet, as Globerman, Ries and Vertinsky (1994) show, the gap vanishes once they control for size or capital intensity. Oulton (1998a) provides two reasons why FOFs may be more capital intensive than DOFs, and both of them are related to higher costs of capital: (1) DOFs face higher costs of capital than FOFs; and (2) DOFs are more exposed to the home market, while FOFs are better able to spread risk globally (but this applies to globalized DOFs as well and depends on the environment in a certain nation). Also, DOFs have to rely on credit markets whereas foreign-owned ones have access to cheap sources of credit (e.g., the cash-flow of the MNE network) without paying a risk premium. But this again relates to the question of national versus multinational firms rather than to DOFs versus FOFs.

A fifth source of productivity gaps that has been identified by the literature concerning acquisitions is that FOFs may be particularly good at 'picking winners' (Oulton, 1998a and 1998b). The 'restricted matching hypothesis' (McGuckin and Nguyen, 1995), that firms with above average productivity are more likely to be taken over, is supported by many studies, but it is difficult to establish cause and effect and also in most cases it is not clear whether DOFs or FOFs are involved in the acquisition. An exception is evidence provided by Moden (1998), who reports that in Sweden it is primarily high-productivity firms which are acquired by FOFs. (There is also a size effect, in that lower productivity firms are acquired if they are larger firms: cf. Feliciano and Lipsey, 1999, p. 1.)

Profitability gap

Profitability gaps between firms can be attributed to accounting factors, to managerial explanations and to economic factors. Among the *accounting* factors, the motivation of MNEs to minimize their tax burden may be responsible for the low performance of FOFs. On the other hand, the *management* in a foreign-owned affiliate may feel more pressure than the management of a DOC, especially after a take-over. Therefore these managers 'set their sights higher' (Ylä-Antilla and Ali-Yrkkö, 1997), and normally they also seek to have a co-operative relationship with the workers in order to pursue the objectives set up by their foreign parent company. Among the *economic* factors, the higher capital-intensity (see above), which is a primary force behind an increase in labour productivity, may lead to higher profit margins. Higher market power of firms in MNE networks might be another source.

On the other hand, the higher capital-intensity may make the firm accept lower profitability abroad, in case the FOFs have lower costs of capital at home. The more global the financial markets are and the lower the barriers to sourcing funds abroad, the smaller will be the interest differentials and the easier will be access to capital. Moreover, connected to firm size, market share has been identified as being a major explanatory variable of profitability (Mataloni, 2000).

The role of age (see also below) as a determinant of profitability is twofold. On the one hand, young affiliates of FOFs entering a new market may have to be cross-subsidized by their parent for some time. Such FOFs may have high start-up and restructuring costs. Blonigen and Tomlin (1999) maintain that newly acquired firms have a higher debt burden which is responsible for low profitability. On the other hand, established affiliates which operate profitably may motivate the firm to use transfer pricing to shift profits (see above). This depends very much on the maturity of the market, as profits are generally declining in mature industries.

The type of entry is important, since a greenfield investment enjoys all the advantages of a newcomer: that is, it has the advantage of the choice of the optimum location, the implementation of state-of-the-art technology and the choice of the optimum plant size. Established firms, on the other hand, may be located in marginal locations, and so on. Thus, a performance gap may arise simply from the different age of FOFs and DOFs. This information is hardly available and only few studies are able to introduce age as a control variable (see, e.g., Blonigen and Tomlin, 1999).

Growth gaps

How is firm growth related to industry structure and ownership of FSAs? Empirical studies reveal that plant size and plant growth are not independent. Blonigen and Tomlin, (1999) reject Gibrat's Law on the basis of evidence of FOFs in the USA.

There are several reasons why FOFs may grow more slowly than DOFs. Blonigen and Tomlin provide an argument for slower growth rates of FOFs in the case of first entry into a market, because of uncertainties such as (1) inefficiencies; and (2) obtaining material inputs. Such inefficiencies may arise from monitoring problems of workers (see below) or other factors. Another factor behind a slower growth of FOFs is their lower capital-intensity if they start as small plants. In this case the growth process may take a long time. This argument is again not connected to ownership, but to optimum plant size in an industry. Blonigen and Tomlin also report that prior experience and learning are substantial for FOFs' subsequent investment and growth performance.

As growth is related to learning, the type of FDI (greenfield versus M&A) is important. It makes a huge difference whether an investing firm acquires a certain stock of know-how instantaneously and has to adapt it or whether this has to be built from scratch, not reaping any benefits of path-dependence. Mataloni (2000) also studies the lower experience of greenfield investors versus acquirers in the case of FDI in the USA.

Wage and skill gap

Wage gaps between firms in general arise for a number of economic and institutional reasons. Possible sources of earnings differentials in FOFs and DOFs are as follows (some of them relate to ownership, but most relate to industry-specific and institutional factors).

1 The organization of production by DOFs may lead to the fact that FOFs employ more skilled employees (Doms and Jensen, 1998, p. 240). While empirical results on wage gaps determined by skills are not unequivocal, they have been established in many studies (see below).

2 Also, higher wages may give rise to higher levels of effort by workers. The high capital-intensity of FOFs that has been found in many empirical studies (see above) encourages firms to pay efficiency wages, since it is more costly for capital-intensive firms to suffer employee shirking or absenteeism (Globerman, Ries and Vertinsky, 1994, p. 153).

3 The main institutional argument relates to the role of labour unions. On the one hand, FOFs may pay a wage premium to deter unionization (Doms and Jensen, 1998, p. 243). On the other hand, where DOFs enter an industry with a high level of unionization, the higher degree of unionization leads to higher wages. Such evidence is produced by Feliciano and Lipsey (1999) on the distribution of FOFs in the USA by states.

4 If there is resistance against a foreign management – for example, in the case of a take-over – higher wages may provide an incentive for domestic workers to accept foreign management.

5 There is clearly another variable that has to be controlled for with regard to wages. Since larger firms pay higher wages, the size effect is important here. The size effect loses considerable importance once the comparison is shifted from DOFs as against FOFs to DOFs^{MNEs} as against FOFs^{MNEs}.

6 An ownership-related argument builds on FSAs. In this view, the higher wage in FOFs is the outcome of a bargaining game, in which workers share the extra rents generated by the superior technologies (Head, 1998, p. 257). He maintains that 'workers are not the same'. Even comparable DOFs in the same industry may pay lower wages than FOFs, if the latter consider themselves less capable of monitoring workers in a foreign environment.

The main source of skill gaps rests on the fact that FOFs, through their FSAs, use superior technology. Such technology may require fewer workers of higher skill. This argument is clearly related to ownership of FSAs and horizontal integration of production internationally.

Despite the conceptual separation of the effects here, it must be emphasized that they are, of course, inter-related. For example, a skill gap may be related to higher capital-intensity, which reflects a newer technology, which consequently might lead to a growth gap, and so on.

What is the appropriate level of analysis: firm, establishment, plant or enterprise level?

Empirical evidence is still constrained by a lack of meaningful data,[3] particularly on the firm level, and methodological problems; therefore comparative studies are scarce. Most of the theoretical arguments refer to *firm* or *company* level, while empirical analysis is often on the *plant* level. Plant-level analysis generally excludes spillovers between plants of the same company (an exception is Maliranta, 1997). Plant-level analysis also misses the crucial point of multinationality and the creation and use

of FSAs. Doms and Jensen (1998, p. 238) mention 'auxiliary establishments' as an additional source of performance gaps. Such establishments
(such as R&D units, controlling departments and so on) create overhead
costs, which may reduce the comparability between plants.

Another related constraint is the aggregation level of industries. The
heterogeneity across companies within industries is considerable (Doms
and Jensen, p. 236), which is reflected by intra-industry variances which
are sometimes larger than inter-industry variances. Also, there may be
substantial variation across sectors in the within-industry changes in
foreign-affiliate presence (Blonigen and Slaughter, 1999, p. 3). Industry
analysis would therefore hide important information. Moreover, the level
of disaggregation is inversely related to the number of observations, yet a
shift from firm to plant level analysis not only allows the use of more
observations,[4] but also reveals the firm-level heterogeneity within the
groups of DOFs and FOFs. For example, plants can be classified in more
disaggregated industries compared to firms, where all plants are consolidated and classified in a single industry. It is therefore desirable to link
plant level and company-level data, yet this is hardly possible.[5]

Also, a change of ownership of firms in long-run time series may
result in a loss of usable data.

Is the gap correlated by parent country? (mostly USA versus non-USA)

Parent country distribution matters. Davies and Lyons (1996) point out
that the firm productivity gap is correlated with international productivity differentials between parent country and host country. Also
Oulton (1998a) emphasizes an *additional* productivity advantage of US
affiliates in the UK of 9–20 per cent. In contrast, Globerman, Ries and
Vertinsky (1994) find no significant difference between parent countries. These results may also derive from a different mix of activities of
affiliates from adjacent or far-away parent countries. As has been
pointed out above, geographical proximity is a driver of FDI, because it
lowers the costs of establishment. Also, the level of economic integration of countries has an effect on the organization of production (geographic centralization or dispersion), so that integrated countries may
be served via exports from larger plants, while production will be set
up in outsider countries, where firms face entry-barriers such as tariffs.
Similar arguments apply in the case of high transport costs.

Overall, the survey has shown the importance of the theoretical
arguments set out in section 2. We now turn to the empirical part
which focuses on productivity and growth gaps.

5 Empirical estimates

The empirical investigation into the effects of foreign ownership for Austrian manufacturing firms is based on the Spring Investment Surveys of the years 1997 to 2000, which WIFO conducts annually in co-operation with the EU Directorate-General II (see European Commission, 1997, for details of the design of these surveys). The Investment Survey is not compulsory and includes about 700 respondents who regularly supply complete answers for most of the questions. It is not a random sample of firms, but rather follows the development of a fixed 'test group' of mainly large and mature firms over the course of the years. Due to the small number of newly-founded firms and new entries in the panel the test group is not representative for the whole population but only for the larger size classes. In addition, it was not always possible to attain a clear picture on mergers and acquisitions which may be partially hidden in the database and cannot be controlled for in all cases.

Formerly, the WIFO Investment Survey had defined the plant as the basic unit of measurement. However, in recent years the majority of firms have preferred to respond at the corporate level so we have skipped all responses at the plant level and base our comparison at the corporate level. For enterprises with multi-layered organizations, the (incorporated) subsidiaries active under the control of the headquarters and responsible for particular branches are included, rather than the whole consolidated enterprise. However, this is not possible for all firms and depends on the degree of integration and consolidation of the individual firm. In this sense our basis of comparison is also second best, although, as argued above, from a conceptual point of view the unit of comparison is the correct one. Additionally, we excluded all firms with fewer than ten employees on average, as well as those with fewer than two observations for the period 1996–9.

The Survey provides information on employment, sales, investments,[6] export propensity (EU and countries outside the EU), market shares in the EU, and cash flow. The last four variables are evaluated on an ordinal scale, according to size classes. For example, the question on export propensity asks for the share of exports to EU countries in sales from domestic production and is formulated as follows: 'no exports, up to 10 per cent, 10–20 per cent, 20–30 per cent, ... , 90–100 per cent'. This form of questioning greatly increases the general acceptance of the questionnaire by firms, but on the other hand implies that some information is lost. With exception of the cash-flow variable, which has open intervals at the tails of the distribution, we valued all stages at the middle of the interval. For all the figures we calculate averages over the period 1996–99 and relate them to the status of ownership at the beginning of the estimation period (1996). The averages of the cash-flow variable – as it is not continuous – have been mapped into three size classes: less than 6 per cent, 6–12 per cent and more than 12 per cent.

The status of ownership has been inferred from various other sources and refers to the year 1996 (1997 if 1996 was unavailable). First, we used information on the top 500 Austrian firms published by Trend. A second source is Dun & Bradstreet's *Who owns Whom*. We classified a firm as foreign-owned if the ultimate owner held a majority share and was based in a foreign country. Additionally, we classified only those firms as foreign-owned if, according to the information at hand, the foreign owner was the operative headquarters which controls the affiliate and not just a shareholder. Despite having no exact definition as to what makes up an MNE, the foreign ownership dummy indicates whether an Austrian firm is part of a foreign MNE network. Additionally, we checked whether a firm belonged to a German MNE. As argued above, there are some arguments that the benefits of foreign ownership – if they exist at all – might be higher if the foreign owner operates in a similar business environment. Additionally, we have information from the investment survey as to whether the firms operate foreign affiliates. Thus, concerning the form of ownership, we are able to distinguish four types: domestically-owned non-MNEs (DOFs$^{non\text{-}MNEs}$), domestically-owned MNEs (DOFs^{MNEs}), foreign-owned non-German companies (FOFs$^{non\text{-}German}$) and foreign-owned German companies (FOFs^{German}). These four groups of firms allow us to compare DOFs^{MNEs} to FOFs and hence to discriminate between pure ownership effects and those arising from FSAs and membership of an MNE network.

At the descriptive level, the Kruskal–Wallis test (which is based on the comparison of ranks) in Table 2.1 indicates marked differences in firm characteristics of DOFs$^{non\text{-}MNEs}$ and FOFs. On average the latter are significantly larger both in terms of employment and sales, more productive (according to the nominal sales/employment ratio), and more capital-intensive (by at least at 10 per cent, measured in terms of the average of the investment to employment ratio). They exhibit higher export orientation and, according to their subjective estimate, hold a higher share in the European market. Compared to DOFs^{MNEs}, the FOFs differ only marginally with exception of labour productivity, where the FOFs again show a superior performance.

In contrast, with respect to growth in size there are no significant differences between FOFs and both DOFs^{MNEs} and DOFs$^{non\text{-}MNEs}$. Instead, growth seems to be mainly randomly determined in all groups of firms. The gap in the growth of productivity between FOFs and DOFs is not significant.

As a measure of profitability in Table 2.2a and 2.2b the average cash flow over the period 1996–9 is classified in three stages (less than 6 per cent, 6–12 per cent and more than 12 per cent). The cross-tabulation with the foreign ownership variable indicates that the share of firms with medium and high cash flows is somewhat higher for firms which belong to MNE networks. A simple chi-square test on independence of these two variables, which is admittedly a rather crude test, does not reject the null hypothesis of any differences (or association of these two variables). However, comparing domestically-owned MNEs

Table 2.2a   Cash flow by type of ownership

Cash flow	DOFs	FOFs	Total
<6%	111	50	161
	32.0	*26.5*	*30.0*
6–12%	103	61	164
	29.7	*32.3*	*30.6*
>12%	133	78	211
	38.3	*41.3*	*39.4*
Total	347	189	536
	100	*100*	*100*

Pearson chi^2(2) = 1.78, p = 0.41
Source: WIFO Investment Surveys, own calculations.

Table 2.2b   Cash flow: DOFs[MNEs] versus FOFs

Cash flow	FOFs	DOFs[MNEs]	Total
<6%	50	33	83
	26.5	*23.8*	*25.3*
6–12%	61	39	100
	32.2	*28.6*	*30.4*
>12%	78	67	145
	41.3	*48.2*	*44.2*
Total	189	139	328
	100	*100*	*100*

Pearson chi^2(2) = 6.59, p = 0.04
Source: WIFO Investment Surveys, own calculations.

to FOFs shows that the share of firms in the low and medium cash-flow classes is lower for the former (however, again the null hypothesis of no association cannot be rejected). So we conclude that – if there is any descriptive evidence at all – the DOFs[non-MNEs] perform worse than FOFs, but not the DOFs[MNEs].

German-owned firms do not show any *additional* difference to the Austrian-owned companies. The hypotheses of higher gaps arising from the cultural proximity does not find support. Instead, German-owned firms largely exhibit the same characteristics as the other FOFs. Only firm size forms an exception, as German-owned firms are on average larger than FOFs from other parent countries.

As is often the case with firm level data, the distributions of the performance variables, especially the growth rates, exhibit long flat tails, including a considerable number of extreme values which would have to be classified as outliers with OLS estimators. Hence in the regressions below we use the LAD estimators (least absolute deviation) or median regressions. The LAD estimator is more robust with respect to outliers and minimizes the sum over absolute errors and weighs extreme values lower than the ordinary least squares (OLS) estimators do. It achieves almost the same efficiency as OLS in situations with independent, but non-normal errors (Hamilton, 1998). In order to account for possible heteroscedasticity which would lead to underestimated standard errors using the standard estimation approach (Rogers, 1992), the standard errors are calculated by bootstrap resampling with 100 replications.

Table 2.3 provides regression results for labour productivity, investment propensity and cash flow as dependent variables. As mentioned above, cash flow is coded in three size classes, so we estimate an ordered probit model to predict the probability that a firm belongs to one of the three categories.

With respect to productivity, here measured as labour productivity in nominal terms (sales over employment), we follow the large literature on productivity and use a simple Cobb–Douglas framework (see, e.g., Maliranta, 1997 among others for a detailed discussion of the proper econometric set-up). We regress the log of labour productivity on the log of employment, the average investment to sales ratio as a proxy of the stock of capital and 16 industry and two regional dummies as additional control variables. As a measure of the productivity gap, which can be directly associated with foreign ownership, we introduce our ownership dummies using DOFs[MNEs] as the baseline. The difference between the German ownership dummy and that of the non-German foreign ownership dummy measures the additional direct effect from cultural

Table 2.3 Regression results on levels

	Labour productivity[a]		Investment propensity[b]		Cash-flow[c]	
	β	t	β	t	β	t
Foreign non-German ownership	0.12	1.6	0.04	0.3	0.03	0.2
German ownership	0.02	0.2	−0.04	0.0	−0.07	−0.3
Domestic[non-MNE]	−0.09	−1.4	0.16	1.4	−0.36	−2.2 **
Log employment	0.07	2.2 **	−	−	−	−
Log investment/employment (in 1000)	0.19	6.1 **	−	−	1.42	3.1 **
Sales growth (log differences)	−	−	0.01	2.6 **	−	−
Cash flow: medium	−	−	0.23	1.5	−	−
Cash flow: high	−	−	0.34	3.0 **	−	−
Export share (EU)*100	−	−	0.83	4.1 **	−0.04	−0.2
Export share (non-EU)*100	−	−	−0.03	−0.1	−0.05	−0.2
Market share (EU)	−	−	−	−	−	−
Observations	521		491		409	
Pseudo-R^2	0.25		0.18		0.11	
Test on						
Non-German FOFs vs DOFs[Non-MNEs], F-test	5.7	**	0.6		6.6	**
German FOFs vs DOFs[Non-MNEs], F-test	1.7		1.4		1.7	
Industry effects, chi^2(16)	4.5	**	4.2	**	43.5	**
Regional effects, chi^2(2)	0.0		0.3		2.1	

Note: extreme values of the lowest and highest percentile have been skipped.

[a] Dependent variable: log(sales/employment), median regression
[b] Dependent variable: log[(investment/employment)/(1 − investment/employment)], median regression
[c] Dependent variable: cash flow in three size classes (see Table 2.2a and b), ordered probit
** significant at 5%
− insignificant
Source: WIFO Investment Surveys, own calculations.

proximity. The estimation results indicate a productivity gap between FOFs[non-German] and DOFs[MNEs] of approximately 12 percentage points. The estimate is not significant, however, and due to the approximation of the stock of capital by the average investment to sales ratio, this is only a rough estimate. For FOFs[German], there is no additional ownership effect. Similar to other studies (Davies and Lyons, 1991; Maliranta, 1997; Oulton, 1998a; Pfaffermayr, 1999[8]) which, however, mostly do not control whether the domestic firms are MNEs or not, our results indicate that DOFs$^{\text{non-MNEs}}$ perform worse. Compared to FOFs$^{\text{non-German}}$ the gap is approximately 0.21 per cent and significant (F(1.496) = 5.73 with p = 0.017). Note, the difference from FOFs^{German} is approximately 11 per cent, but insignificant.

In the productivity growth equation (Table 2.4) the foreign-ownership dummies are insignificant, suggesting no systematic difference from the baseline (DOFs^{MNEs}). The gap between FOFs and DOFs$^{\text{non-MNEs}}$ is likewise higher than that to the baseline but not significant. Therefore, with respect to the productivity gap there is some evidence

Table 2.4   Regression results on growth

	Employment growth[a]		Sales growth[b]		Productivity growth[c]	
	β	t	β	t	β	t
Foreign non-German ownership	0.03	0.0	–0.64	–0.6	0.55	0.6
German Ownership	0.01	0.0	–0.98	–0.9	–0.36	–0.4
Domestic non-MNE	–0.86	–1.2	–0.69	–0.8	–0.28	–0.4
Log initial employment	–0.52	–2.7 *	–	–		
Log initial sales	–	–	0.10	0.4	–	–
Investment/sales	0.30	4.6 **	0.20	1.8 *	–	–
Export share in % (EU)*100	0.21	1.9 *	0.30	1.8 *	–	–
Export share in % (non-EU)*100	0.31	1.9 *	0.31	1.4	–	
Log difference employment	–	–	–	–	–0.23	–3.6 **
Log (investment/employment)	–	–	–	–	0.69	2.1 **
Observations	497		495		521	
Pseudo-R^2	0.1		0.1		0.1	
Test on						
Non-German FOFs vs DOFs^{MNEs}, F-test	1.4		0.0		1.1	
German FOFs vs DOFs$^{\text{Non-MNEs}}$, F-test	0.9		0.0		0.0	
Industry effects, Chi^2(16)	0.9		1.5	*	2.7	**
Regional effects, Chi^2(2)	2.2		2.0		0.6	

Note: extreme values of the lowest and highest percentile have been skipped.
[a]   Dependent variable: log difference of log(employment), median regression
[b]   Dependent variable: log difference of log(sales), median regression
[c]   Dependent variable: log difference of log(sales/employment), median regression
** significant at 5%
* significant at 10%
– insignificant
Source: WIFO Investment Surveys, own calculations.

that not foreign ownership *per se* is important, but that belonging to or operating a MNE network in order to exploit the FSAs optimally is one important factor behind the productivity gap.

To explain investment behaviour we use the investment to sales ratio as the dependent variable and transform it by the logit-transformation to ensure that the prediction lies in the [0,1] interval. Following the huge literature on investment we introduce growth in sales, dummies on the two upper cash-flow size classes and the degree of export orientation as explanatory variables. With exception of the export ratio to non-EU countries, all variables are significant and, after controlling for a number of influences, the direct impact of foreign ownership vanishes. This is an indication that it is mainly firm performance and other characteristics such as sales growth, export orientation and profitability (the access to high cash flows as cheap source of finance) which determine investment behaviour.[7] The different form of ownership *per se* has no direct effect, although the DOFs[non-MNEs] exhibit a higher, but insignificant, investment to sales ratio than the base. However, since FOFs differ according to characteristics used to explain the profitability gap, we conclude that ownership effects are mainly indirect and more pronounced for FOFs[non-German].

The ordered-probit equation explains the probability that a firm belongs to one of the three cash-flow classes (low, medium and high). It is based on the standard specification used in industrial economics which introduces market share and capital-intensity (which is to some extent endogenous and should be interpreted with care) as the main explanatory variables (Martin, 1993). Both are highly significant. The dummy for DOFs[non-MNEs] is significantly negative, while the two foreign-ownership dummies are not, implying that their profitability does not systematically deviate from the base line (domestically-owned MNEs). Setting the foreign-ownership dummy counterfactually to one holding all else equal results in a 33.4 per cent chance of being in the highest profitability class as compared to the actual prediction of 21.6 per cent. This result again emphasizes that foreign ownership *per se* does not explain the gap.

Table 2.4 refers to average firm growth measured both in terms of sales and employment growth. The econometric specification is based on the traditional approaches which test Gibrat's Law of proportionate growth and introduces initial size, export and investment propensity as well as industry dummies and two dummies for the western and the southern region as explanatory variables (see, e.g., Bloningen and Tomlin, 1999). Consistent with the descriptive evidence we do not find any impact of foreign ownership (either in general or in case of German ownership) after controlling for these growth determinants. Instead, firm growth is mainly randomly determined and idiosyncratic with systematic influences being of minor importance.

6 Summary and conclusions

The empirical evidence for a sample of Austrian manufacturing firms suggests that the direct positive effect of participating in a foreign MNE's network can mainly be found in productivity and profitability. This is in line with the hypothesis that these firms can draw on FSAs and receive spillovers from the network which DOFs could not, or only to a lower extent. Distinguishing between DOFs[MNEs] and DOFs[non-MNEs] proves important in this respect in order to discriminate between the effects of foreign ownership *per se* and the gains of MNE networks. The productivity and profitability gaps refer to the former but not to the latter. Concerning investment propensity and firm growth there seem to be no direct effects (gaps) after controlling for the most important determinants. However, as FOFs are significantly different with respect to several important characteristics such as size, capital-intensity, export propensity and market share there may be important indirect effects which could explain the gap. For example, an increase of the cash flow may be mainly due to a firm's growing market share; or the productivity gap could be partly explained by the higher capital-intensity. We find no additional effect of cultural proximity as it would materialize for German-owned companies. In contrast, there is weak evidence that other foreign firms perform better, although effects could not be estimated precisely. Future research should look at the channels and size of spillovers in more detail to find more evidence about the advantages of operating in an MNE's network.

Several empirical studies distinguishing the type of FDI (horizontal as opposed to vertical integration) or the market entry strategy (greenfield versus acquisition) revealed different impacts on the gaps examined. Affiliates reap variegated advantages from being part of an MNE's network, such as access to firm-specific human capital, information exchange, technology transfer, transfer pricing and so on. Little is known so far about the role of the affiliates within MNEs' networks and the economic nature of the interactions and exchanges between affiliates.

On the basis of the evidence presented, three aspects are of interest for economic policy. First, economic policy should enforce inter- and intra-company spillovers to improve the performance of the manufacturing sector, and the structure of ownership is important in this respect. Based on the evidence of significant spillovers within MNEs one option is to support *foreign entry* by take-overs or by greenfield investment (i.e., to promote the direct effects of foreign ownership.). However, due to the rather small direct ownership effects this may not be very efficient and it is also not attractive to many governments, as public concern over foreign ownership is widespread. Also, the danger that locational competition may bid away most of the benefits after subtracting the costs of local incentive packages cannot be denied (Head, 1998, p. 256). A more efficient approach would focus on DOFs and seek to increase their degree of internationalization (e.g., by providing information about foreign markets, through state insurance packages and so on). This should induce more investments in FSAs, a catching-up and a reduction or even closing of the gap. Still another option is to stimulate indirect effects, most prominently the industry composition, through structural policies and the encouragement of inter-firm spillovers. The second important aspect focuses on rents accruing to the host country from successful FOFs. Since these companies usually engage in transfer pricing to avoid this, the capacity for rent extraction by the host country is often limited. A third concern for economic policy is the effect of FOFs on competition, especially if FOFs enter the domestic market by a take-over. This is an important aspect of competition policy, which has not been subject of the present chapter.

Table A2.1 Earlier studies on performance gaps between DOFs and FOFs

Country; author (year)	Research problem	Performance indicator viz. dependent variable	Explanatory variables for gap	Sample	Main results	Superior group of firms
[1] UK Davies and Lyons (1991) PR	To decompose a productivity gap into a structural and an ownership effect.	Productivity	Structural effect Ownership effect	UK firms 1971–87	Structural effect more important than ownership effect Productivity differential of 20% Random advantage model vs 'best practice' Catching-up possible (management)	FO
[2] UK Oulton (1998a) IN, WA, PR, GR, CI	Studies physical investment in UK manufacturing from the viewpoint of the individual establishment. Studies reasons for differences between businesses in the levels of labour productivity.	Gross output (and net output, value added)	Wages (for skill levels); administrative, technical and clerical employees; operative wages; intermediate inputs	N = 1,752* 1973–93 Plant Level Manufacturing sector *of which 176 US-owned and 235 other foreign-owned	FO establishments are more capital intensive, more human-capital intensive, value added per worker (LP) is 38% higher (Table 8, p. 38) Human and physical capital-intensity differences are a significant determinant of productivity gaps. US-owned plants have additional productivity advantages over other FO plants. 3 explanations for the higher capital-intensity of FO are provided (pp. 45, 50)	FO

Country; author (year)	Research problem	Performance indicator viz. dependent variable	Explanatory variables for gap	Sample	Main results	Superior group of firms
[3] UK Oulton (1998b) PR	Do foreign-owned companies have a productivity lead over domestically-owned ones? (gap, because (a) some companies use more inputs per worker; and (b) some companies may have access to superior technology, etc.)	Productivity Input intensity	Physical capital-intensity, human capital-intensity and size; age, US, Non-US, UK-subsidiary	N = 49,009 companies Non-manufacturing	After controlling for industrial composition and other factors, FO was found to raise productivity by about a third in non-manufacturing Explained by higher capital intensity and more skilled labour force (FO generally positively correlated with input intensity)	FO
[4] USA Howenstine and Zeile (1992) SK, CI, RD, Plant scale	Examines the characteristics of manufacturing industries with substantial foreign investment intensity	Capital-intensity, skill level and plant scale (R&D activity)	only descriptive	N = 66,878 FO establishments Establishment vs enterprise data (levels of disaggregation)	FO account for 1 per cent of all US businesses and 4 per cent of employment and tend to be larger on average FO are more active in industries characterized by higher capital-intensity FO are more concentrated in manufacturing industries that require a higher level of employment skill	FO

Table A2.1 Earlier Studies on Performance Gaps between DOCs and FOCs (*continued*)

Country; author (year)	Research problem	Performance indicator viz. dependent variable	Explanatory variables for gap	Sample	Main results	Superior group of firms
					No significant relationship between foreign ownership activity and the average scale of plant operations. On a more aggregate level: significant tendency for FO establishments to operate in industries with the most R&D activity Compares 2-digit to 4-digit levels in order to examine the structural effect Explanations for wage gap: FO tend to be located in high-wage areas; or labour market shortage for specific skills demanded by the FO	

Country; author (year)	Research problem	Performance indicator viz. dependent variable	Explanatory variables for gap	Sample	Main results	Superior group of firms
[5] USA Doms and Jensen (1998) PR, WA, SK	How do foreign plants compare to domestically-owned plants in terms of wages and productivity? Differentiate by national ownership, firm size, and whether US-owned plants belong to firms that have significant assets outside the USA, i.e. compare plants of foreign MNEs to plants of US MNEs. Hypothesis is that no gap exists between these plants.	Labour productivity (capital / employment; value added / employment); and capital / labour ratio	Control for: plant size, industry; plant age, plant location and capital / labour ratio; production and non-production workers; and their wages. Number of technologies	N = 4,463 FO N = 110,676 DO establishments	Control variables reduce the observed differences, but they persist (inclusion of the capital/ labour ratio further reduces the gap, but remains statistically significant). FO MNEs vs US-owned MNEs: are the most similar → firm-specific advantages By parent country: no country compares favourably with plants owned by US MNEs Use of technology (hypothesis: might produce spillovers, p. 248ff): negligible gap	DO: US MNEs as a group by PR, SI, WA, PR, followed by large domestically-oriented plants FO follow closely in terms of WA, PR, followed by large domestically-oriented plants
[6] UK Kumar, M.S. (1984) GR, PF	Do firms with overseas production differ significantly from those with only domestic operations? Effect of overseas activities on growth and profitability			N = 700 UK firms	International firms have slightly higher growth. But have a lower profit rate and lower investment than DO firms. Degree of overseas operations has no strong influence on profitability or growth	FO DO

Table A2.1 Earlier Studies on Performance Gaps between DOCs and FOCs (*continued*)

Country; author (year)	Research problem	Performance indicator viz. dependent variable	Explanatory variables for gap	Sample	Main results	Superior group of firms
[7] Canada Globerman, Ries and Vertinsky (1994) WA, VA	Performance comparisons of Canadian and non-Canadian firms, as well as between non-Canadian firms.	Value-added, labour-productivity, wages	Cost of fuel and electricity (proxy for capital costs); production workforce; share of male workers; scale economies, ownership dummies, industry dummies	All establishments in 21 sample industries Plant level data	FO have higher value-added per worker; pay higher wages FDI improves efficiency and pay levels in Canada Gap vanishes, if controlling for size or capital-intensity	FO

Country; author (year)	Research problem	Performance indicator viz. dependent variable	Explanatory variables for gap	Sample	Main results	Superior group of firms
[8] Finland Maliranta (1997) PR	Explain the differences in productivity levels among plants.	Total factor productivity	Dummy variable for FO, plus 20 other explanatory variables (p. 27)	$N = 5,379$ plants (208 FO, 4,668 DO) Plant level	FO firms appear to be capable of using resources more productively. It is not clear to what extent good performance leads to foreign ownership and vice versa (p. 41).	FO
[9] Japan Blonigen and Tomlin (1999) SI, GR	Gibrat's Law and FO firms Is the relationship between firm growth and firm size for these foreign-owned affiliates similar to that found for domestic plants? Sample: Japanese affiliates are large plants with high growth rates	Employee growth (1987–90)	Plant size 1987 industry dummy; Plant age*; Dummy variable for joint venture with US firm. *distinguishes age of *acquired plant* vs age of *greenfield plant*	$N = 688$ Plant level (subsample on automobile firms)	Reject Gibrat's Law: smaller plants grow faster than larger ones (doubling of plant size reduces growth by one-third). Plant size and plant growth are not independent. Learning effects are substantial for foreign-owned affiliates, because of uncertainties such as (a) inefficiencies; (b) obtaining material inputs. More recent plants grow much quicker (indicates learning effects). Learning through prior investments increase the likelihood of future investments (only new plants are examined): prior investments do not affect plant growth.	

Table A2.1 Earlier Studies on Performance Gaps between DOCs and FOCs (*continued*)

Country; author (year)	Research problem	Performance indicator viz. dependent variable	Explanatory variables for gap	Sample	Main results	Superior group of firms
[10] USA Blonigen and Slaughter (1999) SK	Whether inward FDI flows contribute to within-industry shifts in USA relative labour demand towards more-skilled labour (wage inequality)	Skill upgrading (level-change in the skilled-labour share of the total wage bill)	Relative unskilled wage; capital; value-added output; Dummy variables (industry ...)	US firm data 1977–94; 56 SIC industries	Inward FDI does not contribute to skill-upgrading *within* manufacturing industries distinction between acquired plants (similar factor demand as DO) and greenfield investments Japanese greenfield FDI: *lower* demand for skilled labour	(–)
[11] USA Feliciano and Lipsey (1999) WA	Whether presence of more foreign firms is associated with higher wages in an industry and to higher wages within domestically-owned operations? Whether, if the foreign firms pay more, the difference can be explained by measurable characteristics of the foreign-owned establishments or whether there is some remaining differential associated with foreign ownership?	Wage gap (annual wage per worker)	Ownership of plant; degree of basis unionisation; size; skill; gender. Industry and state dummies	Establishment Manufacturing sector 2 digit SIC and state 1987–92	Manufacturing sector Wage gaps related to industry composition (FO in high-wage industries) Differences within industries: 5–7 per cent without control variables gap disappears with control variables (size, industry, state) extent of FO had no impact in 1987, but positive impact in 1992. Other industries: wage gap remains even after controlling for other factors (8–9%)	FO DO

Country; author (year)	Research problem	Performance indicator viz. dependent variable	Explanatory variables for gap	Sample	Main results	Superior group of firms
[12] Finland Ylä-Anttila and Ali-Yrkkö (1997) PR, PF	Performance of FO firms after strong increase of inward investment in Finland	Productivity Profitability and key balance sheet data	Only descriptive; analysis of balance sheet data	N = 288 Finnish-owned firms and N = 104 Foreign-owned firms Industry, Services and Commerce	Yield on capital invested: 13% (DO) : 23% (FO) Value added per employee (FIM1,000): 366 (DO) : 423 (FO) FO are more capital-intensive Managerial explanations: Mostly takeovers → new managers bring in new know-how → new owners are more demanding	Equal, except profitability and productivity, where FO > DO
[13] USA Mataloni (2000) PF	Explain the profitability gap	ROA	Market share, age, industry, intra-firm imports	N = 2,133 firms 1992 Industry level and company level (US firms)	Only a small portion of the gap can be explained by the industry effect, i.e. FO to be concentrated in low-profit industries (12% of gap) Market share: the larger the market share of FO, the lower the gap between profitability of FO and US-owned firms Profit transfer explanation for unexplained profitability gap: only weak and inconsistent evidence Age effects: some evidence; e.g., the ROA narrows over time,	DO

Table A2.1 Earlier Studies on Performance Gaps between DOCs and FOCs (*continued*)

Country; author (year)	Research problem	Performance indicator viz. dependent variable	Explanatory variables for gap	Sample	Main results	Superior group of firms
					which seems to be related to age effects. Acquiring or establishing a new business can add costs that disappear over time; experience can yield benefits that accumulate over time. All four effects combined: market share and newness are significantly correlated; intra-firm import content not correlated	
[14] India Kumar N. (1990) PF	Examine determinants of profit margin gap (sustained differences in inter-group profitability)	Profit margins	Entry barriers (advertising, technology-intensity, skill intensity), VA: sales ratio, average capital requirements, CR4, growth, size, effective rate of protection, capital-output ratio	$N = 43$ Indian manufacturing industries	MNEs enjoy greater protection from entry barriers MNEs have persistent advantage over local firms, especially in knowledge.	FO

Country; author (year)	Research problem	Performance indicator viz. dependent variable	Explanatory variables for gap	Sample	Main results	Superior group of firms
[15] Austria Glatz and Moser (1989) GR, PR, RD	Comparison of subsidized inward investments to manufacturing sector total in Austria	Employment growth Investment / turnover ratio Value-added per employee, etc.	–	$N = 36$ largest inward FDI since 1970	employment growth: −1.9% (DO) vs + 7.7% (FO) investment/turnover ratio: 6.0% (DO) vs 10.9% (FO) labour productivity: 25% higher in FO than manufacturing sector average R&D-ratio of FO: more than twice as high as manufacturing sector average	FO
[16] Austria Gugler (1998) PF, RD	Analysis of the ownership structure of Austrian firms			$N = 600$ largest non-financial corporations 1996	foreign control increases profitability: FOs' rate of return = 10.4% (compared to overall median = 8.4%) FOs' R&D ratio = 2.6% (compared to overall mean of 1.7%)	FO

Table A2.1 Earlier Studies on Performance Gaps between DOCs and FOCs (*continued*)

Country; author (year)	Research problem	Performance indicator viz. dependent variable	Explanatory variables for gap	Sample	Main results	Superior group of firms
[17] Austria Hahn, Mooslechner and Pfaffermayr (1996) GR, IN, Equity, PR, labour costs	Examine the concentration of ownership and its effects on performance	Investment-sales ratio, equity ratio, labour productivity etc.	Cash-flow ratio, investment-sales ratio, fixed effects (time)	1980–94	No significant difference between FO and DO	No difference
					FO have higher labour productivity, higher value-added per employee and higher wage costs per employee	FO
					DO have large total wage costs	DO
[18] UK Dickerson, Gibson and Tsakalotos (1997) PR, MA	Investigate the impact of acquisitions on company performance.	Pre-tax profits as a proportion of net assets	Size, debt ratio, growth of net assets	N = 2,941 UK firms, of which 613 made at least one acquisition	Acquisitions have a detrimental effect on company performance lower rate of return than growth through internal investment	–

Country; author (year)	Research problem	Performance indicator viz. dependent variable	Explanatory variables for gap	Sample	Main results	Superior group of firms
[19] USA McGuckin and Nguyen (1995) MA, PR	What type of property experiences ownership change? How do transferred properties perform after acquisition?	Relative labour productivity, total factor productivity for subsample	Capital, labour, materials	$N = 28,407$ plants, SIC 20 (food industry) 1977–87	Plants with high productivity are most likely to be taken over ('restricted matching hypothesis', p. 265) (not clear whether by DO or FO (For larger plants, firms tend to acquire plants with low productivity.) Initial productivity and plant size have inverse relationship with ownership change. Post-merger productivity performance: plants experiencing ownership change had higher productivity growth rates than plants that had no ownership changes	–

Table A2.1 Earlier Studies on Performance Gaps between DOCs and FOCs (*continued*)

Country; author (year)	Research problem	Performance indicator viz. dependent variable	Explanatory variables for gap	Sample	Main results	Superior group of firms
[20] Sweden Moden (1998) PR, RD	Examine, whether a firm, or plant, that changes ownership has had a poor productivity performance before the ownership change, and whether it shows an improvement afterwards.	Labour productivity (deviation from average labour productivity)	Firm sales, ownership Dummy	1980–94	Foreign acquisitions have increased the labour productivity, while the development of total factor productvity is more uncertain Foreign MNEs are not particularly attracted to R&D. Results are broadly in line with the predictions of the matching theory.	–

Note: FO = Foreign owned; DO = Domestically owned; SI = Size; GR = Growth; SK = Skill; PR = Productivity; VA = Value-added; WA = Wages; M&A = Mergers and Acquisitions; FI = Finance; LR = Labour relations; PF... Profitability; R&D = Research and Development; ROA = Rate of Return; N = number of observations; IN = investment; CI = Capital intensity; CR4 = Concentration ratio of four largest firms

Notes

1 For example, in our empirical analysis of Austrian manufacturing firms age cannot be observed.
2 To our knowledge, no such evidence has been produced comparing FOFs and DOFs (i.e., whether inward FDI was made in the form of acquisition or greenfield FDI and how this relates to profitability).
3 Large *and* long-run databases (such as long-run database (LRD), annual respondents database (ARD)) are often on the establishment (plant, location) level rather than on the firm level.
4 Often more information is collected at the plant level than at the firm level.
5 For a more detailed discussion, see, e.g., Howenstine and Zeile (1992), p. 45.
6 The survey asks for both realized values of sales, employment and investment which are lagging two years after of the survey date as well as 4 planned figures in four consecutive bi-annual surveys (spring and autumn) afterwards. For missing values and those referring to the year 1999 where the realizations are not yet available the most recent available plan (4th plan in the terminology of these surveys: see European Commission, 1997) of the spring survey has been used.
7 Based on the same data set as a panel, Pfaffermayr (1999) uses the foreign ownership dummy as a control variable to test for effects of foreign affiliates on domestic performance. Since there a capital stock has been constructed and an industry share of intermediates has been imputed, the effect of foreign ownership has turned out somewhat higher but likewise significant.

References

Allan, K. and R. Frances (1999), 'The tangible contribution of R&D spending of foreign-owned plants to a host region: a plant level study of the Irish manufacturing sector (1980–1996)', *Trinity Economic Papers*, No. 7, Dublin.

Bellak, C. (2000), 'Large Multinationals from Small Countries: The Case of Wienerberger Brick Company (Austria)', in T. Almor and N. Hashai, *FDI, International Trade and the Economics of Peacemaking, A Tribute to Seev Hirsch*, Rishon LeZion, Israel, Academic Studies Division, College of Management, pp. 216–35.

Blanchflower, D. (1984), 'Comparative Pay Levels in Domestically-owned and Foreign-owned Manufacturing Plants: A Comment', *British Journal of Industrial Relations*, Vol. 22, pp. 265–7.

Blonigen, Bruce A. and Matthew J. Slaughter (1999), *Foreign-Affiliate Activity and U.S. Skill Upgrading*, NBER Working Paper, No. 7040, Cambridge.

Blonigen, Bruce A. and KaSaundra Tomlin (1999), *Size and Growth of Japanese Plants in the United States*, NBER Working Paper, No. 7275, Cambridge.

Buckley, P. J. (2000), 'Cross-border governance in multinational enterprises', in Peter J. Buckley (ed.), *Multinational Firms, Cooperation and Competition in the World Economy*, Basingstoke, Palgrave Macmillan, pp. 289–304.

Carmichael, F. (1992), 'Multinational Enterprise and Strikes: Theory and Evidence', *Scottish Journal of Political Economy*, Vol. 39, No. 1 (February), pp. 52–68.

Caves, R. (1996), *Multinational Enterprise and Economic Analysis*, Cambridge: Cambridge University Press.

Cousineau, J.-M., R. Lacroix and D. Vachon (1989), *Foreign Ownership and Strike Activity in Canada*, Working Paper No. 8927, University of Montreal, Department of Economics.

Creigh, S. W. and P. Makeham (1978), 'Foreign Ownership and Strike-Proneness: A Research Note', *British Journal of Industrial Relations*, Vol. 16, pp. 369–72.

Davies, S. W. and B. R. Lyons (1991) 'Characterising Relative Performance: The Productivity Advantage of Foreign Owned Firms in the UK', *Oxford Economic Papers*, Vol. 43, pp. 584–95.

Davies, S. W. and B. R. Lyons (1996), 'The Industrial Organisation in the European Union', Oxford, Clarendon Press.

Dickerson, A. P., H. D. Gibson and E. Tsakalotos (1997), 'The Impact of Acquisitions on Company Performance: Evidence from a Large Panel of UK Firms', *Oxford Economic Papers*, No. 49, pp. 344–61.

Doms, M. E. and B. J. Jensen (1998), 'Comparing Wages, Skills, and Productivity between Domestically and Foreign-Owned Manufacturing Establishments in the United States', in R. E. Baldwin, R. E. Lipsey and J. D. Richardson (eds), *Geography and Ownership as Bases for Economic Accounting*, Studies in Income and Wealth, Vol. 59, pp. 235–55.

Dun & Bradstreet's, *Who owns Whom*, various issues.

Egger, P., M. Pfaffermayr and Y. Wolfmayr-Schnitzer (2000), *The International Fragmentation of the Value Added Chain: The Effects of Outsourcing to Eastern Europe on Productivity, Employment and Wages in Austrian Manufacturing*, Vienna, WIFO.

European Commission (1997), 'The Joint Harmonized EU Programme of Business and Consumer Surveys', *European Economy*, Reports and Studies 6.

Feliciano, Z. and R. E. Lipsey (1999), *Foreign Ownership and Wages in the United States, 1987–1992*, NBER Working Paper, No. 6932, Cambridge.

Fors, G. (1997), 'Utilization of R&D Results in the Home and Foreign Plants of Multinationals', *Journal of Industrial Economics*, Vol. XLV, No. 2 (June), pp. 341–58.

Glatz, H. and H. Moser (1989), *Ausländische Direktinvestitionen in Österreich*, Frankfurt, Campus.

Globerman, Steven, John C. Ries and Ilan Vertinsky (1994), 'The economic performance of foreign affiliates in Canada', *Canadian Journal of Economics*, Vol. XXVII, No. 1, pp. 143–56.

Gomes, L. and K. Ramaswamy, (1999), 'An Empirical Examination of the Form of Relationship Between Multinationality and Performance', *Journal of International Business Studies*, Vol. 30, No. 1 (First Quarter), pp. 173–88.

Greer, C. R. and J. C. Shearer (1981), 'Do Foreign-Owned Firms Practice Unconventional Labor Relations?', *Monthly Labor Review*, Vol. 104, pp. 44–8.

Gugler, K. (1998), 'Corporate Ownership Structure in Austria', *Empirica*, Vol. 25, No. 3, pp. 285–307.

Hahn, F. R., P. Mooslechner and M. Pfaffermayr (1996), *Globalisierungstendenzen in der österreichischen Wirtschaft*, Vienna, WIFO.

Hamilton, L. (1998), *Statistics with Stata 5* (Pacific Grove, CA, Duxbury Press).

Head, K. (1998), Comment, in R. E. Baldwin, R. E. Lipsey and J. D. Richardson (eds), *Geography and Ownership as Bases for Economic Accounting*, Studies in Income and Wealth, Vol. 59, NBER, University of Chicago Press, Chicago, pp. 255–8.

Howenstine, N. G. and W. J. Zeile (1992), 'Foreign Direct Investment in the United Stages: Establishment Data for 1987', *Survey of Current Business*, October, pp. 44–58.

Kumar, M. S. (1984), 'Comparative Analysis of UK Domestic and International Firms', *Journal of Economic Studies*, Vol. 11, No. 3, pp. 26–42.

Kumar, N. (1990), 'Mobility Barriers and Profitability of Multinational and Local Enterprises in Indian Manufacturing', *Journal of Industrial Economics*, Vol. XXXVIII, No. 4, pp. 449–63.

Maliranta, M. (1997), *Plant Productivity in Finnish Manufacturing*, ETLA–The Research Institute of the Finnish Economy Discussion Papers, No. 612, Helsinki.

Markusen, J. R. (1984), 'Multinationals, Multi-plant Economies and the Gains from Trade', *Journal of International Economics*, 16 (May), pp. 205–26.

Markusen, J. R. (1995), 'The Boundaries of Multinational Enterprises and the Theory of International Trade', *Journal of Economic Perspectives*, Vol. 9, No. 2 (Spring), pp. 169–89.

Martin, S. (1993), *Advanced Industrial Economics*, Oxford and Cambridge, MA, Basil Blackwell.

Mataloni, R. J. (2000), 'An Examination of the Low Rates of Return of Foreign-Owned U.S. Companies', *Survey of Current Business*, March, pp. 55–73.

McGuckin, R. H. and S. V. Nguyen (1995), 'On productivity and plant ownership change: new evidence from the Longitudinal Research Database', *RAND Journal of Economics*, Vol. 26, No. 2 (Summer), pp. 257–76.

Moden, K.-M. (1998), 'Foreign acquisitions of Swedish companies: Effects on R&D and Productivity', IUI, Stockholm, mimeo.

OECD (1996), *Globalisation of Industry*, Paris.

Oulton, N. (1998a), *Investment, Capital and Foreign Ownership in UK Manufacturing*, National Institute of Economic and Social Research (NIESR) Discussion Paper, No. 141, August.

Oulton, N. (1998b), *Labour Productivity and Foreign Ownership*, NIESR Discussion Paper, No. 143, September.

Pfaffermayr, M. (1999), 'Ownership Advantages, Foreign Production and Productivity – Evidence from Austrian Manufacturing', *Review of Industrial Organisation*, No. 15(4), pp. 379–96.

Porter, M. E. (1990), *The Competitive Advantage of Nations*, Cambiridge, MA, Harvard University Press.

Rogers, W. H. (1992), 'Quantile Regression Errors', *Stata Technical Bulletin*, No. 9, pp. 16–19.

Scherer, F. M., A. Bechstein, E. Kaufer and R. D. Murphy (1975), *The Economics of Multi-Plant Operation: An International Comparison Study*, Cambridge, MA, Harvard University Press.

Sutton, J. (1991), *Sunk Cost and Market Structure: Price Competition, Advertising and the Evolution of Concentration*, Cambridge, MA, MIT Press.

Ylä-Antilla, P. and J. Ali-Yrkkö (1997), 'Foreign owners set their sights higher than local ones', *Unitas*, No. 2, pp. 14–19.

Zeckhauser, R. J. and J. Pound (1990), 'Are Large Shareholders Effective Monitors? An Investigation of Share Ownership and Corporate Performance', in G. Hubbard (ed.), *Asymmetric Information, Corporate Finance and Investment*, Chicago, University of Chicago Press.

3
(Why) do Foreign-owned Firms in Germany Achieve Above-average Productivity?

Lutz Bellmann and Rolf Jungnickel

1 Introduction

The aim of this chapter is to analyse whether productivity differentials between industrial firms can be explained by foreign ownership. The question if and why foreign-owned firms (FOFs) achieve higher productivity than indigenous firms is less ambitious compared with the aim of numerous studies that try to assess the effect of inward foreign direct investment (FDI) on the domestic economy. It is, nonetheless, highly relevant for economic policy. Labour productivity is a key factor for the development of the labour market. It determines both the volume of labour input and the income potential. If FOFs were more productive than indigenous firms, one could assume that more FDI would increase the domestic income level.[1] The effect on the demand for labour is less clear: the demand for labour would be expected to fall to the extent to which the growth of hourly productivity exceeds that of production. In this case, without a reduction in working hours the manpower requirements would decrease. On the other hand, increased productivity can mean improved competitiveness and thereby open up new employment opportunities. To explain the development of productivity is therefore one of the central tasks of labour market research. The question why differences in productivity may exist is of interest since if FOFs have above-average productivity, this is not necessarily because of differing behaviour. It may well be the result of differences in the structure of foreign as compared with domestic firms, or may follow from integration into an international business network regardless of whether it is German or foreign-controlled.

The starting point of our analysis is an overview of the position of FOFs in the German economy in an international comparison (Section 2). We then develop our expectations on the basis of the received theories of FDI and on evidence available from other studies (in section 3). Part 4 gives the description of the database and methodology. In the main part 5 of the chapter, these hypotheses are then confronted with empirical evidence from Germany. We approach our topic both from a sectoral perspective and on the basis of micro data available from the Institute for Employment Research (IAB) establishment panel, a unique data source that allows one to distinguish between foreign-owned and indigenous establishments and provides extensive information on structural characteristics. In the final section we draw some conclusions for economic policy in Germany.

2 Position of foreign-owned firms in the German economy

The position of foreign-owned firms (which is indicated by the level of inward FDI) is of interest in three ways. First, it shows the relevance of the issue in Germany in comparison with the situation in other countries. Second, the sectoral structure can give indications of where FOFs may affect the host economy and, third, differentiating between source countries can be of interest for the implications in the host economy.

With an inward FDI stock of DM472 billion (US$257 billion) at the end of 1999, Germany is an important host to foreign investors. According to the United Nations Conference on Trade and Development (UNCTAD, 2000) compilations it is, along with the Netherlands (whose FDI statistics are heavily pushed up by holdings with few employment effects), the forth-ranked host country behind the USA, China and the UK. The over 12,000 FOFs had sales of more than US$600 billion and over 1.8 million employees. However, German locations seem to have fallen behind in the past decades. Although the FDI stock at the end of 1999 was almost six times the 1980 value, the growth was slower than that of worldwide FDI (Table 3.1) and it was far behind the development of FDI in Western European countries (UNCTAD, 2000) which are the main competitors for internationally mobile investment. The share of Germany in Western European inward FDI (about 12 per cent) is clearly below the share in GDP (23 per cent). However, most of the falling behind took place in the 1980s and not in the early 1990s when fears were raised about the dwindling quality of Germany as a business location *(Standort Deutschland)*. Employment and sales data show a slightly differing picture insofar as Germany's position has declined clearly even in the 1990s.

This development is in contrast not only to the expanding FDI in other countries but also to German outward FDI which showed a rate of increase slightly above the international average. German firms have

Table 3.1   Foreign-owned affiliates in Germany and worldwide, 1980–99

Foreign-owned affiliates	Germany				Worldwide			
	1980	1990	1999	99/90 (%)	1980	1990	1999	99/90 (%)
FDI stock (US$ bn.)	40	113	226	(200)	495	1,761	4,015	(228)
Employment (1000)	1,536	1,789	1,849	(103)	17,433	23,605	40,536	(172)
Sales (US$ bn.)	227	499	686	(137)	2,462	5,503	13,564	(246)

Source: UNCTAD (2000); Deutsche Bundesbank.

employed more persons abroad (outward employment) than foreign firms in Germany (inward employment) since 1980 and the sales value of German affiliates abroad surpassed that of FOFs in Germany in 1995. While inward employment developed roughly in line with the domestic employment level, outward employment increased much faster. The relation of the two to domestic employment figures therefore shows a fundamentally different development (Figure 3.1). The question underlying our discussion of the productivity of FOFs as against domestic firms therefore is if and to what extent Germany forgoes income gains as a consequence of the gap in inward FDI. In other European economies the question is rather about the effects of the expansion of existing FDI.

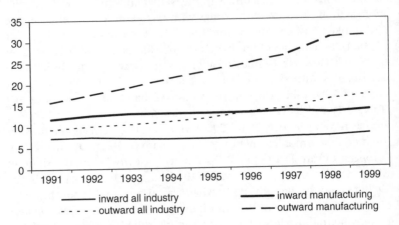

[a] Employment with FOFs in Germany and German affiliates abroad in per cent of employment in Germany, manufacturing and all enterprises.
Source: Deutsche Bundesbank; Statistisches Bundesamt; own calculations.

Figure 3.1   Employment with foreign affiliates of German firms and foreign-owned affiliates in Germany[a]

The operations of FOFs in Germany are characterized by two trends:

• the growth of services at the expense of manufacturing; and
• the growth of intra-European FDI at the expense of US investors.

Manufacturing has lost much of its formerly dominant position (Table 3.2). This process is exaggerated in the FDI statistics since the rapid expansion of holding companies[2] drives up the share of services although they often are busy in manufacturing. However, data on sales and employment (which are more relevant for economic development in Germany) also display a bias towards services although at a slower rate. FDI and employment data are not always consistent. For example, FDI in trade increased at a rate clearly below average while employment in these affiliates increased by 30 per cent above average. In the finance sector the reverse development took place: employment receded while FDI expanded rapidly. In terms of employment, manufacturing is still the dominant field of activity of FOFs.

Table 3.2 Sectoral structure of inward FDI in Germany, 1990 and 1999[a]

Sector	FDI stock (DM bn.)			Sales (DM bn.)			Employment (1000)		
	1990	1999	99/90 %	1990	1999	99/90 %	1990	1999	99/90 %
Total	183	471	257	806	1,260	156	1,789	1,849	103
Manufacturing	96.8	167	173	464	613	132	1,242	1,070	86
Services	84.8	299	354	339	626	185	543	738	136
Trade	37	70	185	256	415	162	264	356	135
Finance	18	79	443	28	44	160	71	52	73
Transportation communication	1.7	6.4	380	16	39	243	34	69	203
Business services	(4.0)	11	265	14	26	182	64	134	209
Holdings	13	105	800	1.6	34	2,139	7	5	71

[a] Development 1990 to 1999 calculated on the basis of rounded figures.
Source: Deutsche Bundesbank; own calculations.

The distribution of manufacturing employment across industries is much less concentrated than in foreign affiliates of German firms. While the big sectors – chemical industry, mechanical engineering and automobiles – are in the lead in absolute terms, smaller sectors, such as tobacco, mineral oil and office machinery/computers, display much higher shares of FOFs (see Table A3.1 in the Appendix). Foreign

investors have a stronger position in human capital-intensive industries than in those industries characterized by low human capital-
intensity, as can be seen from Figure 3.2. However, FOFs in Germany
are much less concentrated in these industries than foreign affiliates of
German firms (outward FDI).

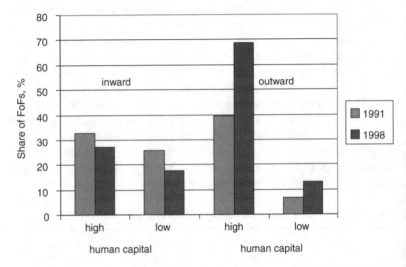

[a] Sales of foreign affiliates in Germany (inward) and German affiliates abroad (outward) in
per cent of total sales of the respective German industries. Human capital intensity defined
as average wages and salaries per employee.
Source: Deutsche Bundesbank; Statistisches Bundesamt; own calculations.

Figure 3.2   Internationalization in human capital intensive industries,[a] 1991
and 1998

Over 97 per cent of all inward FDI is from industrialized countries
with the EU (15), the USA and Switzerland accounting for as much as
92 per cent. The former dominance of US investors has been overcome
since the 1980s.[3] It was succeeded by a 'Europeanization' of the inward
investment links. While the integration of production lagged behind
the integration of markets in the EC for a long time, it took off in the
1980s when the companies prepared for the internal market, and it
continued to intensify in the EU of the 1990s. Western European
investors dominate both in terms of sales and employment of the
affiliates as they are published by the Bundesbank (Table 3.3).
Although the trend towards Europeanization is overrated in these statistics since third-country firms investing in Germany often do so via
holdings in the Netherlands,[4] it seems clear that about two-thirds of

the activities of FOFs in Germany is intra-Western Europe and roughly half is intra-EU. The high share of European investors may have implications for the productivity differentials of FOFs as compared to German firms if the home country matters for the productivity level, as has been suggested by a study on FOFs in the UK (Oulton, 1998).

Table 3.3 'Europeanization' of foreign-controlled production[a] in Germany

Source country	All industries				Manufacturing			
	1990		1999		1990		1999	
	absol.	%	absol.	%	absol.	%	absol.	%
All countries								
No. employees	1,789	100	1,849	100	1,242	100	1,070	100
Sales	806	100	1,260	100	464	100	613	100
Western Europe								
No. employees	1,277	71	1,331	72	829	67	750[b]	70[b]
Sales	537	67	939	75	278	60	431[b]	70[b]
USA								
No. employees	505	28	493	27	405	33	314	29
Sales	237	29	277	22	178	38	172	28

[a] Sales in DM bn.; no. of employees in 1,000s
[b] Partly estimated
Source: Deutsche Bundesbank; own calculations.

3 Hypotheses

The prevailing theoretical approaches to explain FDI focus on the point that FDI is undertaken in order to exploit more fully the investor's existing competitive advantage (or 'knowledge capital') at foreign locations or to develop such advantages by combining domestic and foreign resources (Dunning, 1980; Markusen, 1998). Therefore it is associated with a transfer of those factors that make up the competitive strength of the companies involved (the ownership or O-factor in Dunning's terminology). Competitive advantages can consist of proprietary knowledge, such as technology, management or organizational know-how. Since those O-factors are often of a public good character within the respective firm (Caves, 1996), their transfer to, and additional use in, foreign subsidiaries does not impair their employment at home. The transfer of superior knowledge by way of headquarter services leads to improved productivity at the receiving foreign subsidiary (as well as to spillovers to the host economy). From this, it is often concluded that FOFs achieve a productivity advantage over domestic firms (Davies and Lyons, 1991; OECD, 1994;

Oulton, 1998). Similarly, productivity advantages can be achieved by extended possibilities for specialization within company-wide international production and technological networks that provide good conditions for the exchange and transfer of knowledge.

One could argue against such a conclusion by saying that firms, when they organize their intra-group division of labour, do not necessarily have high-productivity operations in the host countries (Doms and Jensen, 1998, p. 235). These activities could equally be kept in the home country while low-income assembly operations are located abroad. If high-productivity operations are performed abroad, it is far from clear that what is 'high productivity' within the foreign multinationals also is 'high productivity' by German standards. Furthermore, the individual host countries (or locations) will compete for these operations. Although there is no obvious reason why foreign investors should not locate high-value activities in high-income Germany, it is, therefore, an empirical question whether FOFs in Germany achieve productivity advantages over indigenous firms.

A number of studies have dealt with this question. They almost unanimously confirm a productivity advantage of FOFs over the host country firms. Statistical compilations of the OECD (1999, p. 23) and UNCTAD (1999) for a number of countries clearly support the thesis as well. Howenstine and Zeile (1994) show, on the basis of a joint data set of foreign affiliates and domestic establishments in the USA, that the foreign-owned establishments have a productivity lead of 40 per cent over their domestic counterparts. Oulton (1998), in a study using the British longitudinal database of the Census of Production, ascertains a substantial 60 per cent higher output and 40 per cent higher value added per employee for foreign-owned firms. And Griffith (1999), in a study on foreign ownership in the British industry, finds even larger differences in favour of FOFs.[5]

The general hypothesis that FOFs achieve a productivity advantage over national firms needs some qualification. If FOFs achieve a high productivity level as a consequence of transfers from the parent company or from other companies of the investor's group, or if proprietary knowledge is mutually exchanged, it cannot be assumed that the subsidiaries are more productive than the parent company; it should be the other way round. Furthermore, there is reason to believe that this should hold true for any multinationals regardless of the countries concerned. This means that the superiority of foreign-owned firms can only be assumed over indigenous firms that are not part of a multinational network (Doms and Jensen, 1998).[6] Why should, for example,

Ford and Opel in Germany be more productive than Daimler, BMW and Volkswagen? The more internationalized the domestic firms, the smaller would be the productivity advantage of FOFs. Doms and Jensen (1998, pp. 245) show that domestic multinationals even in the USA are ahead of FOFs which, in their turn, operate with clearly higher productivity than domestic firms with no foreign assets. The basic hypothesis of our Chapter (H1) therefore reads as follows:

FOFs in Germany enjoy a productivity advantage over purely nationally operating firms but not – or less so – over multinationals headquartered in Germany.

From this, one could conclude that the advantage should be larger in East Germany than in the West since eastern firms are less internationalized. In view of a general lack of managerial resources in East Germany and its less developed business infrastructure and industrial capacities, one would expect that FOFs play a more important role there than in West Germany. In the case of any supply bottlenecks they have the option of falling back on the entire company´s resources. This relation could, however, be blurred to some extent by substantial weight of the high-productivity affiliates of West German investors in the East.

It may be argued that FDI in highly developed countries such as Germany nowadays mostly takes the form of mergers and acquisitions (M&A) instead of greenfield investments (UNCTAD, 2000; Wortmann, 2000) and that M&A are only a transfer of ownership with no substantial knowledge transfer to the acquired firm. Then, a strong performance by the firm to be acquired can be considered a factor that makes it attractive for a foreign investor. Productivity advantage of FOFs could reflect a successful strategy on the side of the foreign investor of picking the winners (Oulton, 1998, p. 42). This causes interpretation problems. Differences in the performance of foreign and domestic firms cannot simply be interpreted as 'effects' of the ownership situation. Such interpretation problems could be aggravated by a change of internationalization strategies from traditional market strategies towards asset-seeking and efficiency-seeking (Dunning, 1998; Borrmann *et al.*, 2001). Asset-seeking can go along with productivity advantages of the acquired firm. Intra-company flows of proprietary knowledge may increasingly be characterized by mutual exchange. There may indeed even be a 'reverse' transfer of knowledge from the acquired firm to the parent company rather than – or in addition to – a transfer from the parent to the subsidiary.

However, from this it cannot be concluded that the foreign owner-ship factor is irrelevant from the outset. First, there is a theoretical argument: the investor has to improve the efficiency of the acquired firm in order to be able to pay a premium above the market price to the former owner to make him sell the company. Second, the evidence available suggests that there is indeed a foreign ownership factor. Griffith and Simpson (2001) show that British firms which were foreign-owned over the entire 23-year period covered not only report an above-average productivity level but also clearly higher productivity growth rates than firms that were taken over during that period. The lead thus cannot (only) be the result of picking-the-winner strategies.

Concerning our second question, why FOFs achieve a productivity advantage, it is obvious that foreign ownership (FO) affects productiv-ity (as well as company performance in general) because of the inflow of resources from the foreign investor, be it labour, capital or know-how. We follow an analysis of these factors suggested by Davies and Lyons (1991) and later extended in a number of other studies, for example, Howenstine and Zeile (1994); Oulton (1998); Doms and Jensen (1998) and Griffith (1999 and 2001).[7] According to these studies, foreign ownership can and does affect productivity in various ways:

1 Influence via industry composition: FOFs are concentrated in knowledge-intensive industries where there are good conditions for the formation of proprietary knowledge and for the international intra-company spread of this knowledge. These industries are pri-marily those which operate at above-average productivity. Even if FOFs, therefore, were not more efficient than their domestic coun-terparts in the same industry, they would show a productivity lead over the average of the host country's firms because of their higher weight in high-productivity industries. This sort of influence was named 'structural effect' by Davies and Lyons (1991).

2 Influence via size: FOFs achieve higher productivity since they are often larger than domestic firms. They can take advantage of the favourable financing opportunities available in big internationally widespread firms. By their integration into the intra-group interna-tional production networks they have an improved chance of spe-cialization and thus of realizing economies of scale. In the following we subsume the size factor under the heading 'structural factors'.

3 Influence via input of other production factors: associated with the development and utilization of company-specific competitiveness is

the above-average input of productivity-enhancing factors such as a qualified workforce and research and development (R&D). For example, the absorption and use of know-how supplied by the parent company will often depend on the use of highly qualified specialists which is tantamount to a respective difference between FOFs and domestic firms as regards wages and salaries per head.

These three kinds of influence have been shown in the various studies mentioned above to be largely responsible for the productivity advantage of FOFs although there are differences in detail. According to Howenstine and Zeile (1994), the productivity lead of FOFs in the USA over national firms is largely attributed to their concentration in high-productivity industries. However, within-industry differences remain. In almost half of the 312 industries the remaining advantage of FOFs is more than 10 per cent. These differences result from the larger plant size, higher capital-intensity, and superior skill level of the employees. Other (not observed) factors which are subsequently subsumed under 'foreign ownership (FO) *per se*' have no additional influence. Similarly, Griffith (1999), in her study on the British car industry, finds that the lead is largely due to differences in factor input. Foreign-owned firms invest more capital, source more intermediate inputs and pay their employees higher wages. However, a 5–10 per cent output-per-employee advantage remains even after differences in factor input are taken into account. Oulton (1998) arrives at similar conclusions. He also produces evidence of a significant influence of FO *per se*, namely in the form of a specific advantage of US-owned establishments in the UK. This suggests that the home country of the investor matters.

Theoretical reasoning and the results of international studies lead to the formulation of the second hypothesis to be examined, which can be expressed as follows:

Productivity advantages of FOFs result from 'structural' factors, input of high-quality production factors and 'FO per se'.

Distinguishing these factors is not without problems since they are not independent of one another. For example, the knowledge-intensity of an industry can go hand-in-hand with above-average employment of qualified labour, and bigger firm size will often mean higher capital-intensity. As such, the statistical distribution of the total ownership effect will always contain a degree of uncertainty.

4 Database and methodology

The testing of our two hypotheses is based on two different sources of information on the internationalization of German firms.

1 The German statistics on international capital links (Deutsche Bundesbank, 2000) which includes – besides the FDI stock – some operating data on FOFs, the number of enterprises, employees, turnover, total assets, although on an aggregate level.
2 The IAB establishment panel, which provides information on German and foreign-owned establishments in Germany. The IAB panel is a unique data set, which allows for the analysis and characterization of foreign-owned firms (or rather plants). It is therefore described here in some detail (see Box 3.1).

Box 3.1 The IAB Establishment Panel

The IAB Establishment Panel supplies information on the labour market´s demand side and some operational data of the establishments surveyed. The Institute for Employment Research of the Federal Labour Services in Germany (Institut für Arbeitsmarkt-und Berufsforschung der Bundesanstalt für Arbeit, or IAB) started the panel in Western Germany in 1993. Since 1996 the survey has been conducted in East Germany, too (cf. Bellmann, 1997a and 1997b; Kölling, 2000).

Proceeding from a base random sample in the first panel wave in 1993 which comprised 4,265 cases, all establishments were, where possible, questioned again in the following years. The East German panel started in 1996 with 4,313 establishments. The number of establishments interviewed in East and West Germany reached approximately 14,000 by 2000. About 11 per cent of total employment in Germany is covered. The large number of units included in the data set allows consistency checks and data cleaning procedures which might not be possible in small firm samples.

Characteristics of the sample

The basis for the German Establishment Panel is the employment statistics register of the Federal Employment Services

---

(Bundesanstalt für Arbeit) which is collected via the compulsory social insurance procedure. That means that all firms with employees who are included in the social security system are covered and not only those that take up loans, as in the samples used, for example, by Birch (1987) and Howland (1988). The unit in the survey is not the company as a legal entity but the establishment as the local entity. This is advantageous, as establishments are normally less affected by restructuring measures than companies. Furthermore, the data needed for the analyses, such as turnover, working times, wage and salary bill, and so on are immediately available to those questioned. Another crucial factor in favour of an 'establishment' concept is that the panel, by linking it to the Federal Employment Institute's establishment data bank, provides a reliable basis for both longitudinal and cross-sectional weighting and projection. This is, however, not important in our context. From those establishments included in the employment statistics register a stratified sample is drawn using selection probabilities which depend on the variation of the number of employees in the respective stratum. All in all, 16 industries and 10 sizes of class are considered.

The project is supported by the tripartite organs of the German Federal Employment Services, including the Federation of German Employer Organizations. The field work is done by Infratest Sozialforschung, Munich. Although the participation of firms is voluntary, the response rates are over 70 per cent. The response rate of repeatedly interviewed establishments in the following waves is higher than 80 per cent.

Identification of foreign-controlled firms

While, in East Germany, the question about foreign ownership has been included each year, for West German plants we have information on foreign ownership in the year 2000 only. In some cases, the identification of FOFs may be not perfect in the panel since the respondents may not know about the ultimate ownership of the firm, or they might not feel 'foreign' although they formally are. However, this should not significantly bias the results.

Although these databases do not allow as detailed an analysis as is possible, for example, on the basis of the Doms and Jensen (1998) and the Griffith and Simpson (2001) data, they enable us to improve significantly the currently available information on the operation of FOFs in Germany. The testing of our basic hypothesis, H1, demands a comparison of FOFs with the average of German firms and with domestic multinational firms. This is possible only to a limited extent since the outward direct investments of German firms were surveyed only in the 1998 wave, when the panel was considerably smaller than in 2000, while the FO question was only included in the 2000 wave.[8] Domestic firms with outward FDI therefore cannot be compared with FOFs in the same year. We can only compare foreign-owned and German establishments for the year 1999 and German establishments with and without direct investments for 1997. In order to reduce this problem we also use a proxy for the multinationality, namely an export quota of at least 30 per cent. This seems to be acceptable since firms with high exports are as exposed to international competition as firms with FDI and – due to their business extending beyond the home country – they can equally realize economies of scale in headquarters services and production.

Unfortunately, no value-added data is available on a sufficient scale[9] so that we are unable to calculate the 'real' productivity. We therefore take 'turnover per employee' as a proxy for productivity. Turnover in manufacturing is, on average, almost three times as high as the value added since it includes inputs and end products purchased from other companies. The explanatory power of this indicator is limited to the extent that there are differences between foreign and national firms in terms of cost of material and other inputs and traded items. Oulton (1998, p. 10) and Griffith and Simpson (2001, p. 15) show that FOFs indeed have significantly higher sourcing ratios than British firms.[10] Turnover productivity would thus overstate their lead. We reduce this problem by a twofold selection. First, we include manufacturing establishments/firms only, so trading companies are thus excluded. Second, we select (from the IAB panel) only establishments with 50 or more employees. In this way, we intend to exclude most of those FOFs which realize the bulk of their sales through the distribution of products from other companies in the group rather than through their own production.

The analysis of the determinants of the productivity advantage starts with some comparative characterizations of the FOFs´ structure and performance compared with domestic firms. We then focus on multivariate regressions in order to explain productivity and control for variables other than foreign ownership. When doing this, it has to be kept in mind, on the one hand, that foreign ownership (or rather the integration into a multinational network) can affect productivity not only in a direct way but also via the structural characteristics of FOFs and via differences in the input of production factors. To the extent that foreign ownership exerts an influence on productivity-enhancing factors such as size, sectoral composition, input of qualified labour and capital input, these factors cannot strictly be considered as exogenous variables. On the other hand, they cannot be considered as fully dependent of foreign ownership. Firms can employ qualified labour and operate at a bigger size without being foreign-controlled, and if foreign investors successfully pursue 'picking-the-winner' strategies the good performance of the acquired firms may have little to do with foreign ownership. We therefore proceed in two steps. First, we run regressions in order to find out if foreign ownership *per se* compared with other relevant factors plays a role as a determinant of the level of productivity. Second, we examine the relationship of foreign ownership and those factors that were found to be relevant for productivity in order to get an indication of the more indirect effects on productivity.

This work is based on the IAB panel in order to take into account the heterogeneity of the firms within the aggregate. As has been mentioned above, a problem with this database is that foreign ownership is not observed throughout, which makes it difficult to determine the causality. A statistically significant relation of foreign ownership and productivity may be the result of foreign ownership as well as the outcome of a successful 'picking-the-winner' strategy. This problem can only be dealt with briefly in the following. Some conclusions can be drawn, however, from studies available for other countries.

5 Empirical evidence

Productivity advantage

Theoretical reasoning and evidence from other countries lead to the presumption that foreign-owned firms enjoy a substantial productivity advantage over the average of German firms and that the advantage is non-existent or smaller when FOFs are compared with German multinationally operating firms/plants (H1). This view is indeed strongly supported by the operating data of foreign and domestic firms in Germany, although the evidence concerning the comparison with German multinationals is less clear-cut.

1 The sales per employee (our proxy for productivity) in foreign-owned manufacturing firms as reported by the Bundesbank (DM560,000, Table A3.1, col. 6) show a lead of over 50 per cent over the national average (DM359,000, col. 11)[11] in 1998.

2 The IAB panel shows – for the year 1999 – that the lead is twice as high in East Germany (100 per cent) as in the West (50 per cent, Table 3.4). This is fully in line with our expectation that the FOFs´ advantage diminishes with the multinationality of the host economy. East German manufacturing affiliates of West German firms (not separately shown in the table) report a level of productivity which is nearly as high as that of FOFs in East Germany (Bellmann *et al.* forthcoming, 2002; Wahse, 2001). This does not contradict our argument; it actually supports it since one can expect that most West German investors in the East are indeed multinationals themselves which achieve above-average productivity.

Table 3.4 Productivity[a] in East and West German manufacturing by type of establishment, 1999

	Establishments[b]					
	All		50+ employees		Exports >/= 30% of sales	
West Germany						
German-owned	212	(64)	258	(77)	276	(78)
Foreign-owned	330	(100)	337	(100)	353	(100)
Total	222	(67)	274	(81)	286	(81)
East Germany						
German-owned	125	(48)	179	(59)	208	(77)
Foreign-owned	261	(100)	303	(100)	271	(100)
Total	129	(49)	188	(62)	217	(80)

[a] Sales per employee in DM1,000; figures in brackets are index figures; FOFs = 100
[b] Total number of observations: 3,292; foreign-owned: 294. When export quota >/= 30%, $N = 622$; foreign-owned: 158.
Source: IAB Establishment Panel; own calculations.

3 On the other hand, the sectoral pattern of the FOFs´ advantage gives no real support to our expectation that the advantage decreases with the degree of internationalization of the German firms in the respective sector (Figure A3.2). For example, the productivity of FOFs in the highly internationalized chemical industry is far ahead of the productivity of all domestic firms, while there is only a small lead in mechanical engineering, textiles/clothing, paper and sporting goods and so on although these industries are less-than-averagely internationalized.

4 Firms with FDI have an advantage over firms that have not invested abroad. According to the 1997 data, this holds both for West and East Germany, although the edge is bigger in the East (Table 3.5). However, the lead of German foreign investors over purely domestic firms in 1997 is only half the advantage of foreign-owned firms over domestic ones in 1999. This leads to the presumption that FOFs realize an advantage even over German multinationals.[12] When a strong export orientation (exports at least 30 per cent of sales) is taken as the criterion for multinationality of German firms, we also obtain the expected results (Table 3.4). Strong exporters achieve considerably higher productivity than the firms with few or no exports while, in the case of FOFs, the export orientation does not link up with substantial further productivity increases. The productivity advantage of FOFs over strong domestic exporters is thus about half the advantage over indigenous exporting firms which export less or not at all.

Table 3.5 Productivity[a] of German multinationals in manufacturing compared with domestic firms,[b] 1998 (DM1,000)

Establishments		All	
West Germany	no FDI	193	(73)
	with FDI	264	(100)
	total	207	(78)
East Germany	no FDI	129	(67)
	with FDI	193	(100)
	total	130	(67)

[a] Sales per employee in DM1,000; figures in brackets are indices, FOFs = 100
[b] Total number of establishments: 1,691, 165 of which reported FDI.
Source: IAB Establishment Panel; own calculations.

Reasons

Before discussing the role of foreign ownership, we first ask if the productivity advantage of FOFs is the result of successful picking-the-winner strategies. In view of the high share of M&As, the presence of such strategies would be directly reflected in productivity differences. It could be indicated by the high significance of domestic R&D as a determinant of inward FDI in Germany (Borrmann *et al.*, 2001). It seems, however, that the 'foreign ownership' factor also works in either of the ways outlined above. Two circumstances speak in favour of this: (1) according to aggregated firm data of the Bundesbank, the productivity advantage prevails not only in industries where voluminous M&As

took place but in virtually all industries (see Figure A3.2). All values are in the upper part of the graph. (2) The advantage in absolute terms is rather stable over time (Figure 3.3) although the number of FOFs (and hence of M&As) and their weight in the economy did not increase substantially. Had it been the result of picking-the-winner strategies with no particular influence from the FO factor over time, the advantage should have decreased since there was no flow of productivity-enhancing resources from the investor to the acquired affiliate. The presumption that foreign ownership matters is reinforced by the evidence produced by Griffith and Simpson (2001) for the UK. They find that establishments that were foreign-owned over the entire period (1973–96) showed the strongest increase in productivity compared with establishments that changed ownership during that period or that remained British all the time. Clearly, for Germany similar longitudinal micro analyses are necessary in order to find robust evidence.

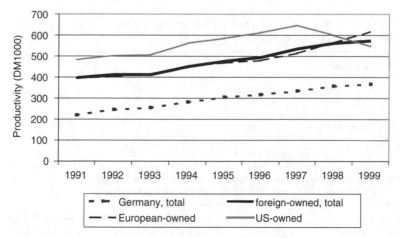

^a Sales per employee
Source: Deutsche Bundesbank; Statistisches Bundesamt; own calculations.

Figure 3.3   Productivity^a in German manufacturing: FOFs compared with the German average

Figure 3.3 also indicates that the home country can matter for productivity differences. US-based firms constantly had a significant advantage over EU-based firms (and even more over firms from other regions which are not incorporated in the graph). This is consistent with the above-mentioned evidence for the UK. However, the disruption from 1998 onwards (probably caused by some major disinvestments) raises doubts with regard to a generalization of a productivity hierarchy.

When dealing with the 'why' question, certain pointers are given by systematic differences between FOFs and DOFs. If there are special features of FOFs, it seems reasonable that these features have an influence on the performance of the firms. From a number of studies, we can presume that FOFs show a particular pattern in the industrial composition and size. We further explore that question by a probit analysis.

The results are displayed in Table 3.6. It can be seen that besides size and industrial composition, high wages, capital investments and exports significantly increase the probability of an establishment being foreign-owned. All this is in line with the results of former studies and with theoretical reasoning: to cover the fixed costs of doing business abroad, a foreign investor has to set up (or acquire) a business of sufficient size; high productivity requires qualified labour which means high wages, and the productivity-enhancing integration into an international business group goes along with increasing international (and often intra-company) transactions.[13] The technological level of machinery, however, turns out to be insignificant in East Germany and is even negatively related with FO in West Germany. The generally lower significance of the coefficients for East Germany is unexpected, but it may be the result of the low number of observations that could be included (53 FOFs).

Table 3.6   Estimate of probit models for foreign control of German manufacturing establishments, 1999[a] (number of employees >/= 50)

Variable	West Germany	East Germany
(log) of number of employees	0.208**(7.83)	0.428*(4.64)
(log) of investments per employee	0.062(2.82)	0.262*(5.08)
(log) of wage per employee	0.940**(11.50)	1.858**(8.43)
proportion of turnover exported	1.164**(14.02)	1.285*(4.23)
Rating of the technical state of the equipment as up to date (yes = 1; other = 0)	*–0.671**(14.84)*	*–0.626(2.00)*
Basis goods industries (yes = 1, other = 0)	0.806**(20.12)	–0.170(0.20)
Consumer goods industries (yes = 1, other = 0)	0.108(0.21)	0.225(0.28)
Intercept	–11.429**(23.53)	–21.676**(16.237)
Log-Likelihood Statistics	997.666	271.15
Pseudo R^2	0.127	0.178
Number of observations	1144	411

[a] Absolute *t*-values in parentheses.
* (**) significant for $\alpha = 0.05$ (0.01)
Source: IAB Establishment Panel; own calculations.

The results of the probit analysis lead to the presumption that the more indirect ways in which foreign ownership could affect productivity (i.e., via structural factors, wages, investment, and foreign trade) are indeed relevant in the case of Germany. According to previous studies, it can be presumed that firm/plant size and sectoral distribution play the most important role for the FOFs' lead in productivity, along with the input of high-quality labour.

First of all, concerning firm size, bigger firms and establishments in Germany operate at clearly higher productivity than small and medium-sized ones (Figure 3.4). The Bundesbank data show that FOFs are indeed larger than the average domestic firm. They employ on average almost twice as many people (318, as against 162) although, on average, they still have to be considered medium sized. The relative size of FOFs varies from sector to sector. In the manufacture of food, for example, FOFs are more than three times as big as the average firm in Germany, whereas in chemicals production the German firms are bigger. Figure 3.6 shows that FOFs have a productivity advantage over domestic medium-sized firms (100–999 employees) of about 60 per cent, and they even show a clear advantage (around 30 per cent) over the bigger firms (more than 1,000 employees) in Germany. The size factor, therefore, cannot explain much of the lead of FOFs. This also follows from a breakdown of the IAB establishment data by size. Foreign-owned plants with at least 300 employees report only slightly higher productivity than German-owned plants of a similar size whereas in the group with fewer than 300 employees the lead is as high as 85 per cent (Figure 3.5). We can thus conclude that although the average advantage of FOFs is to some extent the result of a higher share of bigger plants, the real productivity difference lies in the group of establishments with fewer than 300 employees. Productivity of FOFs does not increase with size.

Second, differences in the industrial structure can be assumed to explain (part of) the productivity difference since FOFs are concentrated on high productivity industries (Figure A3.1). To find out about the significance of this factor, we calculated sector-specific productivities of the FOFs (see Table A3.1, col. 6). These values were then weighted with the share of the respective sector in total manufacturing employment (col. 10) and added up to a hypothetic productivity (col. 7) which would have occurred if there had been no sectoral divergence of FOFs and DOFs. The average productivity of the FOFs then decreases by roughly 15 per cent from the actual DM560,000 to a fictitious DM483,000. The productivity advantage over domestic firms is thereby

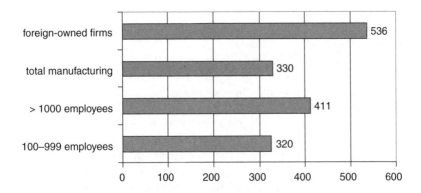

[a] Sales per employee
Source: Deutsche Bundesbank; Statistisches Bundesamt; own calculations.

Figure 3.4 Productivity[a] of foreign-owned manufacturing firms and firm size, 1997 (DM1,000)

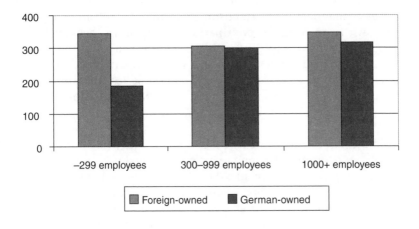

[a] Sales per employee
[b] West German manufacturing only
[c] grouped by number of employees
Source: IAB Establishment Panel; own calculations.

Figure 3.5 Productivity[a] of foreign- and German-owned[b] establishments by group size,[c] 1999 (DM1,000)

reduced by 35 per cent. That means that the concentration of FOFs in high-productivity sectors explains slightly more than one-third of their overall productivity advantage.

The relationship of FO and other important determinants of productivity was further examined by regression analyses reported in Table 3.7. They display a significant influence of the foreign control dummy on the wage level, exports and investments (Table 3.7a). These findings meet our expectations as set out above. Even if we narrow our comparison group of German establishments to those exporting at least 30 per cent of their sales (Table 3.7b), the FO factor exerts a significantly positive influence on the wages.[14] This means that FOFs pay higher wages than German multinationals. However, the effect on investment disappears and the relation to exports becomes negative: among the strong exporters, FOFs are less export-oriented.

These results mean that, in particular, part of the wage level´s statistically displayed influence on productivity has to be assigned to foreign ownership. This has to be kept in mind in the final step of our analysis where we explore the relative influence of the mentioned operating variables and 'foreign ownership *per se*'.

In the respective regressions we first compare FOFs with all German manufacturing establishments with over 50 employees and then with the German 'multinationals' which are defined by an export share of at least 30 per cent of sales (Table 3.8). The regressions are run separately for East and West Germany in order to test our proposition (H1) that FO *per se* should be less relevant in the West and when the comparison is done with multinationals only. They reveal the following:

1. In the model comprising all establishments with over 50 employees, all the factors included tend to increase the productivity and (what is most important in our context) the foreign-control dummy exerts an influence of its own. That means the productivity advantages cannot fully be explained by the above-mentioned indirect effects via structure, factor input and foreign trade. However, the statistical relationship does not necessarily follow from foreign ownership; it can also be a result of the integration into an international business network.
2. This question can be dealt with by restricting the German-owned comparison group to what we call 'multinationals' (export >/=30 per cent of sales). Then, the explanatory power of our estimates is reduced substantially, as was expected. This holds particularly for East Germany where only the wages are statistically significant. The influence of FO

Table 3.7 Regression estimates for the determinants of operating variables of manufacturing firms in Germany, 1999[a]

(a) Establishments with 50 + employees

Independent variable	Export % of turnover	(log) wage per employee	(log) investment per employee
foreign control (yes = 1, no = 0)	0.089** (5.70)	0.114** (5.11)	0.361* (2.05)
(log) of number of employees	0.053** (9.30)	0.057** (7.12)	0.472** (7.46)
East/West Germany (West = 1, East = 0)	0.077** (5.70)	0.275** (14.18)	–0.577** (3.73)
Basic goods industries (yes = 1, other = 0)	-0.024 (1.78)	–0.052** (2.62)	0.358* (2.32)
Consumer goods industries (yes = 1, other = 0)	–0.137** (9.43)	–0.168** (7.00)	–0.127 (0.77)
Intercept	–0.067* (2.14)	7.91** (177.90)	6.174** (17.54)
R^2	0.167	0.219	0.047
Corrected R^2	0.165	0.217	0.045
Number of cases	1,720	1,661	1,715

(b) Establishments with 50 + employees and export quota >/= 30%

Independent variable	Export% of turnover	(log) wage per employee	(log) investment per employee
foreign control (yes = 1, no = 0)	–0.145** (9.08)	0.071** (3.07)	0.066 (0.37)
(log) of number of employees	0.0139 (1.92)	0.031** (2.98)	0.487** (6.10)
East/West Germany (West = 1, East = 0)	0.038 (1.89)	0.240** (8.14)	–1.023** (4.52)
Basic goods industries (yes = 1, other = 0)	–0.0328 (1.91)	–0.086** (3.41)	0.615** (3.22)
Consumer goods industries (yes = 1, other= 0)	–0.131** (5.76)	–0.128** (3.89)	0.184 (0.73)
Intercept	0.429** (9.78)	8.135** (128.60)	6.60** (13.75)
R^2	0.144	0.137	0.068
Corrected R^2	0.139	0.132	0.062
Number of cases	817	775	805

[a] *t*-values in parentheses.
* (**) significant for $\alpha = 0.05$ (0.01)
Source: IAB Establishment Panel; own calculations.

per se on productivity disappears, which is no surprise in view of the strongly increased weight of high-productivity West German affiliates in the sample. They account for roughly half of the observations while there are only 30 per cent East German-owned firms. The still strong significance of FO *per se* in West Germany indicates that it is not only multinationality as such but foreign ownership that matters. This result is unexpected since the strong domestic competitors in West Germany should be able to achieve a productivity as high as FOFs.

Table 3.8　Regression estimates for the determinants of labour productivity in German manufacturing industries, 1999[a]

Variable	No. of employees >/= 50			No. of employees >/= 50 turnover exported >/= 30%	
	Germany	East	West	East	West
Foreign control	0.176**	0.212**	0.168**	0.130	0.175**
(yes = 1, no = 0)	(4.36)	(2.21)	(3.75)	(0.94)	(3.74)
(log) of number	0.054**	0.037	0.057**	0.093	0.035
of employees	(3.47)	(0.847)	(3.43)	(1.12)	(1.71)
(log) of investments	0.025**	0.023	0.026**	0.039	0.028**
per employee	(4.07)	(1.72)	(3.81)	(1.13)	(3.08)
(log) of wage	0.791**	0.807**	0.780**	0.607**	0.487**
per employee	(17.75)	(7.79)	(15.73)	(2.78)	(7.22)
Proportion of	0.334**	0.387**	0.316**	–0.206	0.308**
turnover exported	(5.21)	(2.61)	(4.42)	(0.69)	(3.09)
Rating of the technical state of the equipment as up to date	0.104**	0.166*	0.078*	0.292*	0.082
	(3.18)	2.38	(2.11)	(1.99)	(1.77)
East/West Germany	0.030				
(West = 1, East = 0)	(0.82)				
With 15 dummies for	yes	yes	yes	yes	yes
industrial affiliation	4.919**	4.760**	5.063**	6.194**	7.699**
Intercept	(13.43)	(5.62)	(12.01)	(3.24)	(13.14)
R^2	0.355	0.318	0.337	0.260	0.298
Corrected R^2	0.345	0.279	0.324	0.132	0.272
Number of cases	1,476	397	1,079	136	572

[a] Absolute *t*-values in parentheses.
* (**) significant for $\alpha = 0.05$ (0.01)
Source: IAB Establishment Panel; own calculations.

6 Summary and research perspectives

The foregoing analysis has confirmed the hypothesis that foreign ownership increases productivity. This effect is brought about not only by a concentration in high productivity sectors but also by the input of human and real capital and by integration into the international (and intra-group) division of labour. As opposed to the situation in indigenous firms and the results of other studies (see Chapter 2 in this volume), the productivity of FOFs does not seem to increase with plant size. On the other hand, 'foreign ownership *per se*', which carries unspecified effects, seems to exert a positive influence which is, however, stronger in West than in East Germany. This issue deserves further research in particular for East Germany where the role of West German-owned, compared with foreign-owned, firms should be studied in detail.

We found that in West Germany foreign ownership is linked with higher wages and productivity, even if FOFs are compared with German-based multinationals (defined by an export quota of at least 30 per cent). This tends to support a critical view of the low level of new inward FDI in the 1990s. The FOFs´ advantage is not compatible with the view that foreign investors avoid German locations because of German competitors being too strong. One could rather conclude that FDI flows directed to competing locations in Western Europe probably lead to income losses in Germany.

However, our analysis was only a first step of studying the characteristics of FOFs in Germany. Clearly more evidence is needed to arrive at more robust conclusions, (e.g., value-added data on a broader scale and information on the linkages with and spillovers to the German economy). Data about the development of FOFs and of German multinationals over time would be helpful to resolve the problem of causality and to assess if foreign ownership 'truly' increases labour productivity or if the statistical effect is caused by selective behaviour of firms picking the winners. Also, the methodology could be refined further: using interactive variables to take into account structural interruptions; treating foreign ownership as an endogenous variable; applying the Heckman correction, treatment effect models or matched pair approaches, which could lead to more robust results.

Appendix

Table A3.1   Foreign-owned firms in German manufacturing

1	2	3	4	5	6	7	8	9	10	11
	Foreign-owned firms						Total industry			
	Sales	Employees	Weight in industry		Sales per employee		Sales	Employees		Sales per employee
			Sales ($=2*100/8$)	Employees ($=3*100/9$)	Actual ($=2/3$)	Hypothetical[a] ($=6*10$)			Share	($=8/9*100$)
	DM bn.	1,000	%	%	DM1,000	DM1,000	DM bn.	1,000		DM1,000
All business activities	1,108	1,666	14.5	7.8	.	.	7,612	21,357	3.37	.
Manufacturing	564	1,007	24.8	15.9	560	483	2,276	6,331	1.00	359
Food products, beverages	49	73	21.5	12.7	668	(61)	227	575	0.09	394
Tobacco products	22	8	71.2	61.5	2,725	(6)	31	13	0.00	2,354
Textiles	3	11	9.2	8.7	264	(5)	32	127	0.02	249
Wearing apparel	3	8	11.5	10.1	325	(4)	23	79	0.01	286
Leather products	1	2	13.9	7.7	500	(2)	7	26	0.00	277
Wood, wood products	3	8	9.5	6.7	388	(7)	33	119	0.02	274
Pulp, paper, products	17	40	32.3	26.8	428	(10)	53	149	0.02	355
Publishing, printing, etc.	5	9	6.5	3.4	556	(23)	77	263	0.04	292
Petroleum products	77	9	73.9	42.9	8,600	(29)	105	21	0.00	4,986
Chemical products	77	120	33.3	24.4	639	(50)	230	492	0.08	467
Rubber, plastic products	22	65	23.2	18.7	332	(18)	93	348	0.05	267

Table A3.1 (continued)

1	2	3	4	5	6	7		8	9	10	11
	Foreign-owned firms							Total industry			
	Sales	Employees	Weight in industry		Sales per employee			Sales	Employees		Sales per employee
			Sales (= 2*100/8)	Employees (= 3*100/9)	Actual (= 2/3)	Hypothetical[a] (= 6*10)				Share	(= 8/9*100)
	DM bn.	1,000	%	%	DM1,000	DM1,000		DM bn.	1,000		DM1,000
Other non-metal mineral products	10	30	15.1	12.0	347	(14)		69	249	0.04	277
Basic metals	22	43	21.3	15.9	514	(22)		104	271	0.04	384
Fabricated metal products	20	64	14.1	10.8	308	(29)		140	591	0.09	236
Machinery and equipment	57	157	20.5	16.0	364	(57)		278	984	0.16	283
Office machinery, computers	16	20	55.1	40.8	805	(6)		29	49	0.01	596
Electrical machinery	20	57	13.5	11.9	358	(27)		151	480	0.08	315
Communications equipment	30	56	60.5	41.5	534	(11)		49	135	0.02	366
Medical optical instruments, watches	17	52	33.9	24.6	317	(11)		49	211	0.03	231
Motor vehicles	78	140	19.7	17.7	560	(70)		398	793	0.13	502
Other transport equipment	10	19	25.1	15.2	532	(10)		40	125	0.02	322
Furniture	4	13	6.8	5.8	292	(10)		56	225	0.04	248
Recycling	1	1	34.6	14.3	900	(1)		3	7	0.00	371

[a] Values for individual industries are weights only that add up to the hypothetical productivity in total manufacturing

* via information available

Source: Deutsche Bundesbank; Statistisches Bundesamt; own calculations.

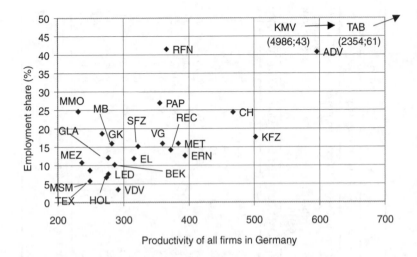

Abbreviations are for individual sectors: ADV – edp hardware; BEK – wearing apparel; CH – chemical industry; EL – electrical machinery n.e.s.; ERN – food, beverages; GK – rubber and plastic products; GLA – glass, ceramics; HOL – wood products; KFZ – car industry; KMV – petroleum products; LED – leather products; MB – machinery and equipment; MEZ – fabricated metal products; MET – metals; MMO – instruments, watches, etc.; MSM – furniture, sporting goods, musical instruments, etc.; PAP – pulp, paper, products; REC – recycling; RFN – consumer electronics; SFZ – other transport equipment; TAB – tobacco products; VDV – printing, publishing, reproduction of recorded media; VG – total manufacturing.

Source: Deutsche Bundesbank; Statistisches Bundesamt; own calculations.

Figure A3.1 Sectoral productivity and share of foreign-owned firms in manufacturing

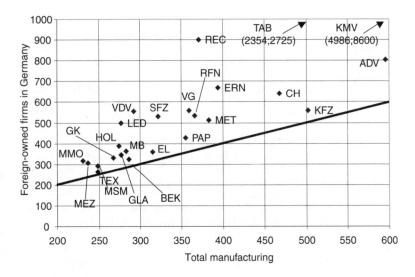

ª Abbreviations for individual sectors as Figure A3.1
Source: Deutsche Bundesbank; Statistisches Bundesamt; own calculations.

Figure A3.2   Productivity of German- and foreign-owned firms in comparison by sectorª

Notes

1 Of course, the underlying question is whether there is a potential for more inward FDI to Germany. This can, however, be presupposed given the high growth and volume of inward FDI in competing European countries (see UNCTAD, 2000).

2 Holding companies account for 23 per cent of the consolidated primary and secondary inward FDI in 1999, up from 7 per cent in 1990. If one considers primary FDI only, they account for as much as 61 per cent (€173 bn. out of €284 bn.).

3 Due to less detailed statistics being available prior to 1989, this process cannot be traced back for a longer period of time. Information of the Bundesbank on primary inward FDI show, however, that US- and Western European-owned affiliates in Germany were about the same size in terms of number of employees and sales in the mid-1980s. In terms of the stock of primary FDI (all industries), Western European investors already had a clear lead in 1985 (45 per cent vs 39 per cent) which thereafter increased significantly by 1999 (70 per cent vs 24 per cent).

4 The Bundesbank puts secondary (or indirect) FDI at 58 per cent of total 'Dutch' FDI in Germany. On the other hand, US FDI in Germany is underestimated by 20 per cent when the direct ownership concept is employed (Deutsche Bundesbank, 2001b, p. 70). According to the ultimate beneficial owner (UBO) concept, US affiliates (all industries) in Germany had 567,000 employees instead of 493,000 according to the German system which ties in with direct ownership. Even according to the UBO concept, the share of the EU 15 in total employment of FOFs in Germany (all industries) would be roughly 50 per cent at the end of 1999.

5 For a survey of the respective literature, see Chapter 2 of this volume.

6 What is subsequently named 'foreign ownership' factor should thus be understood as 'part of a multinational network'.

7 For a detailed literature survey see Chapter 2 of this volume.

8 For East Germany foreign ownership was asked about from the panel's inception.

9 From the information in the IAB panel, value-added data could, in principle, be calculated. However, the firms often did not give numbers for input costs so that value-added data may be not representative. The use of value added instead of sales data would imply a 40% smaller data base.

10 There is evidence that this problem may be less serious in Germany. This can be concluded from a comparison of value-added and turnover per employee of the affiliates of US firms in Germany. On the basis of value-added data, the advantage of manufacturing US affiliates is of a similar order of magnitude as on the basis of sales data (see Borrmann *et al.*, 2001).

11 These figures relate to a comparison with domestic firms with over 20 employees.

12 Multinationals are defined here as establishments that report own FDI activity. Unfortunately, a differentiation by the degree of internationalization is not possible.

13 This would also mean above-average purchases of intermediates and end products. However, this could not be included into the probit model for

reasons of matching data availability. The inclusion of the sourcing ratio would have resulted in a reduction of observations by about 40%.

14 The relationship with exports becomes negative which is a natural consequence of our definition of German 'multinationals' (exports >/= 30% of sales).

References

Armington, C. and M. Odle (1982), 'Small Business. How Many Jobs?', *Brookings Review*, 1, pp. 14–17.

Barell, R. and D. W. te Velde (2000), 'Catching-up of East German Labour Productivity in the 1990s', *German Economic Review*, 1, pp. 271–98.

Belitz, Heike *et al.* (1999), 'Der Beitrag ausländischer Investoren zum Aufbau wettbewerbsfähiger Wirtschaftsstrukturen in den neuen Bundesländern', Berlin, September (mimeo).

Bellmann, L. (1997a), 'Das Betriebspanel des IAB', in R. Hujer, U. Rendtel and G. Wagner (eds), *Wirtschafts-und sozialwissenschaftliche Panelstudien*, Sonderheft des Allgemeinen Statistischen Archivs, Heft 30, Göttingen, pp. 169–82.

Bellmann, L. (1997b), 'The IAB Establishment Panel with an Exemplary Analysis of Employment Expectations', *IAB Topics*, No. 20.

Bellmann, L. And M. Brussig (1999), 'Productivity Differences Between Western and Eastern German Establishments', *IAB Topics*, No. 37.

Birch, D.L. (1987), *Job Creation in America*, New York and London, The Free Press.

Bellmann, Lutz, Peter Ellguth and Rolf Jungnickel (Forthcoming 2002), 'Produktivitätsvorteile auslandskontrollierter Unternehmen?', IAB, Nuremberg.

Borrmann, Christine *et al.* (2001), *Standort Deutschland im internationalen Verbund*, Baden-Baden, Nomos.

Caves, R. (1996), *Multinational Enterprise and Economic Analysis*, 2nd edn, Cambridge, MA, Cambridge University Press.

Davies, S. and B. Lyons (1991), 'The productivity advantage of foreign owned firms in the UK', *Oxford Economic Papers*, Vol. 43, pp. 584.

Deutsche Bundesbank (2000), *International Capital Links*. Special Statistical Publication 10, Frankfurt, May.

Deutsche Bundesbank (2001a), *Kapitalverflechtung mit dem Ausland*, Statistische Sonderveröffentlichung 10, May.

Deutsche Bundesbank (2001b), 'Struktur der Kapitalverflechtung deutscher Unternehmen mit dem Ausland Ende 1999', *Monatsberichte*, April, pp. 61–76.

Doms, Mark E. and Bradford J. Jensen (1998), 'Comparing Wages, Skills, and Productivity between Domestically and Foreign-Owned Manufacturing Establishments in the United States', in R. E. Baldwin, (eds), *Geography and Ownership as Bases for Economic Accounting*, University of Chicago Press., 1998, pp. 235–55.

Dunning, John H. (1980), 'Towards an electic theory of international production: some empirical tests', in *Journal of International Business Studies*, Vol. 11, p. 9.

Dunning, John H. (1998), 'Location and the multinational enterprise: A neglected factor?', *Journal of International Business Studies*, 29, Columbia, pp. 45–66.

Griffith, Rachel (1999), 'Productivity and foreign ownership in the UK car industry', *IFS Working Paper* No. W99/11, London.

Griffith, Rachel and Simpson, Helen (2001), 'Characteristics of Foreign-Owned Firms in British Manufacturing', *Institute for Fiscal Studies*, London, March, mimeo.

Härtel, H.-H. and R. Jungnickel *et al.* (1998), *Strukturprobleme einer reifen Volkswirtschaft in der Globalisierung*, Baden-Baden, Nomos.

Howenstine, N. G. and W. J. Zeile (1994), 'Characteristics of foreign-owned U.S. manufacturing establishments', Survey of Current Business SCB, January, pp. 34–59.

Howland, M. (1988), 'Plant Closings and Worker Displacement: The Regional Issues', W. E. Upjohn Institute for Employment Research (mimeo).

Kölling, A. (2000), 'European Data Watch: The IAB-Establishment Panel, Schmollers Jahrbuch', *Zeitschrift für Wirtschafts-und Sozialwissenschaften*, No. 120, pp. 291–300.

Markusen, James (1998), 'Multinational enterprises and the theories of trade and location', in P. Braunerhjelm and K. Ekholm (eds), *The Geography of Multinational Firms*, Boston, Kluwer, pp. 9–32

Müller, G. (1999), 'Smaller Productivity Gap Between German Regions When Different Producer Prices Are Taken into Account'. Discussion paper, Institute for Economic Research, Halle.

OECD (1994), *The Performance of Foreign Affiliates in OECD Countries*, Paris.

OECD (1999), *Measuring Globalization. The Role of Multinationals in OECD Economies*, Paris.

Oulton, Nicholas (1998), 'Investment, capital and foreign ownership in UK manufacturing', *NIESR Discussion Paper* No. 141, London, August.

UNCTAD (1999), *World Investment Report 1999, Foreign Direct Investment and the Challenge of Development*, New York and Geneva.

UNCTAD (2000), *World Investment Report 2000*, Geneva and New York.

Wahse, J. (2001), 'Beschäftigungsentwicklung in auslandskontrollierten und exportierenden Betrieben Ostdeutschlands', paper prepared for a workshop on the IAB establishment panel, Magdeburg, 26 June 2001.

Wortmann, Michael (2000), *What is new about 'global' corporations? Interpreting statistical data on corporate internationalization*. WZB discussion paper FS 100-102, Berlin, December.

4

Locating Foreign Affiliates in Germany: The Case of Swedish MNEs[*]

Henrik Braconier and Karolina Ekholm

1 Introduction

Sweden is an important home country for multinational enterprises (MNEs). In particular, relative to its size, Sweden is the country of origin of a large number of large and highly internationalized MNEs. The fact that Germany is the largest economy in Europe and lies geographically close to Sweden makes it an attractive location for Swedish firms. Therefore, Germany has consistently been one of the most important host countries for Swedish MNEs.

This chapter examines the foreign activities by Swedish MNEs in Germany. The data used are based on surveys of Swedish manufacturing firms with producing affiliates abroad, which have been carried out by the Research Institute of Industrial Economics (IUI). On the basis of these data, we examine the performance of producing affiliates of Swedish MNEs located in Germany and draw comparisons with producing affiliates located in other countries. Moreover, we perform an econometric analysis in order to analyse how labour costs affect the Swedish MNEs' decision to locate affiliates in Germany and to what extent changes in labour costs in different locations affect the firms' demand for labour in Germany.

The chapter is organized as follows: in section 2, we compare German affiliates to affiliates located in other host countries, with

* We thank Rolf Jungnickel and participants in the HWWA workshop 'Foreign-Owned Firms – Are They Different?' in October 2000 for useful comments and suggestions. Financial support from the Swedish Bank Tercentary Foundation and the European Commission through the Socio-Economic Research (SER) Project on Labour Market Effects of Foreign Direct Investments is gratefully acknowledged.

respect to labour productivity, research and development (R&D) expenditure per employee, skill-intensity and export propensity. Section 3 discusses how the firms' decision to locate activities in a certain country is likely to be affected by labour costs in different locations. Section 4 estimates empirically how Swedish MNEs' decisions to locate in Germany are affected by labour costs in different locations and generates estimates of cross-wage elasticities. These provide information about whether workers employed in German affiliates are substitutes for, or complements to, workers employed in other locations. Finally, section 5 concludes.

2 The performance of German affiliates of Swedish MNEs

The data used in this study are based on a comprehensive survey of Swedish manufacturing firms with foreign-producing affiliates that has been carried out since the early 1970s. To date, the survey has been conducted seven times: 1970, 1974, 1978, 1986, 1990, 1994 and 1998.[1] The most interesting feature of this database is that it contains detailed information about each of the firms' foreign producing affiliates.

Tables 4.1 and 4.2 show the distribution of Swedish MNEs' affiliate employment and production based on these data. The figures in the tables are based on information about employment and production in foreign affiliates with at least some production activities, which means that pure sales affiliates are not included, whereas affiliates with production as well as sales activities are included.

The tables reveal two striking features of the relative importance of Germany as a host country for Swedish MNEs. First, it is evident that the relative importance of Germany has declined substantially since the early 1970s. In terms of employment, Germany's share of affiliate activities has decreased by about 4.5 percentage points (from about 18 to about 13.5 per cent). In terms of production, there has been a decrease of about 8.5 percentage points (from about 21 to about 12.5 per cent).

The tables also reveal that this decrease in relative importance as a host country is mirrored mainly by the increased relative importance of the USA. It is thus not the case that Swedish MNEs have tended to favour low-wage locations over Germany. Instead, they seem to have been much more oriented towards the USA in their locational strategy.

The second striking feature of the development of Germany's share of the foreign activities of Swedish MNEs is that there was a temporary

Table 4.1 The share of affiliate employees in selected countries, 1970–98 (%)

	1970	1974	1978	1986	1990	1994	1998
Developed countries:							
Western Europe	68.5	66.8	65.7	57.9	61.5	56.8	51.8
Belgium	3.3	3.7	4.1	3.4	2.9	3.4	3.6
France	7.1	9.0	10.6	5.8	4.4	4.1	6.0
Germany	**17.9**	**15.3**	**13.5**	**10.7**	**14.2**	**12.0**	**13.3**
Italy	8.5	8.1	6.9	11.6	9.3	11.1	10.0
The Netherlands	4.1	3.8	5.8	3.0	3.6	3.4	2.4
UK	7.6	7.0	9.6	6.2	11.5	8.4	5.3
Other Western Europe	20.0	19.9	15.2	17.2	15.6	14.4	11.2
USA	5.4	6.0	9.2	19.1	21.0	22.4	22.1
Other developed countries	4.3	4.9	4.1	4.9	3.8	3.7	4.8
Eastern and Central Europe	0.0	0.0	0.0	0.0	0.0	3.9	7.4
Developing countries:							
Brazil	11.6	13.0	10.3	6.9	5.9	5.7	4.8
India	6.7	5.7	1.5	1.8	1.4	1.8	2.2
Other developing countries	3.5	3.6	9.2	9.4	6.4	5.7	6.9

Source: Ekholm and Hesselman (2000).

Table 4.2 Percentage distribution of affiliate production in selected countries, 1970–98

	1970	1974	1978	1986	1990	1994	1998
Developed countries:							
Western Europe	72.5	72.5	70.2	67.2	72.0	63.0	53.3
Belgium	7.5	9.2	8.5	10.7	10.9	10.7	13.3
France	10.9	11.6	8.9	7.5	6.6	6.1	4.0
Germany	**21.1**	**20.6**	**17.0**	**14.5**	**20.6**	**14.1**	**12.4**
Italy	9.2	7.2	5.0	12.6	5.7	10.0	9.1
Netherlands	6.2	6.7	9.3	4.7	5.8	4.8	2.0
UK	4.6	4.1	8.6	4.9	10.0	8.3	4.0
Other Western Europe	13.0	13.1	12.9	12.3	12.4	9.0	8.5
USA	9.1	6.6	11.0	18.2	17.3	24.0	29.0
Other developed countries	4.6	6.4	4.8	5.1	3.9	4.0	6.6
Eastern and Central Europe	0.0	0.0	0.0	0.0	0.0	1.0	2.4
Developing countries:							
Brazil	5.1	6.7	8.5	4.9	4.3	4.0	5.8
India	3.0	1.6	0.6	0.6	0.5	0.3	0.4
Other developing countries	4.6	6.2	4.9	4.0	2.0	3.7	2.5

Source: Ekholm and Hesselman (2000).

increase between 1986 and 1990. In terms of employment, the share increased by 3.5 percentage points (from 10.7 to 14.2 per cent) whereas, in terms of production, the increase was about 6 percentage points (from 14.5 to 20.6 per cent). Part of the explanation is probably that the uncertainty about Sweden's status within the European Union which prevailed in the late 1980s gave Swedish MNEs stronger incentives to locate activities in EU countries (see Braunerhjelm and Ekholm, 1999). However, it is interesting to note that there was a particularly large expansion of activities in Germany and the UK, two of the largest EU countries in terms of their markets.[2]

It is evident that Germany's share of affiliate production has been higher than its share of affiliate employment for all years except the most recent one, 1998. One reason for the differences in the two distributions is that some firms have not reported the value of production for their affiliates and hence the distribution of employment is typically based on a larger number of observations than the distribution of production. Another explanation for this difference is that labour productivity differs between affiliates located in different host countries. In the case of Germany, the evidence suggests that labour productivity is, on average, higher than in other locations.[3]

In Table 4.3, we present a direct measure of labour productivity: value added per employee. Here, we have defined three different groups of countries for comparison: high-income Europe, low-income Europe, and high-income non-Europe. High-income Europe consists of all Western European countries except Ireland, Greece, Portugal and Spain. Low-income Europe consists of Greece, Portugal and Spain.[4]

Table 4.3   Value added per employee (SEK thousands)

	German affiliates	Industry	High-income Europe (Aff.)	Low-income Europe (Aff.)	High-income non-Europe (Aff.)
1970	37.5	36.2	33.6	24.5	47.9
1974	74.1	62.7	60.1	36.8	78.9
1978	117.3	110.0	93.4	59.5	103.5
1986	263.9	237.2	195.1	164.1	239.2
1990	343.9	304.1	312.1	269.0	258.0
1994	517.0	454.4	485.2	324.7	398.6
1998	598.8	472.6[a]	541.1	395.6	442.2

Note: All data are from the IUI database except industry figures for Germany which are from STAN (OECD, 1999) and are based on data for the manufacturing sector.
[a] Data for 1997.

High-income non-Europe, finally, consists of the USA, Canada, Japan, Australia and New Zealand.

From Table 4.3 it is evident that average value added per employee has consistently been higher in the German affiliates compared to affiliates located in other high-income European countries (as well as in low-income European countries). However, in the early 1970s, average value added per employee was higher in the high-income non-European countries (a group that is dominated by affiliates located in the USA).

This development is even clearer in Figure 4.1, which presents the average value added per employee in fixed prices.[5] It is evident that from 1978 onwards, the affiliates in Germany show higher average labour productivity than those in any of the country groups included for comparison. However, the gap between Germany and other high-income countries in Europe seems to have decreased during the 1990s. At the same time, labour productivity in affiliates in high-income non-Europe exhibits lower growth than European affiliates.

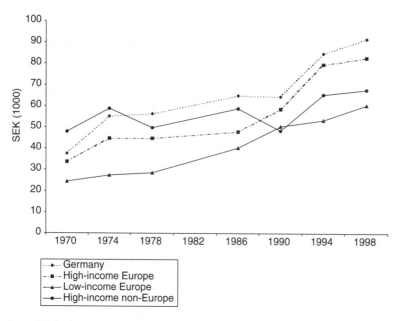

Source: IUI database.

Figure 4.1   Value added per employee in fixed (1970) prices

German affiliates are not only more productive than affiliates located in other high-income countries, but they also exhibit a higher labour productivity than the German manufacturing sector as a whole (Table 4.3). The difference is not very large, however, and we cannot determine whether it is due to higher productivity in affiliates than in comparable firms, or whether affiliates, on average, are located in more highly-productive sectors.[6]

Another interesting issue with respect to differences in characteristics is whether affiliates located in different countries differ systematically with respect to factor intensities. Tables 4.4 and 4.5 present two measures of the skill-intensity of affiliates: average R&D expenditure per employee (Table 4.4) and the share of high-skilled white-collar workers (Table 4.5).

Table 4.4 reveals that there is much more variability in the figures for R&D expenditures per employee than for value added per employee. This is related to the fact that there are far more missing values with respect to information about the R&D expenditures of affiliates. It may

Table 4.4   R&D expenditure per employee (SEK thousands)

	Germany	High-income Europe	Low-income Europe	High-income non-Europe
1970	0.49	1.21	0.08	2.51
1978	3.68	2.31	0.53	3.80
1990	21.4	14.9	14.3	14.0
1994	27.5	32.4	33.7	34.0
1998	28.3	22.1	8.2	20.1

Source: IUI database.

Table 4.5   Share of high-skilled white-collar workers in the total labour force in 1998 (%)

Area	%
Germany	9.3
High-income Europe	6.2
Low-income Europe	2.4
High-income non-Europe	7.3

Source: IUI database.

also be noted that there is no information on R&D expenditures for 1974 and 1986. Moreover, large mergers and acquisitions can easily change the R&D figures dramatically. Still, it is evident that the affiliates located in Germany on average tend to have high R&D expenditures per employee compared to other countries. In 1990 and 1998, in particular, R&D expenditures per employee were higher in Germany than in any of the country groups included in Table 4.4.

Information about the skill-structure in the affiliates is available for only a few years. In 1998, the surveyed firms were asked to indicate not only the number of blue-collar and white-collar workers, but also the number of high-skilled and low-skilled white-collar workers. Table 4.5 shows the average share of high-skilled white-collar workers based on this information. According to this table, about 9 per cent of the German affiliates' employees were high-skilled white-collar workers, which can be compared to about 6 per cent for other high-income European countries and about 7 per cent for high-income non-European countries.

Since Germany is a high-wage country, we would not expect Swedish MNEs to locate production in Germany primarily to cut production costs, but in order to get access to the large German market instead. Before the accession of Sweden to the European Union, the location of affiliates in Germany may also have been motivated by a desire to obtain access to the European market in general. One way of assessing whether there is evidence of German affiliates being more oriented towards selling in the local German market is to examine the export propensities of affiliates. Table 4.6 shows affiliate exports as a share of total turnover. As expected, taking into account the large size of the domestic market,

Table 4.6 Exports as a share of total turnover (%)

Year	Germany	High-income Europe	Low-income Europe	High-income non-Europe
1970	17.3	21.9	53.8	9.2
1974	24.6	32.2	35.1	15.1
1978	25.3	36.0	25.9	10.5
1986	29.5	37.9	45.3	7.9
1990	41.3	39.8	17.6	12.2
1994	35.2	47.2	38.1	12.6
1998	37.0	48.8	44.0	18.9

Source: IUI database.

the export share is lower for the German affiliates than for affiliates in other European countries in all years except 1990. As would also be expected, the export share of German affiliates is still substantially higher than that pertaining to affiliates located in high-income non-European countries, which primarily relates to affiliates located in the USA. It seems reasonable to assume that Swedish MNEs locate affiliates in the USA primarily to supply the large domestic US market.

The fact that the export orientation of German affiliates seems to have been particularly high in 1990 suggests that Swedish firms were investing in Germany in the late 1980s in order to obtain access to the larger European market.

Tables 4.7a and 4.7b provide information about the intra-firm trade pattern of foreign affiliates. Table 4.7a shows imports from the Swedish parents as a share of total turnover, while Table 4.7b shows the share of these imports accounted for by intermediate inputs. As can be seen in Table 4.7a, the German affiliates consistently have a lower share of imports from the Swedish parent firms than affiliates in other high-income European countries; hence it seems as if the German affiliates are less dependent on imports from the foreign parent than affiliates located in other high-income countries in Europe. Moreover, the share of imports from the Swedish parents is lower for the German affiliates than for affiliates located in low-income European countries and high-income non-European countries in most of the survey years. It should also be noted that there seems to be a general decline in the share of imports from the parent firms. For all country groups, the share of imports from the Swedish parents is substantially lower in the late 1990s than in the early 1970s.

Table 4.7b reveals that some of this decline in the share of imports from the parent firms may be explained by the reduced importance of imports of final goods for resale by the affiliates. The share of intermediate inputs of total imports from the Swedish parents is considerably higher in the late 1990s than in the early 1970s for all country groups. The German affiliates do not in any systematic way differ from other affiliates with respect to the share of imports from the parent accounted for by intermediate inputs. In 1998, about 80 per cent of total imports from the parent firms consisted of intermediate inputs for all country groups. One implication of the German affiliates' small share of imports from the Swedish parents, combined with the fact that most of these imports are intermediate inputs, is that the German affiliates rely fairly strongly on the supply of intermediate inputs from local German producers.

Table 4.7a Imports from Swedish parents as a share of total turnover (%)

Year	Germany	High-income Europe	Low-income Europe	High-income non-Europe
1970	13.2	17.7	15.5	18.7
1974	10.7	17.8	13.8	19.7
1978	11.2	19.7	8.9	19.1
1986	11.5	16.2	10.2	10.2
1990	8.2	13.9	13.8	9.4
1994	8.4	15.9	13.0	9.1
1998	5.5	14.6	6.8	10.3

Source: IUI database.

Table 4.7b Imports of intermediate inputs as a share of total imports from Swedish parents (%)

Year	Germany	High-income Europe	Low-income Europe	High-income non-Europe
1970	25.3	40.4	35.8	42.3
1974	45.1	43.0	65.5	51.5
1978	36.3	53.2	45.0	44.0
1986	53.9	51.3	45.1	43.7
1990	49.7	77.2	66.8	56.6
1994	67.2	74.6	43.5	44.5
1998	80.5	78.7	78.3	78.0

Source: IUI database.

Table 4.8 Mode of entry for affiliates in 1998 (shares)

Category	Greenfield	Merger or acquisition	Former sales affiliate
Germany	0.14	0.73	0.14
High-income Europe	0.14	0.78	0.09
Low-income Europe	0.12	0.84	0.05
High-income non-Europe	0.14	0.70	0.15

Source: IUI database.

Finally, we look at whether the mode of entry into the German market differs from entry into other markets. As shown in Table 4.8, the IUI database distinguishes between three ways of setting up a producing affiliate: greenfield investment, merger or acquisition, and the transformation of a former sales affiliate. In general, the bulk of producing affiliates are the result of mergers or acquisitions, whereas greenfield investment and former sales affiliates are less common. The stock of existing affiliates in 1998 in Germany follows the same pattern as comparable locations, with the possible exception of mergers or acquisitions being somewhat less common, while the transformation of former sales affiliates is somewhat more common.

3 The effect of labour costs

In order to analyse the determinants of the decision to establish foreign affiliates empirically, we use an unbalanced panel based on the IUI database, where we have eliminated all firms appearing only once in the time series.

As has been shown previously (e.g., Brainard and Riker, 1997; Braconier and Ekholm, 2000b), for a given configuration of the firm in terms of foreign affiliates, the relationship between labour costs in one location and labour demand in another location can be either substitutionary or complementary. A relationship of substitution is said to prevail if an increase in the level of labour costs in one location leads to an increase in the demand for labour in another. In this case, the firm increases employment in one location while reducing employment in the location where costs have increased. This may reflect a relocation of activities from high-cost to low-cost locations. A complementary relationship, on the other hand, is said to prevail if an increase in the level of labour costs in one location leads to a decrease in the demand for labour in another location. In this case, the firm decreases employment not only in the location where costs have increased, but in other locations as well. This may reflect complementarities in production which make the firm react to cost increases in one location by downscaling activities in locations that are now experiencing either a decrease in the demand for intermediate inputs or a higher cost of intermediate inputs supplied by other production units within the corporation.[7]

The effect of labour costs on the entry decision may, however, very well differ from the effects on labour demand when the MNE has activities in given locations. For instance, a firm that is considering setting up a new plant in a certain foreign location is likely to compare the product and factor market conditions not only in that location and other locations where the firm has existing production units, but also in other potential foreign locations. A Swedish firm, selling in the European market, that is considering setting up an additional plant will not only compare the product and factor market conditions in Sweden and, say, Germany, but also in France, the UK and other European countries. Thus, it is important to study the determinants of the decision to invest in a particular location as well as the effect of changes in labour costs on the level of employment in the locations where the firm is already established (cf. Braconier and Ekholm, 2000a).

In our empirical specification, we therefore distinguish between the selection process and the effect on employment within existing affiliates. We specify the selection model as:

$$P(A_{it} = 1) = f(w^G_{it}, w^S_{jt}, w^{HE}_{it}, w^{LE}_{it}, w^{min}_{it}) \tag{4.1}$$

where A_{it} denotes whether MNE i has an affiliate in Germany at time t or not. In this equation, w stands for labour costs in the host country, Germany (w^G); the home country, Sweden (w^S); in locations in high-income and low-income Europe, respectively, where the firm already has activities $(w^{HE}$ and $w^{LE})$; and in the lowest-cost location in high-income Europe where the firm does not have activities (w^{min}).

In order to reduce potential problems of endogeneity, labour costs in Sweden are not measured by labour costs reported by the Swedish parents, but by industry-distributed average labour costs in Swedish manufacturing instead.[8] The variables w^{HE} and w^{LE} are calculated in the following way: first, we construct a wage rate for each location in the sample by taking the average over all affiliates of all the firms in the sample that are located in that particular host country. Then, we compute a firm-specific exogenous wage rate by excluding the MNE's own affiliate wages in that particular host country. Based on this wage, we construct employment-based averages for each of the MNE's affiliates, distinguishing between high- and low-income Europe.

We expect the level of labour costs in Germany to affect negatively the probability that an MNE will produce in Germany. Wages in locations where the firm already has activities may affect the likelihood of operating an affiliate in Germany either way, depending on whether affiliate employment in Germany tends to substitute or complement employment in the other locations. Labour costs in alternative locations where the MNE is not producing should affect the likelihood that the MNE will operate in Germany positively, as entry in one location is likely to be a substitute for entry in another location.

Determinants of the level of employment in existing affiliates are modelled in the following way:

$$\ln L_{it} = \alpha + \delta_i + \beta_0 \ln w_{it}^G + \beta_1 \ln w_{jt}^S + \beta_2 \ln w_{it}^{HE} + \beta_3 \ln w_{it}^{LE} + \varepsilon_{it} \qquad (4.2)$$

where L_{it} is the number of employees in German affiliates belonging to firm i.

We now omit the variable capturing the level of labour costs in other potential locations, since there is no obvious reason why this should affect the level of employment in existing production units. The estimates from this regression may be interpreted as wage-elasticities. Any non-observable features of the firm that influence the firm's demand for labour but are constant over time are accounted for by the fixed-effect coefficient, δ_i.

4 Results from the econometric analysis

Table 4.9 presents the results from an estimation of (4.1), using a logit approach. The estimated coefficient for the level of labour costs in Germany is negative and significant at the 10 per cent level in two of

Table 4.9 Results for logit estimation. Dependent variable: $P(A)$

	(1)	(2)	(3)
$\ln w^G$	−18.6	−28.8*	−62.7*
	(−1.19)	(−1.79)	(−1.74)
$\ln w^S$	0.51	0.77	0.38
	(1.38)	(1.57)	(0.36)
$\ln w^{HE}$	−	2.84***	6.12**
		(3.23)	(2.14)
$\ln w^{LE}$	−	−	0.51
			(1.00)
$\ln w^{min}$	6.79***	9.94***	11.8***
	(6.23)	(6.87)	(4.00)
Log likelihood	−372.3	−270.0	−53.9
Observations	613	467	121
Pseudo R^2	0.08	0.14	0.30

Note: Figures within parentheses are *t*-statistics. Asterisks denote significance levels: *** (1%), ** (5%), * (10%). The regressions also include time dummies. The estimations are based on the assumption that observations are independent across, but not necessarily within, firms.

the three specifications. The level of labour costs in Sweden, however, does not have a statistically significant effect in any of the specifications. The variables that seem to assert the strongest influence on the likelihood that Swedish MNEs decide to produce in Germany are labour costs in locations where the firms are already established and in the lowest-cost location within high-income Europe where they are not yet established. The estimated coefficients of both these variables are positive and significant at the 5 per cent level. This means that the higher the labour costs in these other locations, the higher the likelihood that Swedish MNEs decide to produce in Germany. In particular, the coefficient of the variable capturing labour costs in potential locations where the firm does not already have production units is strongly significant; it is significant at the 1 per cent level in all specifications. This suggests that although the primary motive for Swedish MNEs to invest in Germany may not be to produce at lower costs, the level of production costs does matter for their locational decision. Moreover, it suggests that Swedish MNEs regard Germany and other high-income countries in Europe as alternative locations for similar activities, thereby creating a relationship of substitution between investments in Germany and other high-income European countries.

Table 4.10 presents the results from an estimation of (4.2). The regressions now include fewer observations since we use only the ones for which there are affiliate activities in Germany. In these regressions,

Table 4.10 Estimated wage elasticities based on fixed-effect ordinary least squares estimation. Dependent variable: $\ln L$

	(1)	(2)
$\ln w^G$	7.44	5.30
	(1.08)	(0.54)
$\ln w^S$	0.20	−0.27
	(0.56)	(−0.40)
$\ln w^{HE}$	2.25***	3.58*
	(2.83)	(1.98)
$\ln w^{LE}$	–	0.06
		(0.16)
Observations	188	81
T-bar	2.7	2.9
R^2 (within)	0.24	0.25

Note: Figures within parentheses are t-statistics. Asterisks denote significance levels: *** (1%), ** (5%), * (10%). The regressions also include time dummies.

the coefficient of German labour costs is estimated with very low precision. The estimates are positive, but insignificant. The estimates of the coefficients of labour costs in Sweden and in locations within low-income Europe where the firm is active are insignificant as well. In fact, the only wage-elasticity whose estimate is statistically significant is the one for locations within high-income Europe where the firm is active. This estimated cross-wage elasticity is positive, implying that increases in labour costs in other high-income countries in Europe lead to increased demand for German labour by Swedish MNEs. This is additional evidence of a relationship of substitution between German workers and workers in other high-income countries in Europe.

As is well known, when estimating a regression equation in a selection model, the estimates may be biased. In order to gauge the potential source of bias, we also use the Heckman estimation procedure to estimate the wage elasticities in the labour demand equation (4.2: see Table 4.11). In the selection model, we include the wage costs in Germany, in other high-income countries in Europe where the firm is active and in the lowest-cost location in high-income Europe where the firm is not already active. In the labour demand equation, we include wage costs in

Table 4.11   Results for Heckman Estimation (maximum likelihood)

	Selection model	Labour demand equation
$\ln w^G$	−2.66***	−23.4**
	(−8.43)	(−2.28)
$\ln w^S$	–	0.82
		(0.99)
$\ln w^{HE}$	0.23	1.11
	(0.79)	(0.51)
$\ln w^{LE}$	–	−0.42
		(−1.42)
$\ln w^{min}$	2.54***	–
	(7.73)	
lambda		0.83***
		(5.04)
Log likelihood		−309.5
Observations (total/censored)		362/81

Note: Figures within parentheses are *t*-statistics. Asterisks denote significance levels: *** (1%), ** (5%), * (10%). The regressions also include time dummies. The estimations are based on the assumption that observations are independent across, but not necessarily within, firms.

Germany, Sweden and high-income as well as low-income countries in Europe where the firm is already active. The labour demand equation now also includes an additional variable, lambda, which is the inverse of the Mill's ratio (or the non-selection hazard) and is calculated based on the parameter estimates of the selection model. The inclusion of this variable yields consistent estimates of the wage-elasticities in the labour demand equation on the assumption that the selection model is correctly specified and disturbances are homoscedastic and normally distributed.

Table 4.11 presents the results from maximum-likelihood estimation of a Heckman selection model. The estimated coefficient of lambda is highly significant, indicating that selection bias is indeed a problem in our data. The results pertaining to the selection model are similar to the ones in Table 4.9; the level of local labour costs affects the probability that Swedish MNEs produce in Germany negatively, while the level of labour costs in other high-income locations in Europe affect this probability positively. The results pertaining to the labour demand equation differ from the ones in Table 4.10 in that the cross-wage elasticity for other high-income European countries is insignificant. Altogether, the results from the estimations suggest that relative labour costs do matter for the Swedish MNEs' decisions to enter and employ workers in Germany.

In many ways, it would be preferable to estimate the equations in (4.1) and (4.2) using unit labour-cost data instead of the firms' reported average cost per employee. It would greatly reduce problems related to endogeneity and would take into account the fact that differences in labour productivity between countries are likely to be reflected in average wages. One problem with using unit labour-cost data in our estimations, however, is that the labour-cost variables contain very little variation and are highly correlated with each other. The results from estimations using unit labour-cost data are presented in Table A4.1 in the Appendix. As can be seen, the estimates are generally very imprecise and the goodness of fit low. None of the estimated coefficients is significant, but the sign pattern seems to be essentially consistent with the results using data on average cost per employee.

5 Concluding remarks

This chapter has examined German affiliates of Swedish MNEs in the manufacturing sector. We have used data that have been collected at the affiliate level in order to assess whether German affiliates differ systematically from affiliates located in other countries and whether labour-costs play a role in the Swedish MNEs' decision to locate production in Germany. We have found that the German affiliates do differ from affiliates located in other European countries as well as other high-income countries outside Europe with respect to labour productivity, R&D intensity, skill-intensity, export propensity and the propensity to import from the Swedish parent. German affiliates are, on average, more R&D and skill intensive and exhibit a higher labour productivity. At the same time, they seem to be more oriented towards selling their output in the local German market rather than in foreign markets. Furthermore, they seem to be less integrated with the Swedish parent in terms of intra-firm imports of intermediate inputs.

We have also found some evidence suggesting that labour-costs do play a role in the Swedish MNEs' decision to locate in Germany. According to our results, both the level of wage costs in Germany and in other potential locations in high-income Europe where the firm has not already set up production plants affect this decision. In this respect, relative wage costs have an influence on whether the Swedish firms invest in Germany or in other European countries.

Furthermore, we have estimated positive cross-wage elasticities with respect to other high-income countries in Europe where the firm is already producing. This implies that from the point of view of the Swedish MNEs, German workers are substitutes for workers in other high-income countries in Europe. However, the results pertaining to the cross-wage elasticities are relatively weak, indicating that the decision to invest is more sensitive to relative labour-costs than the demand for workers by existing production units. This is not very surprising, since investments in manufacturing plants often are, at least partly, sunk costs, which cannot be retrieved if the firm were to relocate production elsewhere.

A possible interpretation of the results is that the activities of Swedish MNEs contribute to a certain 'lumpiness' in the relation between overall labour demand in Germany and relative labour-costs; changes in relative labour-costs seem to lead to changes in labour demand mainly through their effect on investments rather than through their effect on employment in existing plants. However, it should be kept in mind that most of the German affiliates of Swedish MNEs are the results of mergers and acquisitions, which makes it very difficult to assess the appropriate counterfactual with respect to overall labour demand in Germany. When a Swedish MNE is discouraged from investing in Germany on account of high labour-costs, this will often simply lead to a reduction in the Swedish firm's willingness to pay for an acquisition. To analyse the consequences of this for the overall labour demand in Germany is, however, beyond the scope of this chapter.

Appendix

Table A4.1   Results for estimations based on unit labour-cost data

Selection model	Logit	Heckman
$\ln w^G$	–0.57	–0.15
	(–1.19)	(–0.54)
$\ln w^{min}$	0.54	0.17
	(1.13)	(0.58)
Log likelihood	–418.6	–718.4
Observations	628	582
Pseudo R^2	0.001	–

Labour demand equation	OLS	Heckman
$\ln w^G$	0.26	–0.14
	(0.75)	(–0.26)
$\ln w^{HE}$	0.39	0.47
	(1.35)	(1.14)
lambda	–	0.49***
		(5.08)
Observations	186	186
T-bar	2.8	–
Adj R^2 (within)	0.17	–

Note: Figures within parentheses are *t*-statistics. Asterisks denote significance levels: *** (1%), ** (5%), * (10%). The regressions also include time dummies. The logit and Heckman estimations are based on the assumption that observations are independent across, but not necessarily within, firms. The OLS estimations are based on a model with firm-specific fixed effects.

Notes

1 A description of these data can be found in Braunerhjelm and Ekholm (1998). An account of the results from the latest survey can be found in Ekholm and Hesselman (2000).

2 It should be noted that although the aim of the survey of Swedish MNEs has always been to collect data from the whole population of Swedish manufacturing firms with producing affiliates abroad and the response rate has generally been very high, there is extensive exiting and entering of firms in the database. This means that the sample of firms on which the figures presented is based has changed over time. An assessment of the relevance of exiting and entering firms for changes over time in the foreign share of production and in the average share of parent exports to affiliates can be found in Ekholm and Hesselman (2000). In general, the effect of exiting and entering firms seems to be fairly low, with the exception of the last survey, the one for 1998, where there are large changes compared to 1994 due to changes in the firm sample.

3 A third reason for differences in the two distributions is that exchange rate movements affect production figures. The strong value of the US dollar in the mid-1980s is, for instance, likely to be the reason why the US share of foreign production was higher in 1986 than in 1990 whereas, with respect to its share of foreign employment, it is the other way around.

4 Ireland is excluded because, according to our criteria, it should have been included in the low-income group at the beginning of the time period and the high-income group at the end of the period.

5 The current prices in SEK have been deflated using the GDP deflator.

6 Due to secrecy, we are unable to compare relative productivity levels in specific sectors.

7 For a more detailed account of the possible effects on employment in one location of changes in the level of labour-costs in another location, see Braconier and Ekholm (2000b).

8 Wage data have been collected from *Industristatistiken* (Statistics Sweden), while information on payroll taxes has been supplied by the Swedish Employers' Confederation.

References

Braconier, H. and Ekholm, K. (2000a), *Competition for Multinational Activity in Europe: The Role Played by Wages and Market Size*, IUI Working Paper.

Braconier, H. and Ekholm, K. (2000b), 'Swedish Multinationals and Competition from High- and Low-Wage Locations', *Review of International Economics*, 8, pp. 448–61.

Brainard, S. L. and D. Riker (1997), *US Multinationals and Competition from Low Wage Countries*, NBER Working Paper No. 5959.

Braunerhjelm, P. and K. Ekholm (1999), 'Recent Trends in the Foreign Activities of Swedish Multinational Corporations: The Role Played by Large European Host Countries', in R. Barrell and N. Pain (eds), *Innovation, Investment and the Diffusion of Technology in Europe. German Direct Investment and Economic Growth in postwar Europe*, Cambridge, Cambridge University Press.

Ekholm, K. and M. Hesselman (2000). *The Foreign Operations of Swedish Manufacturing Firms: Evidence from a Survey of Swedish Multinationals 1998*, IUI Working Paper No. 540.

OECD (1999), STAN Database.

5
Foreign-Owned Firms and UK Economic Performance*

Nigel Pain and Florence Hubert

1 Introduction

In the UK, as in other European countries, successive governments have attached considerable importance to inward investment and significant levels of public funds have been spent in order to attract foreign firms. This reflects an assumption that such firms transfer new technologies and knowledge across international borders with significant positive externalities for indigenous firms. If this was the case, the location of economic activity would be an important endogenous influence on the size of national economies. The Competitiveness White Paper issued by the UK Department of Trade and Industry in 1998 argued that foreign direct investment (FDI) is one of the main transmission mechanisms behind the diffusion of knowledge, both codified and tacit, across national borders (DTI, 1998). Previous Competitiveness White Papers suggested that the high level of inward investment into the UK during the 1980s helped to encourage the transfer of innovative production and managerial techniques to UK-owned companies, and improved the efficiency of their operations by enhancing product market competition (Eltis, 1996).

The desire to attract inward investment is one of the few industrial policies pursued consistently by successive UK governments over the past 25 years. Despite this, there has until recently been little evidence about the potential size of the net benefits of inward investment for

* We are grateful to the ESRC for financial support (grant numbers L138251022 and R000223590) and to worshop participants for helpful comments and suggestions. This work was undertaken whilst Florence Hubert was at the National Institute of Economic and Social Research. The views expressed in the paper are those of the authors alone and do not necessarily reflect those of the Bank of England.

the economy or the national policies and institutions that could help to maximize the potential size of those benefits. Indeed the UK does not even have a comprehensive official data source on the activities of foreign-owned firms throughout the economy as a whole.

We begin by briefly reviewing the long-term trends in the level of inward investment in the UK and the particular characteristics of inward investors. This serves to highlight some of the most important channels through which inward investors might influence the performance of indigenous companies. We then discuss the evidence regarding the existence of spillovers from inward investment and outline some of the policies available to affect location choice.

2 The pattern of inward investment in the UK

The UK has been relatively successful in attracting inward direct investment over the past 40 years, as can be seen from Figure 5.1.[1] Inward investment grew especially rapidly in the second half of the 1980s. Although the proportion of total global investment located in the UK has fallen since 1990, the UK share of the global stock of inward investment in 1999 was still over 8 per cent, approximately 2 1/2 times the share of UK output in global GDP measured on a purchasing power parity basis.

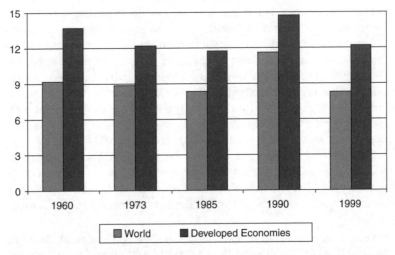

Source: Authors' calculations based on Dunning (1988, Table 3.2) and UNCTAD (2000, Annex Table B3).

Figure 5.1   The UK share of the global inward investment stock (%)

The long-term trends in the stock of inward foreign direct investment in the UK economy as a whole and in the manufacturing sector
are shown in Figure 5.2, expressed as a proportion of gross domestic
product (GDP) and gross value added in manufacturing respectively.
By the end of 1999 the whole economy stock was equivalent to
27 per cent of GDP, compared to approximately 6.5 per cent of GDP
in 1960. This is considerably larger than the share of inward FDI in
most other large industrialized economies, although comparable to
that seen in a number of small, open European economies. There are
two periods in which the UK inward stock has risen especially rapidly
in real terms, these being the latter half of the 1980s and, more
recently, since 1997. Total FDI inflows averaged 2.25 per cent of GDP
per annum over 1985–89 and just under 3.5 per cent per annum over
1995–99, compared to a long-run average of 1.6 per cent per annum
since 1960.

The ratio of inward investment to output in the manufacturing
sector has always been above that for the economy as a whole, in part
because there are some sectors of the economy (such as public administration) where there is no inward investment at all. However, it can be
seen that the long-term trend in the manufacturing sector is very
similar to that for the overall economy.

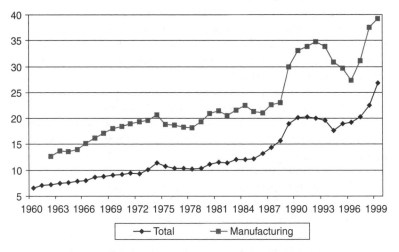

Source: Authors' calculations from Business Monitor MA4 and UK National Accounts,
various issues.

Figure 5.2 The inward FDI stock (per cent of value-added output)

Table 5.1   The composition of the UK inward FDI stock (%)

		1968	1978	1988	1998
Sector:	Manufacturing	58.6	46.3	32.8	30.1
	Energy	29.7	29.4	27.2	18.5
	Financial services	4.8	8.0	17.2	23.6
	Other non-manufacturing	6.9	16.3	22.8	27.8
Source:	USA	66.8	59.5	39.4	47.4
	Western Europe	21.8	29.7	39.8	38.7
	Asia	0.1	1.2	5.5	4.8
	Rest of the world	11.3	9.6	15.3	9.1

Source: Pain (2000, Table 1.2) updated using Business Monitor MA4 (1999).

The composition of the inward FDI stock is summarized in Table 5.1. Thirty years ago inward investments were concentrated in the manufacturing sector. Although there has since been a marked decline in the relative importance of this sector, the share does appear to have stabilized in recent years at just under one-third. Inward investors still remain relatively concentrated in manufacturing activities, since the manufacturing sector now accounts for about only one-fifth of UK GDP. The importance of inward investment in the energy sector is also clear, with significant investments having taken place in the North Sea and, in recent years, in the privatized public utilities in the electricity, gas and water supply industries. Nonetheless the relative level of investment in this sector has also begun to decline, coinciding with the decline in the relative share of oil production in total UK GDP. In recent years there has been strong growth in investments in non-manufacturing activities, such as financial and business services and telecommunications.

The ownership data highlight the long-standing importance of inward investment from the USA. Despite the popular attention given to inward investment from Japan, Korea and other Asian economies, it continues to represent a small minority of total inward investment. It is clear that the rapid growth in inward investment in the 1980s was driven by the growth of inward investment from Western European and Asian investors. In contrast, investment from US-owned companies has been the most important force behind the upturn in the late 1990s. As we highlight below, the empirical evidence from a variety of studies suggests that it is US investors who have brought the largest benefits with them.

Inward investment in knowledge-intensive sectors in the UK has grown more rapidly than in other activities over the past decade. From the available data it is possible to identify four separate sectors that contain many knowledge-intensive activities: chemicals, transport equipment, electronics and business and financial services. In 1987 these sectors accounted for approximately one-third of the total inward investment stock; by 1998 their share had risen to just over 43.5 per cent of the stock. Between 1987 and 1998 the combined stock of inward direct investment in knowledge-based activities rose by an average 13.5 per cent per annum compared to growth of 9.1 per cent per annum in other industries.

Foreign direct investment is just one means of financing the activities of inward investors. Once foreign investors have established a presence in the host country, tacit and codified firm-specific knowledge can be transferred continually from parent companies independently of other financial transactions. Equally, productive facilities can be established and expanded using capital raised outside the home country of the parent firm. Such capital will not be included in the direct investment statistics. Thus there is a strong argument for focusing on the activities undertaken by foreign-owned firms, as well as the level of inward direct investment, in assessing the impact of inward investors on the UK economy.

A further distinctive feature of inward investment in the UK lies in the methods through which new foreign investment takes place. Investment can be via cross-border mergers and acquisitions or by investment in greenfield sites. The latter has a direct influence on the level of domestic demand in the economy, whereas the former does not. But new ideas, products and knowledge can be introduced as easily in the former as in the latter, at least in principle. Inward investment is much more likely to take place through take-overs in the UK than in other European countries. Over the period 1994–99, cross-border mergers and acquisitions in the UK accounted for 39.1 per cent of the total in the European Union, whereas inflows of FDI into the UK represented 23.7 per cent of the EU aggregate.[2] Indeed the total value of cross-border mergers in the UK over this period exceeded the total value of FDI inflows by over $100 billion. This again suggests that the FDI data are providing only a partial indication of the influence of foreign-owned firms in the UK. Griffith and Simpson (2001) report that take-over was the dominant form of foreign entry in 14 out of 16 two-digit manufacturing industries in the UK over the period from 1980 to 1996.

However, there are no official data on the activities of foreign-owned firms throughout the UK economy as a whole. It is difficult to understand why such data are not collected given the importance attached to inward investment by successive governments. Detailed statistics are available on the output, employment and fixed capital formation of foreign firms in the manufacturing sector, but outside the manufacturing sector comprehensive data can be obtained only from commercial databases of company accounts.

The long-term trends in the share of foreign-owned firms in the UK manufacturing sector are summarized in Table 5.2 and Figure 5.3. It can be seen that their share of total output, employment and investment has risen over time. As with the foreign direct investment data, the dominance of US-controlled affiliates is clear. They continue to account for over half of the value-added output produced in foreign-owned firms, even though their relative importance has declined over time as the share of Western European and, to a lesser extent, Japanese firms has risen.

The figures in Table 5.2 highlight some of the key stylized facts about foreign firms:

- labour productivity, measured in terms of value added output per employee, has been continuously around 40 per cent higher on average than in UK-owned firms;
- foreign firms are more capital intensive than domestic ones, accounting for a larger share of investment than output (this difference has risen over time);
- foreign firms employ a higher proportion of skilled labour than domestic firms.

Table 5.2   Foreign-owned firms in UK manufacturing (annual averages)

	1973–79	1981–89	1990–97	1997
Share of foreign-owned firms (%)				
Gross value added	17.4	18.5	23.9	25.2
Net capital expenditure	18.1	22.2	30.9	33.1
Total employment	12.8	13.8	17.4	17.4
Employment of operatives	12.0	12.8	16.0	n.a.
Employment of non-operatives	15.2	16.4	19.9	n.a.
Nationality of investor (%)				
USA	72.9	65.2	53.1	52.7
Western Europe	18.7	20.3	29.8	32.7
Japan	0.1	1.0	6.6	6.6
Rest	8.3	13.5	10.5	8.0

Source: Pain (2000), Table 1.3.

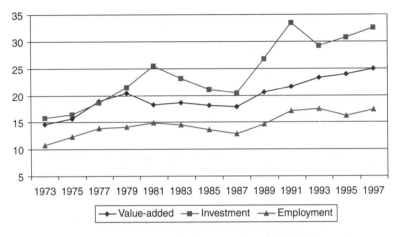

Source: Authors' calculations from Annual Census of Production, various issues.

Figure 5.3   Foreign firms' share of UK manufacturing (%)

These differences appear to stem from more than just differences in the scale of operations or a concentration of foreign firms in capital-intensive sectors with high value added. Using a sample of establishments drawn from the longitudinal database of the Annual Census of Production, Oulton (2000) finds that, controlling for industrial structure, labour productivity in establishments owned by US companies in 1993 was 32 per cent higher than in UK-owned establishments. Other foreign-owned establishments had a productivity advantage of 15 per cent. Differences in the mix of inputs could account for 61 per cent of the higher labour productivity of US-owned establishments and 97 per cent of that of other foreign-owned ones. Other studies, such as Davies and Lyons (1991), Girma *et al.* (2000) and Griffith and Simpson (2001) have also found evidence that labour productivity in foreign-owned manufacturing firms is higher than in domestic ones after controlling for factors such as scale, industrial structure and age. Girma *et al.* also find that the level of total factor productivity in foreign-owned firms is 5.25 per cent higher than in UK-owned ones using a sample of manufacturing firms for 1991–96 drawn from the OneSource database.

Evidence for the non-manufacturing sector is also presented by Oulton (2000), using OneSource data for 1995. The labour productivity advantage of foreign firms is estimated to be 49 per cent and 46 per cent respectively for US and other foreign-owned companies.

Table 5.3 Foreign firms' share of manufacturing, UK and France (%)

		1973/74	1987	1997
Output	UK	14.7	17.9	25.2
	France	22.2	25.2	34.4
Employment	UK	10.8	12.8	17.4
	France	17.5	21.6	29.2
Investment	UK	15.8	20.4	33.1
	France	21.8	25.6	35.3

Sources: Annual Census of Production (ONS) and L'implantation étrangère dans l'industrie (Ministère de l'Economie, des Finances et de l'Industrie, Paris).

Differences in capital-intensity and labour quality are found to account for only two-thirds of these differentials.

Thus it seems clear that foreign firms have some important firm-specific advantages that allow them to achieve higher levels of productivity than their UK counterparts. These may reflect factors such as better organizational efficiency, greater exposure to international competition and the quality of knowledge-based assets. If foreign firms did not possess such firm-specific advantages, it would be difficult to explain why they are able to take advantage of profitable opportunities in the UK whilst UK-owned firms are not, especially as there is little evidence of any significant difference in the provision of public financial incentives for inward investors and indigenous firms (House of Commons 1998, 1999).

Indeed it should be noted that the UK is far from unique in having a steadily growing population of comparatively high productivity foreign-owned firms in the manufacturing sector. Table 5.3 provides some comparable statistics for France, and shows that the degree of foreign penetration in the manufacturing sector is larger than in the UK. On average foreign firms also have a higher level of productivity and are more investment-intensive than indigenous firms in France, but the gap between them is smaller than in the UK.

3 Productivity spillovers from inward investors

Given that foreign firms in the UK possess specific advantages, it is natural to ask whether these spill over and become available to domestic companies. If that were to prove the case, then inward investment would be associated with significant positive externalities for the economy as a whole, providing a justification for government intervention in the form of investment incentives and promotional activities designed to attract potential foreign investors. There are two broad categories of spillovers that can be distinguished:

- direct spillovers, whereby domestic firms can acquire knowledge of new technologies and working practices from foreign firms;
- indirect spillovers: examples include the impact of greater competition in product markets, the impact on national innovation and research and development (R&D), and the impact on export performance.

All of these are potentially important sources of productivity growth. Blomström, Kokko and Globerman (2000) provide a comprehensive overview of the literature on spillovers from inward investment in developed economies.

Direct spillovers

The modelling approach

It is important to be clear about how direct spillovers from inward investors are best evaluated. All too often the focus of investment promotion activities is on the number of jobs associated with inward investment, yet there is little evidence that the long-run level of unemployment in the UK and other industrialized countries is affected by the industrial structure of the economy. Instead emphasis is placed on supply-side factors and labour market institutions (Layard, Nickell and Jackman, 1991).

In an economy such as the UK, with flexible real wages, inward investment should affect only the types of jobs available rather than the quantity, unless it can be shown that it has wider effects on the growth process. There would obviously be significant adjustment costs if all foreign firms suddenly left the economy, but ultimately employment could be expected to recover in the economy as a whole provided the real cost of labour fell. Thus a more appropriate means of judging the benefits from inward investors is to look at the overall level of national income. Even if inward investment does not affect the long-run level of employment, it might still affect the productivity of those employed, their wage levels and the organizational efficiency of the companies in which they work.

There is some survey evidence which indicates that new technologies and standards have been adopted by UK producers as a result of inward investment. In a study of the impact of technology transfer by US multinational companies, Mansfield and Romeo (1980) found that over half of the UK firms in their survey had introduced new products or processes more quickly because of a transfer of a new product or process by a US-based firm to its overseas subsidiary, with around two-thirds of the UK firms indicating that their technological capabilities had been raised by such transfers. Inward investment in the UK has also helped to bring about a significant improvement in the product quality of suppliers (PA Cambridge Economic Consultants, 1995). The quantitative importance of such qualitative findings is not clear. Recent empirical research has begun to fill this gap by providing a comprehensive overview of the relative performance of foreign-owned firms in the UK and the extent to which their presence has had a sustained impact on the performance of UK-owned firms over time.

The extent of direct spillovers from foreign-owned firms in the manufacturing sector has been investigated by Hubert and Pain (2000 and 2001), using an econometric approach first applied by Barrell and Pain (1997). This allows for endogenous technical progress within labour demand relationships derived consistently from an underlying production function. Suppose output *(Q)* is produced using labour *(L)* and capital *(K)*, consistent with a CES (constant elasticity of substitution) production function of the form:

$$Q = \gamma \left[s(K)^{-\rho} + (1-s)\left(Le^{\lambda t}\right)^{-\rho} \right]^{-(v/\rho)} \tag{5.1}$$

Here *v* denotes returns to scale, γ and *s* are production function scale and distribution parameters, and the elasticity of substitution (σ) is given by $1/(1 + \rho)$. Technical progress is assumed to be labour-augmenting at rate λ_t. The first-order condition that in a competitive market the marginal product of each input should equal its real price can be used to derive a log-linear 'desired' labour demand function:

$$\ln(L^*) = \underline{1 + \sigma\,(v-1)}\,\ln(Q) - \sigma\ln\,(w/p) - (1-\sigma)\lambda t + k \tag{5.2}$$
$$v$$

where *k* denotes a constant. The coefficient on the real producer wage *(w/p)* provides a direct point estimate of the elasticity of substitution, allowing the technical progress parameter(s) and returns to scale to be identified. Technical progress can be endogenized by allowing the level within any given industry to be dependent on various factors, including indicators of the scale of the activities of foreign-owned firms *(F)*, imports *(M)*, the R&D stock *(R)* as well as an exogenous deterministic time trend *(T)*:

$$\lambda t = \lambda_T T + \lambda_F \ln(F) + \lambda_M \ln(M) + \lambda_R \ln(R) \tag{5.3}$$

This specification implies that technical progress will grow at a constant rate if the key driving factors also grow at a constant rate. The parameters of the technical progress function can be estimated jointly with those of the labour demand schedule by substituting (5.3) into (5.2). Allowance can also be made for the costs of adjusting labour by estimating a dynamic model for employment in which the factor demand expression implied by the combination of the marginal productivity condition (5.2) and the technical progress function (5.3) is embedded as the long-run steady-state solution. This has the form:

$$\Delta\ln(L_t) = \beta_0 + \beta_1\Delta\ln(Q_t) - \beta_2\ln(L_{t-1}/L_{t-1}^*) + \varepsilon_t \tag{5.4}$$

Failure to allow for any cyclical effects would imply the strong assumption that companies always use the minimum inputs necessary to produce a given level of output.

Setting $\lambda_M = 0$ and $\lambda_R = 0$, substituting (5.3) into (5.2) and the resulting expression into (5.4) gives:

$$\Delta\ln(L_t) = \beta_0 + \beta_1\Delta\ln(Q_t) - \beta_2\ln(L_{t-1}) + \theta_1\ln(Q_{t-1})$$
$$- \theta_2\ln(w_{t-1}/p_{t-1}) - \theta_3 T_{t-1} - \ln\theta_4(F_{t-1}) + \varepsilon_t \tag{5.5}$$

where $\theta_2 = \beta_2\sigma$, $\theta_3 = \beta_2(1 - \sigma)\lambda_T$, and $\theta_4 = \beta_2\sigma\lambda_F$. An equation of this form is used to obtain the parameters reported in column (A) in Table 5.5 below. The implied estimates of the elasticity of substitution and returns to scale can be recovered from the estimated equation using $\sigma = \theta_2/\beta_2$ and $v = (\beta_2 - \theta_2)/(\theta_1 - \theta_2)$.

There are important differences between our approach and other methods which are commonly used to examine the impact of absorbed technology on growth. Typically, the production function used in exercises of this type is assumed to have a Cobb–Douglas form:

$$Q = A\,L^a\,K^b \text{ with } \alpha + \beta = 1 \tag{5.6}$$

where *A* is an indicator that will pick up changes in technology, scale economies and organizational efficiency. Equation (5.6) can be rearranged to 'back-out' an estimate of total factor productivity (TFP) levels (or, in first differences, growth):

$$\ln (A) = \ln (Q) - \alpha \ln (L) - (1 - \alpha) \ln (K) \qquad (5.7a)$$

with α given by the share of labour in national income. Since the weights on capital and labour are imposed to sum to unity, measures of TFP constructed in this fashion will include any scale economies. They may also include the impact of gradual changes in organizational efficiency that raise the level of output produced with given inputs and technologies. Hence TFP may be very different from technical progress. The constructed measure of TFP can be regressed on a number of factors which are thought to determine it using a specification such as (5.3). Coe, Helpman and Hoffmaister (1997) provide a well-known recent example of this approach, with TFP levels related both to the domestic R&D stock and foreign R&D stocks embodied in trade.

A related strand of the literature seeks (often implicitly) to use the production function to model labour productivity directly. Examples include Caves (1974), Globerman (1979), Blomström (1986) and Blomström and Sjöholm (1999), all of whom find that the presence of inward investors can affect the productivity of local firms. Re-arranging (5.7a) gives an expression in which labour productivity is related to the capital–labour ratio and technical progress. A technical progress function such as (5.3) can again be substituted into (5.7b) in place of $\ln(A)$ to derive an empirical model:

$$\ln(Q / L) = \ln(A) + \beta \ln(K / L) + \varepsilon_j \qquad (5.7b)$$

There are a number of difficulties with these two alternative methods. One general problem is that the Cobb–Douglas function imposes an elasticity of substitution of unity. If this is invalid, then the constructed measures of TFP will be biased. Rodrik (1997) demonstrates that the biases can be significant when the elasticity of substitution is less than one and technological change has a labour-saving bias. Use of a Cobb–Douglas function also forces technical progress to be neutral, excluding the possibility of factor biased technical change. The TFP approach and the production function approach also both make an assumption that firms are always on their production frontier.

Our approach allows the long-run restrictions required to yield a factor demand model consistent with a Cobb–Douglas structure to be tested directly in (5.5). Four restrictions are required: a unit elasticity on output and real wages ($\theta_1/\beta_2 = \theta_2/\beta_2 = 1$) and a zero coefficient on the proxies for technical progress ($\theta_3 = \theta_4 = 0$). Imposing these gives a constant long-run nominal factor share (wL/pQ), which is what is implied by the Cobb–Douglas structure.

Hubert and Pain (2001) examine the impact of inward investment on the pace of technical change in UK-owned firms in 15 manufacturing sectors between 1983 and 1992.[3] This encompasses two factors: new advances which serve to push out the production possibility frontier and demonstration effects which serve to eliminate technical inefficiencies. Their indicator of the activities of foreign firms (F in equation 5.3) is based on value added at constant prices. A panel data analysis is undertaken, with the dynamic term in output in (5.5) and the lagged level of employment both treated as endogenous. Fixed effects are included for each industry. Labour input is measured in terms of employee hours. Some summary statistics for the industries considered are reported in Table 5.4. Further details on the comparative characteristics of foreign and domestic firms in each of them can be found in Hubert and Pain (2001).

It can be seen that there were considerable differences in the rate of labour productivity growth in domestic firms across these industries between 1983 and 1992. Eight of the industries had average annual productivity growth of more than 3 per cent; three of them had annual growth of under 1 per cent. The extent of foreign penetration also exhibits considerable variation, with a peak of 44 per cent in the motor vehicles sector, but just 4–5 per cent in furniture manufacturing, other transport equipment (primarily aerospace) and clothing. In all industries it can be seen that the average productivity of foreign firms exceeded that of domestic firms both at the start and the end of the sample. Griffith and Simpson (2001) find a similar pattern using establishment level data. There is little evidence of convergence in labour productivity levels. The gap between foreign and domestic firms narrowed in only four out of the 15 sectors between 1983 and 1992. Of course one explanation for this might be that new foreign firms with productivity-enhancing practices are continuously arriving, so that the production possibility frontier facing domestic firms is continuously shifting. However, in five sectors (non-metallic mineral products, metal manufacturing, food/drink/tobacco, clothing, and furniture) the labour productivity levels of domestic firms in 1992 remained lower than those of foreign firms in 1983. Griffith and Simpson (2001) find that labour productivity improves faster with age in foreign-owned establishments than in UK-owned ones, suggesting that the productivity

Table 5.4   Selected characteristics of foreign and domestic firms

Industry	SIC(80)	Domestic firms' labour productivity growth (% p.a.)	Foreign firms' output share (1983–92 average, %)	Foreign firms' labour productivity (domestic firms = 1)	
				1983	1992
Basic metals industries	22	3.97	15.7	1.397	1.208
Non-metallic mineral products	24	0.93	8.7	1.120	1.050
Chemicals and man-made fibres	25 + 26	3.59	33.6	1.165	1.096
Metal manufacturing	31	1.66	12.1	1.356	1.482
Mechanical engineering	32	2.09	21.7	1.219	1.270
Electrical engineering and office machinery	33 + 34	3.12	25.1	1.170	1.231
Motor vehicles	35	3.31	44.0	1.493	1.150
Other transport equipment	36	3.82	4.1	1.029	1.089
Instrument engineering	37	2.97	24.7	1.081	1.426
Food, drink and tobacco	41 + 42	0.97	17.4	1.421	1.810
Textiles	43	3.01	5.0	1.195	1.253
Footwear and clothing	44	2.63	4.5	1.466	1.548
Timber and furniture	46	0.58	3.7	1.403	1.689
Paper and publishing	47	3.54	17.6	1.155	1.378
Plastics and rubber	48	3.09	24.7	1.193	1.302

Source: Authors' calculations from Annual Census of Production, various issues.

gap between foreign and UK-owned firms reflects more than just the continual arrival of high productivity foreign-owned entrants or the take-over of high-productivity UK-owned firms by foreign ones.

A simple cross-sectional regression of domestic productivity growth in the 15 industries over 1983–92 on the size of foreign penetration and the productivity gap in 1983 yields the following (heteroscedastic-consistent t-statistics in parentheses):

Productivity = 4.928 + 0.036* Foreign Share – 2.340* Productivity Gap
Growth   (2.0)   (1.9)   (1.2)
               $R^2 = 0.23$

This indicates that productivity growth in domestic firms tended to be highest in those sectors with the highest level of foreign penetration, with the coefficient implying that each rise of 1 percentage point in the foreign share was associated with an increase in the average annual labour productivity growth rate of 0.036 per cent. However, this was smaller if the initial productivity gap between foreign and domestic firms was large, with each extra 1 percentage point on the initial gap associated with a reduction in productivity growth of 0.023 per cent. Although the overall fit of the regression is limited, suggesting that strong conclusions should not be drawn, it is consistent with the notion that greater competition from foreign firms accelerates the introduction of new ideas and technologies in domestic firms. But if the technologies used, or possibly the scale of operations, are very different from those required by domestic firms then they may be less likely to be adopted.

Econometric evidence

The results from estimating (5.5) with technical progress modelled solely using a deterministic time trend and the volume of output produced by foreign-owned firms are reported in Table 5.5.[4] In the first column we use the total output produced by foreign firms in all manufacturing. In the second we split this into own-industry output and spillovers from investors in other industries. The foreign-output term is split into two components using a logarithmic transformation. Letting ΣF_j denote the total output of all firms:

$$\ln(\Sigma F_j) = \ln\left(F_i + \sum_{j \neq i} F_j \right) = \ln(F_i) + \ln\left(1 + \frac{\sum_{j \neq i} F_j}{F_i} \right) = \ln(F_i) + \ln(FS_i) \quad (5.8)$$

The first term captures intra-industry spillovers from foreign firms, whilst the second allows for inter-industry spillovers.

The panel data set appears broadly consistent with the sort of aggregate data set utilized in Barrell and Pain (1997) and confirms that inward investment has indeed had a positive effect on the performance of domestic firms. The long-run elasticity of substitution is estimated to be a little over one-half, and there is some weak evidence of increasing returns to scale. It is also possible to accept constant returns to scale, although this restriction has not been imposed in the reported regression. However, the restrictions required to ensure a Cobb–Douglas production function are strongly rejected (Wald(4)=42.3). The lagged total value-added output of foreign-owned firms is found to be significant, and there is also a negative coefficient on the deterministic trend, which is significant at the

Table 5.5   Panel data results for industry labour demand
dependent variable: $\Delta \ln(L_{it})$ (sample period 1984–92)

	(A)	(B)	(C)	(D)
$\Delta \ln(Q_{it})$	0.2490 (3.1)	0.2426 (2.9)	0.1997 (1.8)	0.2413 (2.9)
$\ln(L_{i,t-1})$	−0.2541 (4.4)	−0.2519 (4.4)	−0.2056 (2.3)	−0.2409 (3.9)
$\ln(Q_{i,t-1})$	0.2245 (4.6)	0.2234 (4.8)	0.1966 (3.6)	0.2240 (3.4)
$\ln(W_{i,t-1}/P_{i,t-1})$	−0.1196 (4.6)	−0.1188 (4.7)	−0.1341 (4.2)	−0.1162 (4.8)
TIME	−0.0031 (1.9)	−0.0030 (1.9)	0.0055 (1.3)	−0.0028 (1.7)
$\ln(F_{t-1})$	−0.1413 (3.2)			
$\ln(F_{i,t-1})$		−0.1450 (3.2)		−0.1524 (2.0)
$\ln(FS_{i,t-1})$		−0.1483 (3.3)		−0.1496 (3.4)
$\ln(FDI_{i,t-1})$			−0.1452 (2.7)	
$\ln(FDIS_{i,t-1})$			−0.1449 (2.6)	
$\ln(FSHARE_i)_{t-1}$				0.0071 (0.1)
No. of observations	135	135	99	135
$\bar{R}^2$	0.730	0.727	0.703	0.724
Standard Error	2.43%	2.45%	2.11%	2.47%
Serial Correlation	Chi(1) = 0.04	Chi(1) = 0.06	Chi(1) = 0.41	Chi(1) = 0.14
Returns to scale (v)	1.281 (0.276)	1.272 (0.276)	1.145 (0.211)	1.157 (0.333)
Elasticity of substitution (σ)	0.471 (0.023)	0.472 (0.024)	0.652 (0.057)	0.482 (0.083)

Notes: heteroscedastic-consistent *t*-statistics in parentheses, apart from returns to scale and the elasticity of substitution which are long-run standard errors.
Source: Columns (A) and (B) from Hubert and Pain (2001). Columns (C) and (D) are new results.

10 per cent level. The implied impact of foreign firms on technical progress in column (A) is large, with a sustained 1 per cent rise in the total output of foreign-owned firms estimated to eventually raise technical progress by 1.05 per cent (standard error 0.44). The exogenous rate of technical change is estimated to be 2.28 per cent per annum (standard error 1 per cent).

The model reported in column (B) helps to assess whether the externalities from inward investment are felt within the industry in which investment occurs, or whether they spread into many different sectors. Both the intra-industry term (denoted F_i) and the inter-industry spillover term (denoted FS_i) have significant negative coefficients, and although that on the inter-industry term is marginally larger than that on the intra-sector one, the hypothesis of common coefficients cannot be rejected (Wald(1)=0.07).

This finding is of considerable interest, as it raises the possibility that there may be particular ideas or working practices brought in by individual investors in particular sectors which are more widely applicable throughout the economy. Historical examples of this include the diffusion of mass production techniques and just-in-time inventory control techniques which originated in the motor vehicles sector and were transmitted across international borders by investments from Ford and other US manufacturers, and by Japanese multinational firms. The evidence of significant inter-industry spillovers suggests that industrial policies designed to facilitate the dissemination of new business practices across a wide range of industries may be of equal benefit to policies targeting selected industries.

In column (C) we provide some preliminary evidence about the question of whether the results obtained using direct information on the scale of operations of foreign firms are very different from those that would be obtained if we reverted to using the stock of inward foreign direct investment at constant prices. An immediate difficulty is that industry level data on inward FDI is not available for such a large number of two-digit manufacturing industries. We use the same 11 industries as Hubert and Pain (2000), with basic metals and metal products, motor vehicles and other transport, and textiles and clothing being combined together. Instrument engineering was dropped from the panel. The FDI stock was deflated using the industry producer price series. The two output-based measures of the activity of foreign-owned firms are replaced by equivalent series for the stock of inward FDI (denoted FDI_i and $FDIS_i$ respectively).

The use of the FDI data makes some difference to the estimated production function parameters, with the elasticity of substitution rising to 0.65. However, both direct investment measures have significant coefficients and it is not possible to reject the joint imposition of the coefficients from column (A) in the model in column (C) (Wald(7) = 6.89). This suggests that use of the stock of inward FDI would not, in this instance at least, provide a misleading indication of the impact of inward investment on technical efficiency. This is an important finding since, outside the manufacturing sector in the UK, it is possible only to undertake an equivalent time series analysis using information on the stock of inward investment.

There are some important differences between the methodology used here and in Hubert and Pain (2000 and 2001) compared with that used in related studies by Girma *et al.* (2000) and Girma and Wakelin (2000), who find weaker evidence of spillovers. We use the level of foreign firms' output as a measure of their influence, since the intention is to model the factors driving the level of technical progress over time. Girma *et al.* use foreign firms' share of total intra-industry employment. This provides a good indicator of the current degree of competition faced by domestic firms in a data field with a large cross-sectional element, but over a long time horizon it is less likely that the *share* of foreign firms in either employment or output can be an important determinant of the *level* of productivity in domestic firms. This is illustrated in column (D) in Table 5.5 where we extend the model in column (B) to include one additional term: the share of foreign-owned firms in total output in each sector i (denoted $FSHARE_i$). This term is not statistically significant and is clearly dominated by the other terms based on the level of output produced by foreign firms.

Extensions

Hubert and Pain (2001) extend this model further by also including intra- and inter-industry measures of the volume of imports and the stock of R&D expenditure. They find that the results reported here are robust as to the inclusion of R&D and imports. However, the magnitude of the spillovers from inward investment is reduced, with a 1 per cent rise in foreign firms' output (1990 prices) in all sectors now estimated to raise technical progress in UK-owned firms by 0.5–0.6 per cent. Intra-industry import volumes are found to be significant, but not inter-industry imports. A 1 per cent rise in imports raises technical progress by 0.3 per cent. Imports bring new technologies (and competition) that are industry-specific, and inward investment also brings ideas that can be applied across industries.

Hubert and Pain (2000) examine the impact of spillovers from foreign firms by nationality of ownership, using a version of the model reported in column (A) of Table 5.5. They find that US-owned firms have a larger effect and EU firms a statistically smaller effect than others.

In a separate exercise using aggregate data for the manufacturing sector, public services and three market service sectors – distribution, business services and transport and communications, over 1972–96, Hubert and Pain (2000) examine the impact of inward investment on technical progress using the (constant price) sector-specific stock of FDI as an indicator of the influence of foreign-owned firms in sector-wide labour demand equations of the form of (5.5). Their results reflect both compositional and behavioural effects from inward investors.

1. Using a panel data estimator they find that for the three market services sectors a 10 per cent rise in the stock of inward investment

is estimated to raise technical progress by 1.35 per cent. Technical progress also has an exogenous trend component worth 1.9 per cent per annum. In the individual industries the effects are largest in business services.
2. The equivalent figures for manufacturing were 3.2 per cent and 2.9 per cent respectively, and were statistically different from those for services.
3. There was no evidence of technical progress in public services.

Thus the direct benefits from inward investment appear to be larger in the manufacturing sector than in non-manufacturing ones, although much more research is required in this area. One explanation might be that some inward investments in non-manufacturing are asset-augmenting ones, with foreign firms seeking to benefit from agglomeration economies. An obvious example is provided by the rapid growth in financial services investment in the City of London. The impact of inward investment in the manufacturing sector also appears to have strengthened over time. The benefits from foreign firms in the sample from 1983 to 1992 are larger than the benefits found in the longer data set stretching back to the early 1970s.

Given estimates of the underlying production function parameters it is possible to estimate the contribution of the growth in inward investment to overall output growth over a period of time. Barrell and Pain (1997) illustrate how this can be done. Hubert and Pain (2000) estimate that the growth of inward FDI accounts for about one-third of average annual output growth in the combined manufacturing and market services sectors of the UK economy (accounting for approximately two-thirds of GDP) from 1972 to 1996 and on the subsample from 1984 to 1996. This should probably be regarded as an estimate of the upper limit of the contribution of inward investment to output growth given the number of other potential determinants of growth which were not included in their analysis.

The wider economic impact of productivity spillovers from inward investment on host economies is also considered for the UK economy by Pain and Young (2000), who use the National Institute macroeconometric model of the UK (NiDEM), and for the Scottish economy by Gillespie *et al.* (2000), who use a computable general equilibrium model. Both studies show that a permanent rise in the level of inward investment generates a permanently higher level of GDP and national income than would otherwise have been enjoyed.

The distribution of spillovers

Even if there are positive spillovers from inward investment, there is no necessary reason why the gains should benefit all factors of production. If there are important complementarities between fixed capital and skilled labour, the factor-bias of the new technologies introduced by foreign firms might also help to raise the relative demand for skilled labour in host economies and potentially widen wage inequality. Whilst there is a considerable body of literature on the relative demand for skills, there has been little empirical work undertaken on the role of inward investors, especially in the UK. One means of assessing whether there may be an important factor bias from inward investment is to undertake an accounting decomposition of the skilled labour share of employment or the wage bill (see, for instance, Berman, Bound and Griliches, 1994). The aggregate change in the skilled proportion over a given time period can be decomposed as:

$$\Delta P = \Sigma_i \Delta S_{di} \bar{P}_{di} + \Sigma_i \Delta S_{fi} \bar{P}_{fi} + \Sigma_i \Delta P_{di} \bar{S}_{di} + \Sigma_i \Delta P_{fi} \bar{S}_{fi} \qquad (5.9)$$

where P_i = share of skilled labour in total employment or wage bill of industry i, S_i = share of industry i in total manufacturing employment or wage bill, and d, f = domestic and foreign firms respectively.

A bar over a term denotes a mean over time. The first two terms capture 'between' effects arising from shifts in the composition of demand between industries with different skill intensities and firms of different nationalities, and the second pair of terms capture 'within' effects arising from skill upgrading within industries. If foreign and domestic firms raise their skill proportions by equal amounts then the 'within' contribution from domestic firms should be $(1 - \alpha)$ times the 'within' contribution of foreign firms, where a is the share of total output produced by foreign firms.

We measure skilled and unskilled labour using data on non-operatives and operatives from the Annual Census of Production in the UK.[5] The long-term trends in the employment and wage-bill shares of non-operatives in the total population of foreign and domestic firms in the UK manufacturing sector are shown in Figure 5.4. In both cases foreign-owned firms are, on average, more skill-intensive than domestic ones, although both groups show a comparatively similar amount of skill upgrading over time.

Using two-digit industry data for the UK manufacturing sector between 1981 and 1992 we obtain the results reported in the upper

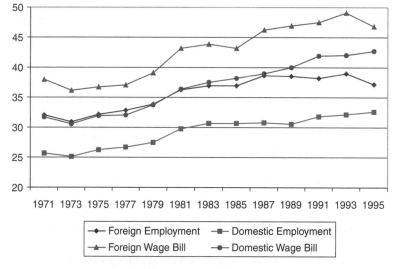

Source: Authors' calculations from Annual Census of Production, various issues.

Figure 5.4   Share of non-operatives in UK manufacturing (%)

Table 5.6   Accounting for skill upgrading in UK manufacturing 1981–92 (%)

	Annual growth (%)	'Between' contribution		'Within' contribution	
		Foreign	Domestic	Foreign	Domestic
Wage bill	1.36	0.55	–0.38	0.23	0.96
Employment	0.77	0.39	–0.30	0.13	0.55

Decomposition of 'Between' contribution

	Ownership		Upgrading	
	Foreign	Domestic	Foreign	Domestic
Wage bill	0.50	–0.45	0.05	0.07
Employment	0.35	–0.30	0.03	–0.00

Source: Authors' calculations using equations (5.9) and (5.10).

panel of Table 5.6. Foreign firms can 'account' for approximately two-thirds of the aggregate rise in the share of skilled labour in total employment, and approximately three-fifths of the rise in the wage bill share of skilled labour.[6] Much of this can be attributed to a shift in the composition of ownership towards more skill-intensive foreign firms, as captured in the 'between' effects, rather than a general switch in the pattern of demand towards more skill-intensive industries within manufacturing. The weighted 'within' contribution of foreign firms is broadly in line with what might have been expected given their share in output.

Aggregating across foreign and domestic firms yields the familiar result that most skill upgrading can be accounted for by within industry shifts rather than between industry ones, implying that the reported 'between' contributions largely reflect changes in the ownership structure. To see this more clearly, it is useful to further decompose the first pair of terms in (5.9) to give:

$$\Delta R_d \Sigma_i \bar{D}_i \bar{P}_{di} + \bar{R}_d \Sigma_i \Delta D_i \bar{P}_{di} + \Delta R_f \Sigma_i \bar{F}_i \bar{P}_{fi} + \bar{R}_f \Sigma_i \Delta F_i \bar{P}_{fi} \tag{5.10}$$

where F_i = share of industry i in total foreign firms manufacturing employment or wage bill, D_i = share of industry i in total domestic firms manufacturing employment or wage bill, and R = share of firms of nationality j in total manufacturing employment or wage bill.

The first and third terms in (5.10) capture ownership effects arising from the general change in the shares of foreign and domestic-owned firms in the total manufacturing sector. The other two terms reflect skill upgrading as a result of a switch in the composition of demand towards more skill-intensive industries. The results of this decomposition are shown in the lower panel of Table 5.6. It is clear that there has been little overall effect from a shift towards skill-intensive industries amongst either domestic or foreign firms. Most of the aggregate 'between' contribution reflects ownership changes and the rising share of more skill-intensive foreign-owned firms in the total population.

The within industry changes in the demand for skills by domestic and foreign firms are positively and significantly correlated, suggesting that common technological developments have occurred in foreign and domestic firms. Cross-sectional regressions of the (weighted) changes in domestic firms on the changes in foreign firms yield (t-statistics in parentheses):

Employment: Domestic   = $0.0004 + 2.7728^*$ Foreign $R^2 = 0.52$
                                   (1.1) (4.1)

Wage Bill: Domestic   = $0.0012 + 2.0988^*$ Foreign $R^2 = 0.62$
                                   (2.9) (5.2)

Since Table 5.6 indicates that the domestic industry contributions are approximately four times the size of the foreign ones (allowing for weighting by industry shares), the lower coefficient obtained in the regression analysis indicates a wide dispersion in the different effects from foreign and domestic firms across industries.

Inward investment and R&D

Foreign firms have come to play an increasingly important role in both the financing and performance of research and development in the UK. Table 5.7 summarizes the trends over the last decade for business enterprise R&D. The share of business enterprise R&D expenditure performed by foreign-owned firms more than doubled between 1989 and 1999. Of the total level of R&D expenditure by foreign firms in 1998 and 1999, some 47.4 per cent was undertaken by US-owned affiliates, and 27.1 per cent by EU-owned affiliates. Japanese affiliates accounted for just 7.8 per cent.

The importance of foreign firms in total R&D becomes even more apparent if expenditure is converted into constant prices using the GDP deflator from the UK national accounts. In 1995 prices total expenditure on R&D declined for three successive years in the mid-1990s, and even after a recovery in 1999 was still only 4.2 per cent higher than in 1989. Expenditure by foreign firms at constant prices almost doubled between 1989 and 1999, whereas expenditure by UK-owned firms declined by 14.2 per cent during this period.

One distinctive feature of the UK is that it is the only major country in which the share of foreign firms in manufacturing R&D is greater

Table 5.7 Business enterprise R&D expenditure

	1989	1993	1994	1995	1996	1997	1998	1999
Total R&D (£m)	7,650	9,069	9,204	9,254	9,431	9,680	10,261	11,302
UK-owned	6,394	6,729	6,630	6,555	6,588	6,547	7,179	7,779
Foreign-owned	1,256	2,340	2,574	2,690	2,843	3,133	3,082	3,523
Total R&D (£m, 1995 prices)	9,684	9,457	9,469	9,245	9,139	9,124	9,396	10,092
UK-owned	8,094	7,017	6,821	6,555	6,384	6,171	6,574	6,946
Foreign-owned	1,590	2,440	2,648	2,690	2,755	2,953	2,822	3,146
Foreign-owned Share (%)	16.4	25.8	28.0	29.1	30.1	32.4	30.0	31.2
Memorandum GDP Deflator	79.0	95.9	97.2	100.0	103.2	106.1	109.2	112.0

Source: Research and Development in UK Business, Business Monitor MA14 (various issues).

than their share in production (OECD, 1998). Put differently, their average R&D intensity is higher than that of domestic firms. Canada is the sole G7 economy in which the foreign contribution to R&D is similar to that in the UK, but there is an important difference between the UK experience and that of Canada: the R&D expenditure of domestic firms in the UK has fallen in real terms, whereas it has risen rapidly in Canada.

A further dimension of the contribution of foreign-owned firms is provided by their research output in the form of patentable products and processes. Cantwell, Iammarino and Noonan (2000) show that foreign-owned firms received 45 per cent of the patents granted by the United States Patent and Trademark Office (USPTO) to large firms resident in the UK between 1991 and 1995, compared to just over one-third of the patents granted in the 1980s. There has been a steady upward trend in the foreign firm share since the 1960s, as Figure 5.5 illustrates.

The research activities of foreign firms in the UK also have a comparatively narrow regional dispersion, with some 60 per cent of the patents granted by the USPTO to large foreign firms resident in the UK between 1969 and 1995 being granted to firms located in the South-east. The corresponding proportion for domestic firms was 40 per cent. To this extent inward investors may be reinforcing existing regional disparities.

Of course the proportion of R&D funded and undertaken by foreign-controlled entities does not in itself matter, although it probably raises the direct influence of foreign economic conditions on domestic

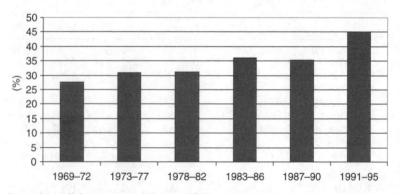

Source: Cantwell, Iammarino and Noonan (2000).

Figure 5.5   Foreign firms' share of US patents granted to UK-resident firms

expenditure. Indeed, part of the explanation for the increase in the foreign share may just be the take-over of R&D-intensive indigenous companies by foreign companies. Whilst the additional foreign funding of R&D in the UK is welcome, there are many areas where further research is needed before the implications for the UK economy are well understood. If it were to prove the case that the magnitude of spillovers from foreign firms was dependent upon domestic firms undertaking additional R&D to facilitate technology adoption, then the decline in the volume of R&D expenditure by UK firms over the past decade is somewhat worrying. A further possibility is that UK-owned firms have simply chosen to undertake their R&D elsewhere in locations that have developed their technological capabilities more rapidly.

Inward investment and exports

Multinational firms dominate merchandise trade and play an increasing role in trade in services. Inward investors can thus have a marked effect on the trade performance of host economies. This will almost certainly be associated with some changes in the industrial structure of the host economy, and possibly also the long-run size of that economy if there are beneficial externalities from exporting. Barrell and Pain (1997) and Pain and Wakelin (1998) both find that inward investment has had a significant positive effect on aggregate UK export performance, with a rise of 10 per cent in the real value of the stock of inward investment estimated to raise the volume of manufactured exports by 0.75 per cent (standard error 0.17), other things being equal.

One important means through which inward investors can expand exports is through sales to their parent companies. Unfortunately there are no official data on the current level of intra-firm trade by the total population of inward investors in the UK. Previous surveys were discontinued in the early 1980s. At that time it was already clear that foreign-owned firms were relatively export-intensive, accounting for 34 per cent of all manufacturing exports in 1981 compared to 18.25 per cent of gross value added output.

However, it is possible to assess the contribution of US-owned companies in the UK to total bilateral trade between the UK and the USA by using the detailed statistics available in the United States on the operations of overseas affiliates of US parent companies. These indicate that in 1998 exports by US non-bank foreign affiliates in the UK represented 28.6 per cent of total UK merchandise exports to the USA, with the proportion having risen from 20 per cent in the mid-1980s. During this period the value of affiliate exports has tripled from $3 billion in 1986 to $9.9 billion in 1998. Figure 5.6 breaks down the exports of the US affiliates into exports to their parent companies (intra-firm trade) and exports to third parties. It is clear that the overall upward trend in the affiliate share is primarily driven by the increasing importance of intra-firm trade. This may reflect the extent to which US multinational companies have been able to exploit informational advantages arising from their (internal) network connections (Rangan and Lawrence, 1999).

A further important question is whether the presence of multinational firms who are successful exporters helps domestic firms to enter foreign markets: for instance, foreign companies can provide knowledge and expertise that can help domestic firms to overcome the fixed costs of entry into export markets. Girma *et al.* (2000) obtain evidence that appears to support the existence of knowledge-related export spillovers in the UK. They find that the probability of a firm in a particular manufacturing industry choosing to export has a significant positive association with the share of foreign-owned firms in employment in that industry and the level of R&D expenditure by foreign firms in that industry. There is less evidence in favour of the hypothesis that the effects are strongest in those sectors in which foreign-owned firms

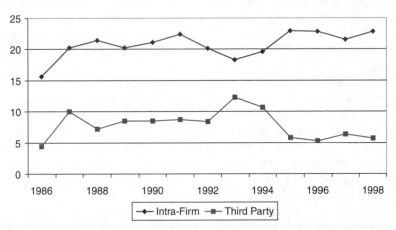

Source: Authors' calculations from US International Transactions and the Operations of US Multinational Companies, Survey of Current Business, various issues.

Figure 5.6   Exports to the USA by US affiliates in the UK (% of total UK exports to USA)

account for the largest shares of total export activity, possibly suggesting that country-specific information from foreign firms may be more important than industry-specific information.

4 Policies to attract inward investment

If inward investment does affect the growth prospects of host economies then it becomes important to understand the policies available to affect location choice. Countries increasingly compete for investments in 'location tournaments' by offering investment incentives. The factors affecting the location decisions of US, Japanese and German companies are studied in detail in Barrell and Pain (1997, 1998, 1999a, 1999b), Hubert and Pain (2002) and Pain and Young (2000). Their results highlight a number of key factors:

- membership of the EU/European Economic Area and participation in the Single Market Programme;
- unit labour costs relative to other European locations;
- government fixed investment as a share of GDP and the effective corporate tax rate; relative to other locations;
- agglomeration economies from large markets and the indigenous research base.

The UK has gained inward investment, particularly in manufacturing, by primarily attracting investments as a result of labour market flexibility and measures to reduce the effective corporate tax rate. Other countries, notably Germany, have attracted investments which aim to tap into the agglomeration economies available from the large domestic research base. It is of interest to note that in the manufacturing sector, US multinational affiliates produce a greater volume of output and undertake greater R&D expenditure in Germany than they do in the UK, although employment is higher in British affiliates. The average labour productivity of US affiliates in the UK is over 15 per cent lower than in all US affiliates in the European Union and 25 per cent lower than in affiliates in Germany (see, for instance, Barrell and Pain, 1999b).

The existence of agglomeration economies has important implications for the structure of proactive inward investment policies. Although the direct impact of fiscal incentives is often found to be small compared to other determinants of location choice, temporary policy initiatives could have permanent effects on inward investment, and hence growth prospects, if they helped agglomerations (or clusters) to become established. Equally, even if the direct benefits from fiscal incentives are limited because all competitors also have them, the losses from their unilateral abolition could be large and difficult to reverse.

There is some potential for tension between the preferences of regional and local development agencies and those of central government. If agglomeration forces are significant, then individual development agencies have a strong incentive to seek to attract as much inward investment as possible. Losing out on one project raises the chances of losing out on subsequent projects, but competition between individual agencies need not produce the optimal outcome for the country as a whole. In principle at least, the losses that could result from excessive local competition which prevents the formation of a single, large agglomeration of related activities might outweigh the benefits to the individual regions. Policies that seek to disperse foreign firms to regions with high unemployment might also lower the potential spillovers that would arise if they were more centrally located close to the majority of existing domestic firms. The issue of regional spillovers from inward investment is addressed by Driffield (2000) and Girma and Wakelin (2000). Both studies indicate that the presence of foreign firms has a positive effect on the productivity of UK firms, but find that the spillovers tend to be confined to the region in which the investment takes place.

Investments also have to fit in with the capabilities of the host location and the state of development. Carefully formulated, proactive industrial policies targeted at particular sectors can be highly successful, as the experience of Ireland indicates (Ruane and Görg, 1999). Complementary public policies designed to improve the contestability of national markets and strengthen the local science base and the adaptability of the local workforce may help to raise the magnitude and speed with which new ideas and technologies spillover to local firms.

5 Summary

Over the years there have been a number of reviews of the impact of inward investment on the British economy. The evidence presented here suggests that foreign-owned firms are making a positive contribution to the economy and that the level of national income is higher than it would otherwise have been if the inward investment seen over the last two or three decades had not taken place. However, it is far from clear that the potential gains from inward investment have been fully realized. The externalities available from inward investment do not always appear to have been distributed equally amongst industries or regions, and there appears to be little evidence that the average productivity gap between foreign and UK firms has been closed over time. Whilst some gap might reasonably be expected to persist, since the average foreign-owned company operates on a larger scale than the average British company, the apparent failure to narrow the gap does suggest that there may be policies or institutional reforms which could help to raise the magnitude of spillovers and the dissemination of best-practice techniques still further.

The research agendas set out in Pain (2000) and Blomström, Kokko and Globerman (2000) highlight a number of areas in which further research might usefully be undertaken. These include the following:

1   Whether spillovers are generic to all inward investors, or whether there are particular types of investor or particular sectors which are more important than others.
2   Whether there are significant inter-industry spillovers from inward investment, as suggested by the econometric results of Hubert and Pain (2001) and, if so, what they are and how they are diffused.
3   The impact of the mode of entry on the transmission of knowledge and technologies to host country firms. Does the re-organization of existing companies have the same impact as the establishment of 'greenfield' sites or joint ventures and strategic alliances?
4   The role of labour mobility in the transmission of knowledge. There is little empirical evidence on the potential existence and magnitude of spillovers resulting from the movement of managers and other skilled employees from foreign-owned firms to domestic ones.
5   The importance of the skills and capabilities of the workforce in assimilating new ideas and technologies from inward investors.
6   Whether the presence of a single inward investor can matter as much as the presence of a number of firms. Greater competition from foreign firms might reasonably be expected to affect the speed with which domestic firms seek to adopt new practices, but a single, high-profile investor could be all that is required to indicate whether new techniques and business methods are viable in the host economy.

All of these issues have yet to be studied in any great detail, either in the UK or in most other industrialized economies. The growing importance of inward investment in national economies and the level of interest displayed by policy-makers make these omissions somewhat surprising.

Notes

1   Data for the global FDI stock and the stock in developed countries (in effect, the OECD) are taken from Dunning (1988) and UNCTAD (2000).
2   Calculated using data from UNCTAD (2000), Annex Tables A.IV.6 and B.1.
3   Attempts to construct a longer data set are hampered by significant changes in the UK Standard Industrial Classification in both 1980 and 1992.
4   We use value-added output deflated by industry-specific producer prices (Q), labour input measured as employee hours (L) and real hourly compensation per employee (W/P). Subscript i denotes an industry-specific measure.
5   Labour quality could also be measured using indicators of educational attainment and training. In practice the lack of time series data on such indicators has led many authors to use data based on occupation. Berman, Bound and Griliches (1994) and Berman, Bound and Machin (1998) find similar shifts in the demand for skilled labour in the USA and the UK using different measures of skills.
6   The results may be sensitive to the level of disaggregation of the data used.

References

Barrell, R. and N. Pain (1997), 'Foreign direct investment, technological change and economic growth within Europe', *Economic Journal*, 107, pp. 1770–86.

Barrell, R. and N. Pain (1998), 'Real exchange rates, agglomerations and irreversibilities: macroeconomic policy and FDI in EMU', *Oxford Review of Economic Policy*, Vol. 14, No. 3, pp. 152–67.

Barrell, R. and N. Pain (1999a), 'Trade restraints and Japanese direct investment flows', *European Economic Review*, 43, pp. 29–45.

Barrell, R. and N. Pain (1999b), 'Domestic institutions, agglomerations and foreign direct investment in Europe', *European Economic Review*, 43, pp. 925–34.

Berman, E., J. Bound and Z. Griliches (1994), 'Changes in the demand for skilled labour within US manufacturing industries', *Quarterly Journal of Economics*, 109, pp. 367–98.

Berman, E., J. Bound and S. Machin (1998), 'Implications of skill-biased technological change: international evidence', *Quarterly Journal of Economics*, CXIII, pp. 1,245–79.

Blomström, M. (1986), 'Foreign investment and productive efficiency: the case of Mexico', *Journal of Industrial Economics*, Vol. 35, pp. 97–110.

Blomström, M. and F. Sjöholm (1999), 'Technology transfer and spillovers: does local participation with multinationals matter?', *European Economic Review*, 43, pp. 915–23.

Blomström, M., A. Kokko and S. Globerman (2000), 'The determinants of host country spillovers from foreign direct investment: a review and synthesis of the literature', in N. Pain (ed.), *Inward Investment, Technological Change and Growth: The Impact of Multinational Corporations on the UK Economy*, London, Palgrave.

Cantwell, J., S. Iammarino and C. Noonan (2000), 'Sticky places in slippery space: the location of technological innovation in the European regions', in N. Pain (ed), *Inward Investment, Technological Change and Growth: The Impact of Multinational Corporations on the UK Economy*, London, Palgrave.

Caves, R. E. (1974). 'Multinational firms, competition and productivity in host-country markets', *Economica*, 41, pp. 176–93.

Coe, D. T., E. Helpman and A. W. Hoffmaister (1997), 'North-South R&D spillovers', *The Economic Journal*, 107, pp. 134–49.

Davies, S. W. and B. R. Lyons (1991), 'Characterising relative performance: the productivity advantage of foreign owned firms in the UK', *Oxford Economic Papers*, 43, pp. 584–95.

Driffield, N. (2000), 'Regional policy and the impact of FDI in the UK', in N. Pain (ed.), *Inward Investment, Technological Change and Growth: The Impact of Multinational Corporations on the UK Economy*, London, Palgrave.

DTI (1998), *Our Competitive Future: Building The Knowledge Driven Economy*, The Competitiveness White Paper: Analysis and Background, London, DTI.

Dunning, J. H. (1988), *Explaining International Production* (HarperCollins, London).

Eltis, W. (1996). 'How low profitability and weak innovativeness undermines UK industrial growth', *Economic Journal*, 106, pp. 184–95.

Gillespie, G., P. G. McGregor, J. K. Swales and Y. Yin (2000), 'A regional computable general equilibrium analysis of the demand and "efficiency-spillover" effects of FDI', in N. Pain (ed.), *Inward Investment, Technological Change and Growth: The Impact of Multinational Corporations on the UK Economy*, London, Palgrave.

Girma, S., D. Greenaway, K. Wakelin and N. Sousa (2000), 'Host country effects of FDI in the UK: recent evidence from firm data', in N. Pain (ed.), *Inward Investment, Technological Change and Growth: The Impact of Multinational Corporations on the UK Economy*, London, Palgrave.

Girma, S. and K. Wakelin (2000), *Are there Regional Spillovers from FDI in the UK?*, University of Nottingham GLM Research Paper 2000/16.

Globerman, S. (1979). 'Foreign direct investment and "spillover" efficiency benefits in Canadian manufacturing industries', *Canadian Journal of Economics*, XII, pp. 42–56.

Griffith, R. and H. Simpson (2001), *Characteristics of Foreign-owned Firms in British Manufacturing*, Institute for Fiscal Studies Working Paper WP01/10.

House of Commons (1998), *Investment in Industry in Wales*, Welsh Affairs Committee Fourth Report, House of Commons Session 1997–98, HC 821.

House of Commons (1999), *Inward/Outward Investment in Scotland*, Scottish Affairs Committee First Report, House of Commons Session 1998–99, HC 84-I.

Hubert, F. and N. Pain (2000), 'Inward investment and technical progress in the United Kingdom', in N. Pain (ed.), *Inward Investment, Technological Change and Growth: The Impact of Multinational Corporations on the UK Economy*, London, Palgrave.

Hubert, F. and N. Pain (2001), 'Inward investment and technical progress in the UK manufacturing sector', *Scottish Journal of Political Economy*, 48, pp. 134–47.

Hubert, F. and N. Pain (2002), 'Fiscal incentives, European integration and the location of foreign direct investment', *The Manchester School*, 70, pp. 336–63.

Layard, R., S. Nickell and R. Jackman (1991), *Unemployment: Macroeconomic Performance and the Labour Market,* Oxford, Oxford University Press.

Mansfield, E. and A. Romeo (1980), 'Technology transfer to overseas subsidiaries by US based firms', *Quarterly Journal of Economics,* 95, pp. 737–50.

OECD (1998), *Internationalisation of Industrial R&D: Patterns and Trends,* Paris, OECD.

Oulton, N. (2000), 'Why do foreign-owned firms in the UK have higher labour productivity?', in N. Pain (ed.), *Inward Investment, Technological Change and Growth: The Impact of Multinational Corporations on the UK Economy,* London, Palgrave.

PA Cambridge Economic Consultants (1995), *Assessment of the Wider Effects of Foreign Direct Investment in Manufacturing in the UK.* Report by PA Cambridge Economic Consultants for Department of Trade and Industry.

Pain, N. (ed.) (2000), *Inward Investment, Technological Change and Growth: The Impact of Multinational Corporations on the UK Economy,* London, Palgrave.

Pain, N. and K. Wakelin (1998), 'Export performance and the role of foreign direct investment', *The Manchester School Supplement,* 66, pp. 62–88.

Pain, N. and G. Young (2000), 'The macroeconomic impact of UK withdrawal from the EU', presented to Money, Macro and Finance Research Group Annual Conference, South Bank University.

Rangan, S. and R. Z. Lawrence (1999), 'Search and deliberation in international exchange: learning from multinational trade about lags, distance effects and home bias', NBER Paper No. 7012.

Rodrik, D. (1997), 'TFPG controversies, institutions and economic performance in East Asia', NBER Working Paper No. 5914.

Ruane, F. and H. Görg (1999), 'Irish FDI policy and investment from the EU', in R. Barrell, and N. Pain (eds), *Investment, Innovation and the Diffusion of Technology in Europe,* Cambridge, Cambridge University Press.

UNCTAD (2000), *World Investment Report,* Geneva, United Nations.

6
Foreign-owned Firms and the Competitiveness of France as a Host Country: A Focus on Foreign Trade and Innovation Issues*

Rémi Lallement

1 Introduction

In France, as in several other developed countries, the public debate on matters related to foreign direct investment (FDI) often leads to intense controversies. At the beginning of the 1990s, the questions raised were mostly related to *outward* FDI and (more precisely) to the phenomenon of relocation abroad. At the end of the decade, however, several discussions were focused on questions dealing with *inward* capital flows, such as the fast growing influence of foreign institutional investors in the capital structure of domestic firms (Morin, 1998) or topics such as 'the nationality of the firm' (Commissariat Général du Plan, or CGP, 1999a) or France's attractiveness as a business location (Lavenir *et al.*, 2001).

Of course, the debate about the link between inward FDI and the economic development of the host country is not a brand new one in France, although it has a shorter tradition there than it has in other major industrial countries such as the USA or Germany, where foreign involvement played a bigger role at earlier stages of the industrial revolution. In the USA, for instance, the ideas submitted to the Congress by Hamilton (1791) reflected the enduring concern shared by many

* This chapter does not necessarily reflect the view of the CGP. The author would like to thank Dominique Francoz (of the Ministry of Education, Research and Technology) for providing some recent data, and Mohamed Harfi (CGP) for useful comments on an earlier draft. The usual disclaimers apply.

Americans about the importance of this topic. The 'Who is Us' controversy launched by Reich (1990) could be considered a mere revival of this debate. As for Germany, the discussion about *Überfremdung* appears to have been recurrent in the 1850s, 1890s, 1920s and 1950s, as recalled by Kindleberger (1987). In 2000, the take-over of Mannesmann by Vodafone-Airtouch showed that the topic remains a key issue. In France, the debate dates back only to the end of the 1960s. The growth of inward (mainly American) FDI in France was then usually considered with mixed feelings by prominent opinion makers, politicians and civil servants, but generally less as a potential source of modernization or as a possible stimulus for competition than as a symptom of a dominated position *vis-à-vis* the investing countries (Servan-Schreiber, 1967), in a tradition of thought implicitly dating back to Hilferding (1955; first published 1910).

As a matter of fact, there still are no clear cut conclusions about the general effects of foreign-controlled firms on the host country's economy. According to the context, two major rival interpretations can a priori be distinguished. A first approach leads us to consider a large number of foreign-owned firms (FOFs) as a sign of a marked attractiveness on the part of the domestic locations. Notably in the form of greenfield projects, inward FDI is then supposed to bring additional financial capital, to give access to foreign markets (Pain and Wakelin, 1998), and to tap into a flow of intangible assets in the form of specific managerial competencies and know-how (Hirschman, 1966) or through technological spillover effects. To that extent, it contributes to the reinforcing of local production and innovation capacities in the host country (Barry and Bradley, 1997). The second approach is more inclined to interpret inward FDI as a sign of a weak competitive ability on the part of the host country's firms compared to competitors based in the investing countries (Hymer, 1976), and nowadays also as a measure of the degree of domestic exposure or vulnerability in the domain of mergers and acquisitions, which have become the primary vehicle behind the growth of FDI. In other words, the inflow of FDI reveals not only the preferences of foreign investors but also the degree of structural competitiveness and openness of the domestic economy (Mazier, 1995). In such a situation, the penetration of foreign capital *eventually* weakens the host economy by reducing its autonomy, the number of its decision centres and the size of its innovation system, *if* the foreign investors choose to concentrate most of their strategic activities in other countries (Dunning, 1993).

In order to shed some light on these effects and, more generally, on the link between inward FDI and the economic performance in the host country, it is necessary to refer to a concrete situation. In this respect, lessons can a priori be learnt from France, a country where the number of FOFs has not only been rapidly growing in the recent years but also has reached an above average level, compared to the other major industrial countries. Both at an analytical and at an empirical level, two related questions then have to be raised and answered: the meaning of the concept of competitiveness at the level of nations, and the choice of the relevant statistical indicators in this domain.

For France, we have chosen here to focus on two particular and complementary aspects. The first concerns the particularities of FOFs as regards foreign trade (section 3). It corresponds to the most usual perspective with regard to competitiveness, and several recent studies based on micro and macro data provide relatively robust results about the contribution of FOFs to France's exports, imports and trade balance. The competitiveness of the host country is then understood roughly as the capacity of its domestic firms to *create value added* though their overall cross-border trade at a given point in time. The second aspect deals with the performance of FOFs with regard to innovation activity (section 4). It is less traditional but allows us to go beyond a mere static approach to competitiveness. It aims to show to what extent the subsidiaries of foreign firms take part in the technological dynamics and, beyond that, in the *creation of competitive advantages* within the domestic economy. Before that, it is necessary to understand basic information about the relative importance of foreign-controlled firms in France and about the reasons why the presence of these firms has recorded an unprecedented growth there during the last 15 years (section 2).

2 The above-average and growing number of foreign-owned firms in France: an overview

In France, the relatively suspicious or restrictive attitude of several governments towards foreign-based multinationals at the end of the 1960s did not bother most foreign investors. Two decades after the Second World War, France had already become one of the main host countries for US-based firms in the EC, although slightly less so than (West) Germany. After the slow but steady increase recorded during the 1970s and until the mid-1980s, the foreign affiliates' profile has been growing strongly in both relative and absolute terms.

Flow and stock data relating to inward FDI in France

The easiest way to emphasize the size and growth of the FOFs' presence during the past decades is to refer to data in terms of inward FDI. At the beginning of the 1970s, the share of France as a host country for worldwide inflows of FDI was only around 3 per cent, and thus much lower than the share of countries such as the UK (12 per cent), West Germany (6 per cent), but also Italy and the Netherlands (4 per cent: Tersen and Bricout, 1996, p. 10). Since then, its share in the total inflows in the OECD countries has gone up from an average of 6.3 per cent during the years 1981–90 to an average of 9.3 per cent in the period 1991–98 (Nivat, 1999, p. 3, Table 2). From 1990 to 1998, France was ranked behind the USA and UK as the third biggest receiver of FDI inflows among the OECD countries, with a cumulated amount of almost US$216 billion, nearly twice as much as the total amount accounted for by Germany (US$116 billion) during the same time (OECD, 2000, p. 29). The stock data confirm roughly the same picture, although France appears in these terms only as the world's fifth largest receiver of inward FDI in 1999, after the USA, the UK, Germany and China, according to UNCTAD's (the UN Conference on Trade and Development) calculations. Given that FDI data remain relatively difficult to compare internationally, it is interesting to consider indicators about the activity of FOFs, although the comparability problems still linger to some extent.

Indicators of foreign-owned firms' activity in the manufacturing industry

In France, institutions such as INSEE (the French statistical office) and SESSI (the Statistical Department of the Ministry of Industry) have developed sophisticated databases concerning the financial links between affiliated firms for years, with data consolidated at the level of groups (Mathieu, 1999; Thollon-Pommerol, 1999). Data on the foreign presence among the domestic manufacturing firms employing more than 20 people have been published every year since 1974. Similar data for other major industrial countries show that the relative share of FOFs is not only comparatively high in France, but also that it has been rising steadily there since the middle of the 1980s.

Between 1989 and 1996, the total number of people employed by manufacturing FOFs diminished in Germany by more than 170,000, while it increased by more than 90,000 in France. Among the 10 industrial countries for which corresponding data are published by the OECD, France appears to be the country where the gain in these terms has been the strongest. It even ranks ahead of the USA, where the absolute number of these jobs was up by around 75,000. Among these 10 countries, moreover, France is (together with the UK, Japan, Sweden and Finland) one of those where domestic manufacturing employment globally *increased* in FOFs (by an average of nearly 2 per cent per year in France) while it globally *declined* in domestic firms (by more than 2 per cent per year in France) (OECD, 1999, pp. 18–19). The share of foreign affiliates in domestic manufacturing employment today reaches a much higher level in France than in bigger countries such as Japan, the USA and Germany, but also in similar or smaller ones such as the UK or Italy. The data collected by the OECD show that this has been the case for 20 years, although to a lower extent with regard to employment data (Table 6.1). Since the end of the 1980s, this growing relative importance of FOFs in France has been observable for the main available indicators (Table 6.2).

The distribution of foreign-owned firms by home country and by industry

For France as for Germany to some extent, the geographic distribution of FDI by countries of origin is relatively concentrated *vis-à-vis* other European countries. This is far less the case for countries like the UK or the Netherlands, which are more diversified in this respect, as shown by Lallement (2001). At the end of 1998 and in all sectors, according to the Banque de France's data, the immediate owners of 65.0 per cent of the total stock of inward FDI in France were located in the EU and 10.5 per cent in other West European countries.[1] In other words, around three-quarters of all inward FDI originated in Western Europe. For the manufacturing industry, the data furnished by the SESSI allow a finer geographical breakdown, on the basis of the ultimate beneficial owner (UBO). In terms of relative share in the total number of people employed by majority foreign-owned manufacturing firms, the main countries investing in France were, at the beginning of 1998, the USA (29.3 per cent), Germany (16.8 per cent), the UK (14.7 per cent), Switzerland (8.2 per cent), Italy (5.8 per cent), Belgium–Luxembourg (5.0 per cent) and the Netherlands (4.8 per cent).

A link can be observed between this geographical distribution and the industrial distribution of foreign-controlled businesses in France. In 1993, for instance, at a time when the relative share of Germany as a home country in the total of the majority foreign-owned manufacturing employment in France was 17.2 per cent on average, this German share was clearly higher in industries such as scientific instruments

Table 6.1 The share of foreign-owned firms in the manufacturing industry of the G-6 countries (%)

	1980[a]		1990[b]		1993[c]		1996[d]	
	Turnover	Employees	Turnover	Employees	Turnover	Employees	Turnover	Employees
France	26.6	18.3	28.4	23.8	30.0[e]	24.3[e]	31.2[e]	25.8[e]
UK[ef]	19.3	14.8	25.1	16.2	29.2	18.1	33.2	19.2
Germany[eg]	15.7	9.0	13.2	7.2	13.3	7.4	12.8	6.9
USA	3.9	5.1	14.9	10.0	14.5	11.6	n.a.	11.4
Italy[e]	16.8	13.5	n.a.	n.a.	13.0	n.a.	11.9	8.9
Japan[e]	4.6[f]	1.6	2.4[f]	1.1	1.2	0.8	1.2	0.8

[a] 1981 for the UK and Italy

[b] 1989 for the USA and Japan

[c] 1992 for the data on turnover in the USA

[d] 1995 for Italy

[e] majority FOFs only

[f] production instead of turnover

[g] Federal Republic of Germany (OECD data in all cases)

Sources: OECD (1999), Dupont and François (1998) for the years 1993 and 1996; OECD (1994) and SESSI (1989) for the years 1980 and 1990.

Table 6.2   The relative share of foreign-owned firms in France's domestic manufacturing industry (%)

	1975	1980	1985	1990	1994	1998
Number of firms	6.5	9.0	10.7	11.8	12.5 (11.5)	(14.2)
Number of employees	17.9	18.3	21.1	23.7	26.3 (24.3)	(30.0)
Turnover	21.6	24.1	26.7	28.4	31.8 (30.0)	(35.8)
Value added	21.9	22.6	25.3	27.1	30.8 (28.7)	(34.7)
Gross fixed capital formation	24.5	29.3	26.2	28.4	32.8 (30.5)	(36.2)
Exports	n.a.	26.8	30.5	31.1	35.6 (33.6)	(40.2)

Note: Share of FOFs among firms employing more than 20 people in France's domestic manufacturing industry (food industry excluded), including the minority FOFs (foreign-owned share above 20 per cent for the years 1975, 1980 and 1985, above 33 per cent for 1994). Figures in brackets show majority FOFs only. Data from SESSI/Trésor.
Sources: Hatem (1995), SESSI (1989), SESSI (1997) and SESSI (2000).

(25.0 per cent), pharmaceuticals (23.6 per cent), non-electrical machinery (21.8 per cent) and electrical machinery (18.8 per cent: Hatzichronoglou, 1998, p. 207, Table 3). These industries belong to the main domains of specialization of the German economy.

In the case of German-owned firms as more generally, the presence of FOFs in France also reflects to some extent certain location advantages and the specialization of the French economy itself. In the French manufacturing industry, the presence of these firms is particularly developed in five domains that represent around two-thirds of the total foreign-owned employment: transportation equipment, electrical and electronic equipment, mechanical engineering, chemicals, and office and computing machinery. In this last case, the share of FOFs in the total domestic performance reached 68.1 per cent in employment, 77.3 per cent in turnover and 85.0 per cent in exports in 1998.[2] Such a dominant presence of FOFs can be considered as a sign of a relative weakness of the French industry in the field of office and computing machinery; however, it does not mean that these FOFs should necessarily have a negative impact on the domestic industry, as will be shown below.

A few possible explanations for the growing presence of foreign-owned firms in France

Before switching to considerations in terms of impact, it is necessary to mention a few explanations for the rising presence of FOFs in France. One the one hand (and this may be more a tautological than a real explanation), the fact that France has tapped into a growing share of worldwide FDI is a sign that this country has intrinsically gained in attractiveness as a business location during the last decades. On the other hand, the increased penetration of foreign capital registered in France since the middle of the 1970s reflects not only the financial vulnerability of the French small and middle-sized firms, but also the quasi-absence of French pension funds. Under the growing pressure of foreign (in France, mostly Anglo-Saxon) institutional investors promoting strict principles of corporate governance, the 'hardcore shareholdings', or *noyaux durs*, which have been built up since the privatization wave started in 1986, have gradually been dispersed since 1994–5. Inspired by some traits of the German model, this network of crossed shareholding was supposed to stabilize the ownership structure of the former state-controlled firms after their privatization, and to prevent them from being the target of hostile take-over bids. Its disappearance made it much easier for foreign investors to purchase small or large shares in the main French firms (Morin, 1998, pp. 28–29; Lallement, 2001, pp. 95–96). The growth of foreign capital in France therefore has to do with the development of both FDI and portfolio investment. It is intrinsically linked with the boom of cross-border mergers and acquisitions (M&As) and stock markets. In France, the relative share of non-residents in stock market capitalization increased from 23.6 per cent in December 1993 to 36.9 per cent in December 1999; in Germany, by comparison, the corresponding share also increased, but at a much lower level, from 11 per cent in 1991 to 16 per cent in 1999 (see Grandjean, 2000, p. 88; Institut der Deutschen Wirtschaft, 2000). No other major developed country has apparently reached a higher share in this domain (Figure 6.1).

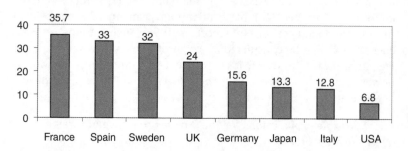

Data: Observatoire européen de l'épargne.
Source: Davydoff (2000), p. 28.

Figure 6.1   The share of non-residents in stock market capitalization in 1999 (%)

Another sort of explanation concerns the role of attractiveness policies and, more precisely, the attitude of the French government towards foreign investors. In contrast to Bonn, Paris has had the reputation of being inclined to hostile practices – or at least to overall restrictive behaviour – for many years; in Europe, this was also true of Rome and even, until the 1970s, of London (Gillespie, 1972, p. 414; Dunning, 1993, p. 389; US Congress, 1993, pp. 7 and 68–9). Since that time, the attitude of the successive French governments has changed significantly in this respect; most administrative controls on inward FDI have been abolished, and a long-lasting commitment to openness has progressively been implemented towards foreign investors. Moreover, a specific attractiveness policy has been developed, including the creation of the 'Invest in France Network' by the French state agency for regional development (DATAR) in 1992. Some scholars go as far as to claim that the French administration in the mid-1980s had *de facto* adopted a policy that was more inclined to support inward FDI than outward FDI (see, e.g., Michalet, 1997, p. 320, for public policy on inward FDI see Hörning, 1998).

On distinctive features of the foreign-owned firms with respect to some performance indicators

Before trying to assess the consequences of inward FDI for the host country, it is necessary to observe that these firms present a series of distinctive features with respect to some performance indicators. In all 13 industrial countries mentioned by the OECD in its report on this topic, the average level of labour productivity (gross production per head) in the manufacturing industry was higher in the FOFs than in domestic firms in 1996. A similar observation can be made for the level of wages and salaries. France appears to be (with the USA and Finland) one of the countries where the difference in labour productivity is relatively small (around 20 per cent), while it is particularly high in countries such as Germany (or Japan and the Netherlands), where it exceeds 100 per cent. In terms of wages and salaries, the average gap is also relatively small in France: 12 per cent in 1996, having been 10 per cent in 1989 (see Hatzichronoglou, 1998, p. 211; OECD, 1999, p. 23). A priori, these higher performances by FOFs can reflect gain due to the superior quality of the foreign management. Generally, in fact, it seems to be largely due to a selection bias, as will be shown later. In the many cases where the foreign presence results from a take-over bid, one reason for such a bias can be a 'picking the winner' effect.

In France, the average 'superiority' of FOFs can also be observed for indicators such as fixed capital formation per head, profit per head or exports per head (CGP, 1992, p. 154). However, it is not the case for other indicators such as the ratio investment/value added. For profit per head, furthermore, this lead only exists *vis-à-vis* independent firms and not compared with firms belonging to *French*-owned groups (Dupont and Mathieu, 1993, p. 4). It is therefore interesting to refer to the study carried out by Houdebine and Topiol-Bensaïd (1999), which compares a sample of FOFs with a sample consisting of firms belonging to French- (or foreign-) owned groups, and, furthermore, which goes beyond the manufacturing industry. When controlling for firm size and industry, a series of significant differences appears, such as a higher labour productivity (notably in small and medium-sized enterprises, or SMEs), higher wages per head (especially in the tertiary sector) and a higher export ratio. In the case of manufacturing firms in 1995, the average export ratio reached 32 per cent in FOFs, which is nearly twice as high as the ratio measured for the firms belonging to French- (or foreign-) owned groups (17 per cent), with the same size and from the same industry. Another interesting result from this study shows that, again when controlling for size and industry, the differences observed in terms of wages per head and productivity (value added per head) cannot generally be explained by the capital-intensity of the firms, but is mainly due to the fact that the FOFs on average employ a workforce with a higher level of qualification. When controlling for qualification structure as well, the productivity and wage level nonetheless appear to be higher in the FOFs.

3 The contribution of foreign-owned firms to France's foreign trade

The stylized facts that have just been mentioned lead to the conclusion that, on average, FOFs in France do not really differ much from other domestic firms in terms of domestic investment, but they do to some extent in other variables such as wages and labour productivity and even more so as regards the export ratio. In order to assess the consequences of inward FDI for the economic performance of France as a host country, it can therefore be considered relevant to focus on the link between inward FDI and foreign trade.[3] For France, two sets of data and studies are available on this issue. The first one is based on the already mentioned database featuring the capital structure of domestic firms. Based partly on 1993 data emanating from a survey carried out by the SESSI and using customs information, it allows detailed insights into the structure of intra-firm trade (see below). The second set of results consists of studies using data on FDI flow and stocks (see below). It is tempting to interpret such results with respect to competitiveness issues at the level of nations, but it must be stressed that such attempts generally remain unsatisfactory (see below) and an explanation should be sought.

Foreign trade activities of foreign-owned firms: the evidence from micro data

In France's domestic manufacturing industry, according to the SESSI, the share of the FOFs in the total value of foreign trade was, in 1990, 32 per cent for exports and 45 per cent for direct imports (Chanut and Mathieu, 1994, p. 1). In 1993, their share in the total *intra-firm* exports and imports in the manufacturing industry reached 40 per cent and 84 per cent respectively (Le Bris, 1998, p. 138). Such data clearly indicate that these firms are more integrated in foreign trade than domestic firms.

Above average export propensity of foreign-owned manufacturing firms

Although the propensity to export is smaller among FOFs than among other domestic firms in countries such as the USA, Sweden, Hong Kong and Taiwan, the contrary can be observed in France, along with Canada, Japan, China and Malaysia (OECD, 1999, pp. 27–9; UNCTAD, 1999, p. 15). With regard to France, this is a long-lasting phenomenon that had already been observed at the end of the 1970s, and it seems that such a gap tends to widen rather than diminish. Among French manufacturing industry, the average export ratio of the FOFs increased from 29 per cent in 1979 to 32 per cent in 1985, while the corresponding ratio of the French-owned firms increased from 26 per cent to 27 per cent respectively (SESSI, 1989, p. 16). An even bigger gap can be observed for the import ratio. Moreover, as shown by Chanut and Mathieu (1994), the fact that the propensity to export and import is higher among FOFs remains when controlling for firm size and industry, and also when only firms belonging to a group are taken into account: that is, when independent firms are excluded. In 1990, the average export ratio was 30.3 per cent among affiliates of foreign firms, 27.9 per cent among affiliates of French groups and only 12.2 per cent among independent firms. In fact, and compared only with firms belonging to French groups, a significant difference exists only in the category of SMEs: that is, for firms employing fewer than 1,000 people (Table 6.3).

Table 6.3 Average export and import ratios: breakdown by category of ownership in the French manufacturing industry (% of turnover, 1990)

Number of employees	Majority FOFs		French-owned affiliates		Independent firms		All categories	
	Export	Import	Export	Import	Export	Import	Export	Import
20 to 49	20.4	23.6	11.3	6.5	6.9	6.3	8.4	7.7
50 to 99	25.3	24.5	13.4	8.8	10.4	8.0	13.5	11.0
100 to 199	26.7	29.3	16.2	8.9	14.4	9.6	18.3	14.9
200 to 499	29.4	26.9	17.4	9.9	16.3	12.3	21.4	16.3
500 to 999	29.6	25.9	23.4	13.4	ns	ns	25.8	19.1
1,000 to 1,999	29.9	26.5	29.2	15.2	ns	ns	29.8	20.1
2,000 and more	35.1	37.8	32.6	14.1	ns	ns	33.2	18.2
All sizes	30.3	29.1	27.9	13.2	12.2	9.0	25.2	16.4

ns: not significant.
Data: customs, SESSI, Trésor, INSEE.
Source: Chanut and Mathieu (1994), p. 2.

A priori, as pointed out by Houdebine and Topiol-Bensaïd (1999, pp. 15–16), there are two possible ways to explain the fact that FOFs export more than affiliates of French groups even when controlling for firm size and industry. The first one says that FOFs benefit from a privileged access to foreign markets, and the second explanation involves the idea that these offshore affiliates tend to be highly involved in *intra-firm* trade: that is, in trade flows within the concerned multinationals. Both explanations can be considered as convincing in the case of France. In the total exports of the domestic manufacturing industry, the share of intra-firm exports is higher on the part of FOFs (53 per cent in 1993) than on the part of firms belonging to French-owned corporations (48 per cent). It is worth noticing that this share is particularly high among affiliates of foreign firms based in the EU (55 per cent) and, moreover, in North American countries (62 per cent: Hannoun and Guerrier, 1998, pp. 124–5). Beyond the single case of intra-firm trade, it is also interesting to notice that, in France, the FOFs with the highest average export ratio are based in the USA and in Japan (Houdebine and Topiol-Bensaïd, 1999). German-owned firms obviously use France much less as an export platform than their American or Japanese counterparts do. In 1998, their relative share among all FOFs was smaller in terms of exports (only 13.3 per cent, while the corresponding share was 36.9 per cent for US-owned firms) than in terms of employment (16.8 per cent) or turnover (15.4 per cent: SESSI, 2000, pp. 31–2).

Another interesting point concerns the destination of these exports, which appears to be only to a relatively small part the home country of these foreign affiliates. In 1990, as shown by Chanut and Mathieu (1994), an average part of only some 20 per cent of the total value of exports made by foreign-owned manufacturing firms in France was shipped back home. This means that the motives behind the location of these affiliates in France are only marginally related to the strict logic of relocation: that is, from the point of view of the home country, with a phenomenon combining 'escape' FDI and additional imports. Certain differences should be mentioned regarding the home country. On the one hand, an average of only 10 per cent of the total exports made by US-owned affiliates was sent to the USA in 1990, which is roughly similar to the share of the USA in the total exports of firms belonging to French-owned groups. On the other hand, the share of Germany as a target country is usually significantly higher for the exports made by German-owned affiliates than for those made by firms belonging to French-owned groups. In France, such differences between US-owned affiliates and German-owned affiliates can be explained by the logic of comparative costs, but also by reasons of spatial proximity.

High import propensity: the importance of intra-firm sourcing

In 1990 in the French manufacturing industry the FOFs' average import ratio was roughly twice as high as that of affiliates of French-owned groups and three times as high as that of independent firms. For firms employing from 20 to 49 people, it was even four times as high as that of independent firms (Table 6.3). A similar calculation confirms these results for 1993, with an average import ratio reaching 30.0 per cent on the part of FOFs and only 13.6 per cent on the part of French-owned affiliates.[4] For the most part, this higher propensity to import can be explained by the specificity of intra-firm trade and also by the fact that the intra-firm imports of FOFs mostly consist of final products destined to be sold as they are, without any further manufacturing.

Of total imports of the domestic manufacturing industry, the share of intra-firm imports reached 58 per cent among FOFs in 1993 but only 32 per cent among firms belonging to French-owned groups (Hannoun and Guerrier, 1998, pp. 124–5). For French manufacturing industry, moreover, the proportion of imported goods destined to be sold as they are was around 36 per cent for FOFs in 1990 (and even 43 per cent for US-owned firms) but only 13 per cent for domestic firms. Differences according to the country of ownership can also be observed for the propensity of firms to import goods from their home country. In France, this is notably the case with US-owned firms and German-owned firms, whether through intra-firm trade or not. The trade relations between the affiliates abroad and their respective home country is much stronger when the home country is Germany than when it is on the other side of the ocean. In 1990, for instance, on average around one-third of total imports made by FOFs in the French manufacturing industry originated in the country of control, but this proportion was much smaller in the case of US-owned affiliates (around one-fifth) and much larger in the case of German-owned firms (nearly two-thirds: Chanut and Mathieu, 1994, p. 3). Some 25 years ago, Michalet (1998, p. 224) had already noticed that the German-owned manufacturing firms located in France had a strong tendency to import goods from Germany. In the total value of their imports, the share of West Germany as a source country reached 69.4 per cent at that time.

Unlike American-owned firms, which on average derive around 29 per cent of intra-firm imports and a mere 18 per cent of extra-firm imports from the USA or from Canada, German-owned firms are much more focused on their country of origin: they purchase up to 85 per cent of their intra-firm imports and slightly more than half of their extra-firm imports from Germany (Table 6.4). As explained by Mathieu and Quélennec (1998), such differences can be attributed both to problems of geographic distance and to the fact that the American affiliates have for a long time been set up in several European countries among which reigns a deeper and more diversified division of labour than in the case of German-owned firms. In connection it can also be noticed that the total value of *intra*-firm imports slightly exceeds the total value *of extra*-firm imports in the case of German-owned firms, while American-owned firms on the contrary import much more through extra-firm channels than by way of intra-firm trade.

As already indicated, a large proportion of the goods imported by the FOFs are sold as they are. In France, nearly half of the total value of these imports (in 1993 it was 47 per cent) are made by *wholesale* affiliates of foreign firms: that is, almost as much as the share of imports made by FOFs classified in the manufacturing industry (53 per cent: Mathieu and Quélennec, 1998, p. 81, Table 4).

The foreign-owned firms' contribution to the French trade balance

When considering the activity of FOFs in France, a clear distinction must thus be drawn between wholesale affiliates and manufacturing affiliates. This distinction allows us to point out that, up to now, the FOFs' activity in France to a large extent consists of mere trade: it often corresponds mainly to a logic of market access and only reflects the existence of domestic location advantages in production to a limited extent. These two different aspects are dealt with successively below.

With respect to manufacturing affiliates, first, FOFs in France usually have a trade deficit *vis-à-vis* their respective home country but a larger trade surplus *vis-à-vis* third countries, so that they are associated with a trade surplus overall. Moreover, this general pattern can be considered as relatively stable over a long period of time. In the past, in fact, the contribution of manufacturing FOFs to the trade balance has been more or less positive from year to year, but it was generally less favourable than that of other domestic manufacturing firms.[5]

In 1990, manufacturing FOFs have globally yielded a small trade surplus (FF 8.6 billion in 1990) which was the sum of a global deficit in bilateral terms (FF 35.7 billion) and of a larger surplus in trade with third countries (FF 44.3 billion). The same year, for instance, the US-owned manufacturing firms in France brought a deficit (FF 10.5 billion) in their trade with the USA, but also a surplus (FF 11.5 billion) with all

Table 6.4 Intra-firm and extra-firm imports of French-, German- and American-owned manufacturing affiliates in France, by country of control, 1993 (%)

Origin of imports	French-owned affiliates[a]		German-owned affiliates		American-owned affiliates	
	Intra-firm	Extra-firm	Intra-firm	Extra-firm	Intra-firm	Extra-firm
Germany	8.9	21.6	**84.8**	50.2	21.1	19.1
Belgium-Lux.	13.1	6.7	2.5	4.1	8.4	10.7
Italy	5.3	11.6	1.4	8.1	7.9	5.2
UK	6.4	7.7	1.7	4.2	14.5	10.8
South of the EU	**41.8**	**10.8**	5.3	7.7	10.6	8.6
USA and Canada	5.0	17.0	0.7	5.9	**28.9**	**17.9**
Other countries	19.5	24.6	3.6	19.8	8.6	27.7
Total	100	100	100	100	100	100

[a] Independent firms are therefore not taken into account.
Data: Customs, SESSI.
Source: Mathieu and Quélennec (1998), p. 80.

other countries. As for the German-owned manufacturing firms, they registered a trade deficit *vis-à-vis* Germany (FF 6.6 billion), but this deficit was almost offset by the surplus shown in trade with the rest of the world (FF 5.9 billion: Chanut and Mathieu, 1994, p. 3). A similar pattern can be observed with the German-owned firms in the USA, where these affiliates produce a noticeable deficit *vis-à-vis* Germany (Pauly and Reich, 1997, pp. 21–2).

In matter of trade balance, of course, there are marked differences according to the industry considered. In 1990, the FOFs were associated with a trade deficit in eight out of the 18 subsectors constituting the French manufacturing industry, including the pharmaceutical industry and the automobile industry (Chanut and Mathieu, 1994, p. 2). At the most aggregate level, the fact that the manufacturing FOFs in France contribute to the French trade surplus is related to the fact that the presence of these firms allows them to reduce the amount of total imports that would occur otherwise.[6] According to estimations made by Chanut and Mathieu (1994), the import-substituting effect due to the presence of these firms is significant and the average substitution coefficient between their domestic turnover and the total imports reaches –0.7.[7]

The situation is quite different on the part of wholesale FOFs, because their trade is almost exclusively made up of imports. Among the 2,000 largest wholesale firms in France, FOFs account for 70 per cent of the *total* value of imports. A similar situation can also be found in the USA, where FOFs strongly contribute to the trade deficit in the wholesale domain, while their contribution shows only a slight deficit in the manufacturing industry. In that country, wholesale FOFs were responsible for nearly 70 per cent of the total trade deficit in 1990 (Chanut and Mathieu, 1994, pp. 1–2).

All in all, when wholesale affiliates are taken into account, it appears that FOFs in France induce a strong trade deficit (FF –215 billion in 1993, compared to a surplus of FF 221 billion on the part of all other domestic firms except for Airbus (Mathieu and Quélennec, 1998, p. 79). While the exports of FOFs globally cover only a part of their imports, with a cover ratio of only 48 per cent in 1993, the exports made by firms belonging to French-owned groups in contrast by and large exceed the value of their imports, with a corresponding ratio reaching 200 per cent on the part of private corporations and 130 per cent on the part of state-controlled groups. When wholesale affiliates are taken into account, German-owned firms in France, for instance, appear to cause a marked trade deficit, which is almost totally due to the bilateral deficit of these affiliates *vis-à-vis* their home country, Germany. Such a strong link between the FOFs and their respective home base cannot actually be observed for all investing countries. According to their nationality, as shown by Boccara (1997, pp. 10, 21, 23), the FOFs are inclined to a different kind of tropism in the domain of foreign trade. In that sense, it seems possible to state that in France these firms form different subsystems according to their nationality.

Links between foreign-owned firms and trade in the light of FDI data

With regard to the link between FOFs and trade balance in the host country, a second set of results concerns in studies using data on FDI flows and stocks. For France, most of these are recent studies carried out by Fontagné at the Centre d'Etudes Prospectives et d'Informations Internationales (CEPII), partly at the request of the OECD. In order to assess the global impact of direct investment flows on French foreign trade, these studies have collected data for the period 1984–94, for 39 partner countries, and on the basis of an *ad hoc* sectoral nomenclature consisting of 19 industries. A priori, the impact of FDI on trade involves not only bilateral relations between the home country and the host country, but also crowding-out effects *vis-à-vis* competitors based in third countries. In the case of France between 1984 and 1994, it appears that these crowding-out effects are statistically significant, but relatively negligible compared to the bilateral effects.

On the sole basis of bilateral relations, the most important results for France during the period 1984–94 are that outward FDI flows show a net trade surplus, while inward FDI flows are on the contrary associated with a net trade deficit. Moreover, this kind of correlation is more obvious at the aggregate level than when the various industries are considered separately. This confirms that the relations between FDI and trade are amplified by inter-industrial linkages: the existence of such externalities or spillover effects illustrates that the relations between FDI and trade apply to a production system made of inter-industrial interactions (Fontagné and Pajot, 1997, pp. 2, 11, 18, 23). The underlying idea is that the degree of complementarity between FDI and foreign trade increases with the level of aggregation, and that the possible substitution effects are more likely on a relatively highly disaggregated level.

When only the bilateral relations are taken into account (effects on third countries are excluded), it is possible to calculate the following elasticities for the marginal relations at the global level of a group formed by 19 sectors in the domain of manufacturing industry, mining and energy:

- $1 of additional outward FDI flow is associated with $2.28 of extra exports and with $1.85 of extra imports, which suggests a 'positive' contribution to the trade balance (around 43 cents);
- $1 of additional inward FDI flow goes hand in hand with $3.52 of extra exports and $4.34 of extra imports, which suggests a 'negative' contribution to the trade balance (around 82 cents: CEPII, 1998, pp. 212–13).

Of course, this calculation only takes into account the goods in the industries mentioned above; it does not include trade in services and ignores the impact FDI made in the tertiary sector. It is therefore very difficult to draw conclusions about the net effect of FDI on the whole economy because of the specific import–export activity of wholesale subsidiaries and also because of the ambiguous role played by holding companies (Fontagné, 1999, pp. 23 and 32). In order to compare the case of France with that of the USA, however, another calculation has been made, once again for the period 1984–94, but this time on the basis of an American sectoral nomenclature. The evidence confirms that, for the USA as well as for France, outward FDI flows usually contribute 'positively' to the trade balance of the home country *vis-à-vis* the host country, while inward FDI flows contribute 'negatively' to the trade balance of the host country *vis-à-vis* the home country. When the calculation is made as the most disaggregated level possible (12 sectors), however, it appears that the complementarity effects between inward FDI flows and trade (exports and imports) are weaker in the case of the USA than for France. On the one hand, the complementarity effect between inward FDI flows and exports is only half as marked in the USA. This corroborates the idea according to which French inward FDI to a large extent has the function of an 'export springboard', notably in direction of other European countries, while inward FDI in the USA is much more likely to be destined for the domestic market. On the other hand, the complementarity effect between inward FDI flows and imports appears as significant in the case of France, but not for the USA. This suggests that the FOFs have a particularly large propensity to import when they are set up in France, but not when they are established in the USA (Fontagné and Pajot, 1997, p. 19; CEPII, 1998, pp. 214–15).

Similar results can also be found on the basis of FDI stock data. For France, over the period 1989–94, it appears that inward FDI stocks in particular are associated with a trade deficit, but that this complementarity is less clear than according to flow data (Fontagné and Pajot, 1997, p. 22; CEPII, 1998, pp. 215 and 218–19). These results are compatible with those found by Pain and Wakelin (1998, pp. 19–21), which are related to goods exported by 11 OECD countries over the period 1971–92. This last study shows that in the long run exports are positively correlated with the level of inward FDI stock for seven (among which are France and Germany) out of the 11 countries considered. This suggests that, for each of these seven countries *ceteris paribus* (for a given volume of trade and production), higher inward FDI goes hand-in-hand with an increased world market share for the host country. Such a correlation appears statistically significant, but relatively modest in the case of France and Germany, with an additional 10 per cent of inward FDI stock associated with 0.75 per cent of extra market share. These effects appear much stronger for the USA and Spain.[8] Unfortunately, Pain and Wakelin (1998) deal only with the link between FDI and export performance. They do not consider the link between inward FDI and *imports*. It is therefore difficult to draw global conclusions from their study with respect to the competitiveness of the host country as a whole, at least with regard to the trade balance.

Some difficulties interpreting FDI data with regard to competitiveness issues

Empirical studies of the impact of inward FDI flows or stocks on national economies often lead to the conclusion that it differs greatly from one country to another. In the case of France, nonetheless, they generally suppose or show that inward FDI tends to stimulate imports more strongly than exports, and that the contrary applies for outward FDI. With such a pattern, the fact that outward FDI increases more (or is higher) than inward FDI seems to enhance the French trade surplus. Some authors draw the conclusion that not only a trade surplus but also an excess of outward FDI over inward FDI is an indication of strong competitiveness at the level of an industry or even of a country. Several examples of this can be found in the case of France.

This interpretation is particularly clear for von Kirchbach (1998, p. 56): 'The French manufacturing sector proved its international competitiveness by registering both a significant surplus of outward FDI and exports.' During the period 1992–4 and with a measure in terms of FDI flows, such a pattern could be observed in particular for the petroleum and chemical sector. The diametrically opposed combination of a trade deficit and of an excess of inward FDI over outward FDI was obtained in the domains of textile and wood, which at that time lacked competitiveness in this country. Another interesting pattern, the co-existence of a trade deficit and of a surplus of outward FDI, could be observed for mining and quarrying (von Kirchbach, 1998, p. 57). It obviously corresponds to the classical phenomenon of resource-based FDI, which is typically associated with a strong import propensity on the part of the home country. In this last case, as also for the combination of a trade surplus and a surplus of inward FDI, it seems more difficult to risk a general interpretation in terms of competitiveness.

Such problems of interpretation also arise when partner countries are considered instead of sectors, as in the case of Hatem (1995, pp. 19 and 22), who refers to trade flow and FDI stock data for the year 1991. It is interesting to notice that the combination of a trade surplus and of a surplus of outward FDI was then found *vis-à-vis* several south European countries and Africa, while the diametrically opposed combination of a trade deficit and of a surplus of inward FDI was found *vis-à-vis* Japan and several countries from the north of Europe, and the combination of a trade deficit and of a surplus of outward FDI was found *vis-à-vis* countries such as the USA and China.

Lastly, several studies carried out at the SESSI also share this approach. They underline that the presence of German-owned firms in France is particularly marked in sectors where German industry is traditionally in a position of worldwide leadership, as with chemicals or machine tools (SESSI, 1989, p. 31). In the French case, according to Mathieu (1998b), a breakdown by sectors and by home countries shows that the underlying FDI globally reflects the competitive strength of the home country's firms and the competitive weakness of the host country's firms. In this interpretation à la S. Hymer, the structure of inward FDI therefore reflects much more the *absolute* competitive advantage of firms than what Dunning (or Ricardo) would call the comparative location advantage of the host country.

Of course, such an approach is basically static. It only gives a view of the link between inward FDI and trade performance at a given point in time. It is not able to give much information on *structural* competitiveness (the ability to hold a strong position in the international division of labour over a period of time). According to a literature survey published by the World Trade Organization in 1996, the empirical evidence shows that the positive impact of inward FDI on the host country's foreign trade is generally stronger on exports than on imports in the short run, and the key question would be whether this additional trade surplus is lasting or not (Organisation Mondiale du

Commerce, or OMC, 1996, pp. 64–5). As already seen, the empirical evidence for France suggests on the contrary that inward FDI is globally associated with a net trade deficit for the host country in the short run, because inward FDI induces a lot of additional imports in intermediates and investment goods. In such a context, the relevant (and up to now unanswered) question seems to be whether this net trade deficit tends to increase or to vanish in the long run. A possible conjecture is that the induced import of investment goods contributes to a modernization of the production system in the host country, so that the initial induced trade deficit tends to be offset in the long run (Fontagné, 1999, pp. 24 and 26). In France, an example of such a positive dynamic process might be found in the paper and cardboard industry (see Box 6.1).

Box 6.1   The foreign presence in the French paper industry: a salutary contribution to domestic competitiveness

In the paper and cardboard industry, which represents 42 per cent of the turnover in the whole wood industry, FOFs nowadays provide 60 per cent of the domestic production in France. Inward FDI, notably from the USA and from North European countries, has helped to revitalize this sector which was nearly bankrupt in the 1980s. These sources contributed strongly to an increase in, and modernization of, its domestic production capacities. As a result, the French trade deficit in this sector diminished by 34 per cent between 1990 and 1997.

The Finnish group, UPM-Kymmene, has played an important part in this process. Since 1988, it has purchased successively the two paper producers Chapelle Darblay (near Paris) and Stracel (Strasbourg), and has decided to invest nearly FF 500 million in each of them in the form of top-class technology and less polluting equipment. The production capacity of these two affiliates is around 600,000 tons of paper, which represents nearly half of the entire French capacity (1.3 million tons) in this industry. Chapelle Darblay and Stracel have become exporters again, with an export ratio of 40 per cent and 80 per cent respectively.

Sources: CGP (1992); Bourgeois and Estival (1999).

In this context, inward FDI can be considered as a way for the host country to strengthen its *future* competitive advantages. Similarly (and at first sight paradoxically), Hirschman (1966, p. 122) considers imports as a means whereby a given country could improve its position in the international division of labour.[9] The questions raised therefore deal not only with the amount or sign of the trade balance, but also (and probably more) with the structure of foreign trade: that is, with the nature of traded goods. As shown by Chesnais and Sailleau (2000), by comparing SESSI figures with data on the revealed comparative advantage (RCA) of French exports in 1993, it appears that the FOFs tend to reinforce French export specialization in domains such as pharmaceuticals or automobile parts, while it only contributes to a consolidation of the French position in industries such as chemicals or perfumes. There are nonetheless also domains in which France is not specialized, but for which the export capacity is almost entirely due to the presence of FOFs, such as pulp and paper (see Box 6.1), as well as data processing equipment (see Box 6.2: see section 4 below) or electronic components, notably through the long-established presence of IBM and Philips, respectively.[10]

Beyond the questions related solely to foreign trade, and given the importance of structural and technological factors, the best way to examine the link between inward FDI and competitiveness in a dynamic approach is probably to focus on innovation issues.

4 The role of foreign-owned firms in the French innovation system

In order to obtain a dynamic perspective on the contribution of FOFs to the global economic performance of France, it is necessary to gain some insights into their innovation activities which play a key role in the genesis and renewal of competitive advantage. To simplify the problem, innovation is considered here mainly in its technological dimension, although innovation also involves social, organizational or managerial aspects. Here it is proposed to examine this question from two successive angles. The first point of view mainly deals with questions related to the generation of technology, evaluating to what extent FOFs contribute to the production of new technological knowledge in France. The second approach has to do with issues related to the transfer and diffusion of technology. One of the main underlying questions is whether the innovation activity of FOFs in France bears a resemblance to a predatory strategy: that is, to a corporate strategy of technology sourcing that mainly benefits the home country of the investor or, more generally, other locations abroad.

The foreign-owned firms´ contribution to the generation of technology in France

A lower R&D intensity in foreign-owned firms than in French-owned firms

In France, the largest part of the manufacturing firms´ total domestic R&D expenditure is made by firms that belong to French-owned groups; the relative importance of these French-owned affiliates is particularly strong in the field of basic research (see Table 6.5).

The share of R&D expenditure that rests with FOFs increased from around 11 per cent in 1985 (CGP, 1999b, p. 140) to 13 per cent in 1993 and 19 per cent in 1998 (Figure 6.2). According to OECD (1999), the corresponding share of FOFs is smaller in countries such as the USA (12.0 per cent in 1996), Germany or Poland, much smaller in Japan (0.9 per cent in 1996), Finland or Greece, but higher in countries such as Italy (23.1 per cent in 1992), the UK (39.5 per cent in 1996) and Ireland (almost 70 per cent in 1993).

The share of FOFs in these R&D expenditures varies greatly according to industry, with only 1 per cent in the aerospace industry at one extreme and with 51 per cent in the pharmaceutical industry at the other extreme. In French manufacturing industry overall in 1994, most of the total R&D expenditure of FOFs was by US-owned firms (34 per cent) and by European affiliates (60 per cent altogether, with Germany ranking ahead

Table 6. 5   The structure of R&D expenditures: breakdown by category of ownership in the French manufacturing industry, 1996 (%)

	Type of R&D expenditure			
	Basic research	**Applied research**	**Development**	**Total R&D**
French private groups	3.2	13.7	31.0	47.8
Public groups	0.7	5.9	22.1	28.8
Foreign-owned groups	0.4	4.6	13.7	18.7
Independent firms	0.1	1.2	3.4	4.7
Total	4.4	25.4	70.2	100

Data: Survey of the French ministry of Education, Research and Technology; LIFI database (INSEE).
Source: study carried out in 1999 by M. Paul, B. Planes and P. Sevestre (Paris 12 University) for the CGP and quoted in CGP (1999b, p. 142).

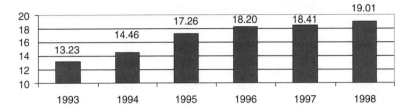

Data: Survey on R&D made by the French ministry of Education, Research and Technology.

Figure 6.2 The foreign-owned firms' share in France's total domestic R&D expenditure (%)

of Italy, the Netherlands, Switzerland and the UK in that order); only 1 per cent was made by Japanese-owned firms at that time. In a few industries, some countries' leadership is particularly obvious; in the domain of computers, for instance, nearly one-third of the *total* domestic R&D expenditure is due to US-owned firms.[11]

For a given country, however, the relevant question is not so much the relative share of FOFs in domestic R&D efforts; at this stage it is rather whether the R&D intensity is higher, equal or lower on the part of FOFs compared with domestic firms. Concerning the manufacturing sector in France, the data collected by the OECD (1999, p. 26, graph 11) show that the average R&D intensity was around 2 per cent for the FOFs in 1996, but around 3.5 per cent for the other domestic firms. In Germany, where similar data emanate from a survey concerning 500 R&D-intensive companies, in 1993 the corresponding figures were around 3.2 per cent and 6.3 per cent, respectively. Another publication gives somewhat different ratios for French industry in 1993: 2.6 per cent in the case of FOFs, 5.6 per cent in the case of firms that belong to French-owned groups and 5.1 per cent in the case of independent firms (Favre and Mathieu, 1998, p. 167). In any case, the same conclusion can be drawn from all this data: in France (and presumably in Germany, too), the R&D intensity on the part of FOFs is only half as high as that of domestically-owned firms. Naturally, such average figures cover in particular strong differences depending on the country of origin. In the case of Japanese-owned firms, for instance, R&D units are often suspected of generally being simple 'alibi-labs', insofar as the Japanese firms seem to maintain nearly all their important research capacities at home. Differences in the distribution of R&D intensity also exist according to the sector considered. Compared to French-owned firms, the fact that FOFs generally have a lower R&D

intensity is particularly noticeable, since foreign affiliates in France are more concentrated in high-tech industries and less in low-tech activities than French-owned firms (Table 6.10 below) and, moreover, because they tend to be larger than average. In France, however, the fact that the relative weight of FOFs is lighter in terms of R&D efforts than in terms of production does not necessarily imply that these firms have a lower propensity to innovate.

A relatively high propensity to innovate

Several studies show that FOFs on average have a relatively high propensity to innovate. According to the SESSI survey on innovation in the French industry in 1990, the proportion of 'innovating products introduced for less than 5 years' in the total turn over was then 18 per cent in the case of foreign-owned SMEs, while it reached 16 per cent in the case of SMEs belonging to French-owned corporations and 16 per cent in the case of independent SMEs too. Among the biggest firms, this proportion reached one-third for FOFs as well as for affiliates of French-owned groups (Dupont and Mathieu, 1993, p. 3). In the French manufacturing sector, furthermore, the proportion of innovative firms (firms having implemented product or process innovation) is on average higher[12] among FOFs than among affiliates of French-owned firms and nearly twice as high as among independent firms (Table 6.6). In the domain of innovation, in fact, the differences are generally significantly marked between FOFs and *independent* firms, but not between FOFs and French-owned *affiliates*. This pattern applies overall for the ratio of product innovation to turnover or for the proportion of firms that registered patents between 1994 and 1996 (Table 6.6).

Compared to affiliates of French-owned firms, in fact, the patent data show that the propensity to innovate is *higher* for the FOFs when we refer to the frequency of firms having registered patents among innovative firms (Table 6.6), but also that it is *lower* when we refer to the number of patents. In the total number of patents that have been registered in Europe on the basis of invention made in France, the share of patents registered by FOFs was 20.5 per cent in 1997 (after 22.5 per cent in 1990[13]). It is interesting to notice that the corresponding share was then 17.2 per cent in Germany (having been 15.0 per cent in 1990) and 38.6 per cent in the UK (having been 33.7 per cent in 1990: Observatoire des Sciences et Techniques, or OST, 2000, p. 256). In this respect, the position of France and Germany are relatively similar, with a much smaller (and more stable) proportion of FOFs than in the UK, where it has been rising rapidly during the 1990s (Table 6.7).

Table 6.6 Innovation activity: a few major differences between foreign-owned firms and domestic firms in the French manufacturing sector, 1996

	Foreign-owned firms	French-owned affiliates	Independent Firms
Product or process innovation between 1994 and 1996 (*% of the number of industrial firms*)	61.9	51.1	33.4
New products from the point of view of the firm (*% of turnover*)	25.7	24.8	11.1
New products from the point of view of the market (*% of turnover*)	8.1	9.8	3.1
Patent registration from 1994 to 1996 (*% of the number of innovative firms*)	39.9	41.1	23.0
Total innovation expenditures (*FF billions*)	36.5	95.8	8.2

Data: SESSI (innovation survey), Trésor, INSEE.
Source: SESSI (2000), p. 8.

Table 6.7 Share of foreign-owned firms in the total number of patents registered in Europe: a breakdown by technological domain for the patents attributed to France, Germany and the UK (%)

Technological domains	France 1990	France 1997	Germany 1990	Germany 1997	UK 1990	UK 1997
Electrical and electronic equipment	30.9	29.5	27.8	25.9	448	51.7
Instruments	23.4	21.4	17.3	18.9	30.4	40.9
Fine chemicals and pharmaceuticals	19.4	14.5	4.8	6.5	29.0	29.1
Process/basic chemicals/metals	14.7	13.9	12.1	11.9	28.9	31.0
Mechanical engineering, transportation equipment	19.5	22.6	14.4	20.6	35.1	43.6
Household consumption/building/ public works	28.9	12.2	18.9	21.2	47.4	41.7
Total	**22.5**	**20.5**	**15.0**	**17.2**	**33.7**	**38.6**

Data: INPI, European Patent Office and OST; OST treatments.
Source: OST (2000), p. 256.

Given that majority FOFs in the French manufacturing industry nowadays represent more than 30 per cent of total employment and more than 35 per cent of total turnover (see Table 6.2), it is clear that their relative weight is on average much lower in terms of patents registered (around 20 per cent) than in terms of production. It reflects the fact that their efforts in the domain of R&D is smaller than those of the other domestic firms. As shown by Patel and Pavitt (1999, p. 97, Table 6.3), on the basis of the SPRU patent database, this pattern can be observed on a worldwide scale, at least concerning the patent activity of large firms. France therefore makes no exception in this respect. On the contrary, the relative weight of FOFs in the German industry is *higher* in terms of patents registered (around 17 per cent in 1997: see Table 6.8) than in terms of turnover (around 13 per cent in 1996; see Table 6.1) or employment[14] (around 7 per cent in 1996). The same patterns apply to the UK.

Furthermore, the US patent database developed by Cantwell at the University of Reading indicates that *'France's world share as a research location for FOFs has globally increased during the last decades.'* In the total number of patents resulting from research carried out by firms outside their respective home country, France represented a higher world share over the period 1987–90 (7.66 per cent) than over all previous periods since the years 1969–72 (6.03 per cent).[15]

In the opposite direction, French firms show a growing propensity to locate their innovation activity in foreign countries. In relation to the total number of patents that have been registered by French industrial firms in France and abroad, the proportion of inventions made abroad has increased from 17.7 per cent in 1990 to 20.0 per cent in 1997, according to OST's database. Therefore, the relative importance of FOFs in France nowadays corresponds roughly to the relative importance of French-owned firms abroad (between 20 and 25 per cent), which was not the case 10 years ago. According to the OST report, it means that France has ceased to 'export' more technology – by way of foreign-owned affiliates in France – than she 'imports' through the opposite channel of French-owned affiliates set up in foreign countries (OST, 2000, p. 151). At this stage of the discussion, it is not clear whether this balanced pattern is more favourable than in the past, when it was relatively asymmetrical. In order to clarify this problem of interpretation, it is necessary to add some complementary elements of diagnosis on sectoral and geographic aspects.

On the sectoral and geographic distribution of the foreign-owned innovation activity

Concerning the country of origin (control), it appears that more than half of all patents registered by FOFs established in France have their

Table 6.8 Share of foreign-owned firms in the total number of patents registered in Europe: a breakdown by country of origin (control) for 7 European countries, 1997 (%)

Country of control	Country of residence of the inventors						
	France	Germany	UK	Netherlands	Italy	Sweden	Switzerland
'National' firms	79.5	82.8	61.4	79.3	56.7	67.3	76.4
Foreign-owned firms	20.5	17.2	38.6	20.7	43.3	32.7	23.6
EU	11.6	6.7	13.5	9.9	30.6	6.4	12.5
EFTA	1.3	2.8	0.8	0.2	1.0	20.6	1.1
USA	6.9	7.1	20.3	9.8	11.3	5.6	9.5
Japan	0.4	0.3	2.2	0.8	0.3	0.1	0.5
Other countries	0.3	0.2	1.8	0.1	0.0	0.0	0.0
Total	100	100	100	100	100	100	100

Data: Institut National de la Propriété Industrielle (INPI), European Patent Office and OST; OST treatments.
Source: OST (2000), p. 220.

home base in another EU country (11.6 per cent of the total patent number in 1997: see Table 6.8). In comparison, the corresponding proportion is smaller for FOFs established in Germany (6.7 per cent). It can also be seen that the share of US-owned firms in this respect is particularly high in the UK, where slightly more than 20 per cent of all patents registered belong to US firms. Last, these data confirm that the Japanese-owned firms in Europe contribute only very little to the number of patents registered. When firms establish R&D activities abroad, according to Patel and Pavitt (1999, p. 98), they generally do so in technological domains that reflect the competitive strength of their home base and, beyond that, of their home country. From the point of view of the host country, moreover, the presence of foreign-owned R&D activities is particularly marked in technological fields where the host country has a relative competitive weakness, at least concerning countries such as France, Germany, Canada and the USA. In such a pattern, the density of the foreign presence in this respect can be explained more by the technological leadership of the investor ('push effect') than by the attractiveness of the host country ('pull effect'). Once again, the underlying logic seems to be more that of the firms' *absolute* competitive advantage than that of the countries' *comparative* locational advantage.

The evidence from the OST database on the whole seems to corroborate this analysis. For example, in the technology-intensive fields of fine chemicals and pharmaceuticals, which belong to the most internationalized sectors worldwide, French, German and British firms have acquired a relatively strong competitive position, while there is only a particularly low level of foreign presence in those countries (Table 6.7).

Beyond the sole evidence brought by patent data, the distribution of the foreign presence by technological domains seems indeed to reflect the specialization of the home country to a large extent. In French industry, for instance, the presence of German firms is mainly developed in the domain of middle technologies, as for example, in mechanical engineering, while the US-owned firms have an above-average presence in the high-tech domain (SESSI, 2000, p. 7). This analysis is also supported by the available data on the distribution of R&D expenditures made by the US firms outside the USA (Table 6.9). These data indicate that US R&D activities abroad in chemicals are much more developed in France, in the UK and even in Japan than in Germany, although this last country has a much stronger specialization in this domain, at least with regard to production. However, these data also show that the US research in Germany is developed to an

Table 6.9 The R&D performed overseas by majority-owned affiliates of US (non-bank) parent companies, by selected industry for the 4 main host countries in the domain of US R&D abroad, 1994, breakdown by industry of affiliate

Share of each country in the total for each industry considered	Germany		UK		France		Japan		All countries	
	$ million	%	$ million	%	$ million	%	$ million	%	$ million	%
Chemicals	296	9.5	616	19.7	543	17.4	397	12.7	31,190	100
Machinery	530	26.1	433	21.3	202	9.9	77	3.04	20,340	100
Electrical equipment	128	16.1	D	D	D	D	136	17.1	7,970	100
Transportation equipment	1,435	51.0	D	D	D	D	6	0.2	2,812	100
Manufacturing	2,630	25.9	1,938	19.1	1,142	11.3	787	7.8	10,147	100
Non-manufacturing	178	9.1	241	12.4	215	11.0	336	17.2	1,950	100
All industries	2,808	23.2	2,179	18.0	1,357	11.2	1,123	9.3	12,097	100

Data: US Bureau of Economic Analysis (includes R&D expenditures conducted by the foreign affiliates for themselves or for others under a contract). D: withheld to avoid disclosing operations of individual companies.
Source: National Science Board (1998); own calculations.

above-average degree in the fields of transport equipment and mechanical engineering, which undoubtedly belong to the core of the German industry, but where US firms also have strong positions. The significant American R&D activities in the German automobile industry reflect the fact that the presence of General Motors in Europe is mainly concentrated in Germany, where its affiliate, Opel, has a very long tradition.

In a given country and beyond the single case of the US-owned firms, it seems that the foreign-owned *R&D* activities usually remain linked to a large extent with foreign-owned *production* activities, although a functional separation between research and production nowadays allows more autonomous location choices for research activities, at least in science-based industries (Gerybadze *et al.*, 1997). This means that the factors determining the location of corporate R&D activities abroad are only partly dependent on the quality of the national innovation system (NIS) in the host country. With respect to France, this analysis is corroborated by the results of several studies. One of them indicates that R&D activities of FOFs in France in general are still mainly aimed at adapting the corporate technology to the national, regional or European peculiarities of the markets involved, rather than at creating brand new products or at introducing major process innovations (Dupont and Mathieu, 1993, p. 3).

Barré (1996) confirms that this analysis is valid, at least for France and Germany, even if other patterns can be observed in other host countries. The question raised in this empirical study is whether or not the technological specialization which characterizes the innovation activities carried out by FOFs in a given country corresponds to that of the NIS concerned. To answer this question, Barré has chosen to measure the possible correlation between, on the one hand, the domestic technological specialization revealed by the patents due to resident FOFs and, on the other hand, the corresponding specialization defined only on the basis of patents due to 'national' inventors in their home country. On the basis of a database related to patents registered in Europe between 1991 and 1993, it appears that such a correlation is significant for neither France nor Germany (and no more than for Switzerland and Japan), in contrast to the situation prevailing in the UK, Italy, Belgium and Canada, where the technological activity of FOFs clearly appears congruent with the technological profile of the NIS in the host country. This is not the case in France and in Germany, where the technological activity of FOFs does not correspond significantly with that of the respective domestic NIS (Barré, 1996, pp. 232–3).

Table 6.10   Manufacturing firms in France: breakdown by level of technology intensity and by ownership (% of turnover in 1998)

Average level of technology intensity	Affiliates of foreign-owned firms	Affiliates of French-owned firms	Independent firms	All firms
High	21.6	15.5	3.9	16.3
Medium-high	32.4	41.7	13.4	35.1
Medium-low	29.8	20.0	34.3	25.2
Low	16.2	22.7	48.4	23.4
Total	100	100	100	100

Data: SESSI, Trésor, INSEE.
Source: SESSI (2000), p. 10.

In the French manufacturing sector, the technological profile of the FOFs is indeed notably different from that of the other domestic firms. The domestic affiliates of foreign firms are relatively more engaged in the domain of high technology, which represents nearly 22 per cent of their total turnover, compared with a corresponding share of only around 16 per cent for all domestic firms. They are also relatively less engaged in the domain of low technology, which represents only slightly more than 16 per cent of their total turnover, compared with a corresponding share of more than 23 per cent for all domestic firms (Table 6.10).

Role of foreign-owned firms in the cross-border diffusion of technology

In France, given that the FOFs have a lower propensity to invest in R&D and to register patents than domestic firms, the fact that their average turnover displays a higher technological intensity suggests that they import technologies from their parent company or from other foreign sources.

Sourcing technology from abroad through intra-firm channels

As shown by the first innovation survey made by the SESSI, the FOFs use more intra-firm channels as a source for their innovation activities. The average share of large firms declaring that their innovations result from R&D carried out by other parts of their respective group (or from patents held by this group) was then 70 per cent, compared to a corresponding share of less than half for their counterparts that belong to French-owned groups (Dupont and Mathieu, 1993, p. 3).

Table 6.11   The technological balance of France: breakdown by nationality of the firm, 1995 (%)

Home country of the parent company	Expenditures	Receipts
France	8.9	63.7
USA	62.2	30.7
Japan	1.1	0.0
Switzerland	7.2	0.2
Netherlands	7.5	2.5
Germany	5.9	2.2
UK	5.0	0.3
Other home countries	2.2	0.5
All home countries	100	100

Data for the manufacturing sector (including the food industry): INPI, SESSI.
Source: Favre and Mathieu (1998), p. 165.

Moreover, 91.1 per cent of all expenditure registered in the French technological balance (patents, inventions and processes) in 1995 was realized by FOFs (Table 6.11). Around 62 per cent of this total expenditure is made by the French affiliates of firms based in the USA; it reveals that these affiliates systematically purchase from abroad knowledge assets owned by their respective parent firm or by affiliated firms. By comparison, the corresponding share of German-owned firms is much smaller (5.9 per cent), which confirms once more that German firms display different types of behaviour.[16] In the opposite direction, almost 64 per cent of the total receipts are registered by French-owned firms. Here, too, the US-owned firms represent a large share (30.7 per cent).[17] This suggests that the American firms concerned use their French affiliates as part of a worldwide strategy of technology sourcing; in other words, they partly repatriate or transfer the technology that they have developed or acquired in France to their other offshore affiliates. Here again, the US firms have apparently developed a behaviour that the firms from other foreign nationalities have not adopted (yet), at least not on such a scale.

According to the data contained in the French technological balance, it is clear that the foreign-owned manufacturing firms in France cover only a little more than one-quarter with their technological expenditures with their receipts, while the domestic firms that belong to French-owned groups display in this domain a cover rate of nearly 200 per cent. For their part, the independent firms hardly have any cross-border technological transfer, at least in these terms. Around 95 per cent of the total flows registered in the technological balance consists of inter-firm relations. If, as shown above, the fact that a firm belongs to a foreign group or not has on average no significant impact on its performance in terms of innovation – as measured by the number of patents registered – it nevertheless has a notable effect on the sources they mobilize to fuel their innovation efforts. In other words, the evidence supports the idea that *ownership generally matters for the origin of the knowledge used* by the firms for their innovative activities, even if it does not matter much for the innovation propensity. More evidence of this pattern is shown by Madeuf *et al.* (1992) on the basis of her own empirical research: in France and compared to French-owned firms, FOFs generally source a smaller part of their R&D expenditures from external partners (Madeuf *et al.*, 1992; CGP, 1999b, p. 143). They rely much more on their respective intra-firm network and, accordingly, on foreign knowledge sources.

A moderate tendency to repatriate the technology developed in France

For France, the technological balance also suggests that the FOFs generally not only have a relatively high propensity to purchase technological knowledge generated abroad, but also a relatively moderate (although probably increasing) tendency to repatriate the technology developed in the domestic innovation system, apart from a few important exceptions in areas such as information and communication technology, notably on the part of several large US corporations (see Box 6.2 below).

Box 6.2   US-owned R&D laboratories within French 'Silicon Valleys': four examples of intra-firm knowledge-based division of labour

In the domain of information and communication technology (ICT), a series of large US firms have chosen certain French regional clusters as locations for specialized R&D centres designed to deliver certain particular technologies to their worldwide affiliates. The following examples concern the four largest French regions in the domain of R&D: Île-de-France, Rhône-Alpes, Provence-Alpes-Côte-d'Azur and Midi-Pyrénées.

Hewlett-Packard (HP) nowadays employs around 2000 people in Grenoble (Rhône-Alpes), where its presence dates back to 1971. The headquarters of its worldwide personal computer (PC) management (including R&D and marketing) has been located there since 1991.

Concerning the European market, the PCs designed in Grenoble have been up to now manufactured in HP's neighnouring industrial plant of l'Isle d'Abeau, near Lyon, but the firm has recently announced that it plans to outsource this assembling facility to the US firm Sanmina-SCI. HP however maintains the business PC department research team HP Labs Grenoble (HPLG) that it created in April 1999, and whose primary role consists of delivering technology to the emerging e-services businesses.

Texas Instruments was established in France in 1962. Near Nice (Provence-Alpes-Côte-d'Azur), its European wireless centre is located in Villeneuve-Loubet, where around 600 people are employed today. In the domain of DSP circuits (Digital Signal Processors), Villeneuve-Loubet, together with Dallas (Texas) and Tsukuba (Japan), is one of the firm's three centres in the whole world. It belongs to the 'Silicon Valley' around Sophia-Antipolis, where altogether nearly 7,000 foreigners are employed and where some 120 FOFs are located, among them Conexant Systems, Lucent technologies, Nortel, Amadeus, Philips, Infineon and SAP. Half of these FOFs are US-owned firms.

As for IBM, a firm established in France since 1914 and whose headquarters for Europe are located in Paris, its French affiliates have been assigned world product mandates since the early 1970s. All the concerned development facilities are coupled with production capacities. In Corbeil-Essonne (near Paris), it has invested billions of francs and produces high-tech dynamic memories for half of the world. In La Gaude (near Nice), IBM has located a telecommunications research centre with 800 engineers.

Last but not least, Motorola chose Toulouse (Midi-Pyrénées) as a location for its very first direct investment abroad, in the year 1967. Today, its Toulouse centre employs 850 engineers and altogether 2,350 people in research and in the fabrication of semiconductors, mainly for the European automotive market as well as for printing and wireless communications products.

Sources: author's compilation from Cambon (1998), *Le Monde* (29 September 1999), *L'Usine Nouvelle* (28 September 2000; 26 October 2000; 7 November 2001; 14 February 2002), *Les Echos* (18 October 2000), Chesnais and Sailleau (2000) and Lavenir *et al.* (2001).

On the basis of another data set and of a quite different approach, Lichtenberg and van Pottelsberghe de la Potterie (1996) confirm this kind of conclusion. For a series of countries, they test the hypothesis that inward FDI operates as a sort of siphon, through which technology is transferred from the host country back to the home country where it improves the total productivity of factors. They find that this 'boomerang effect' plays a significant role in the case of inward FDI in the UK and in the USA. For these two countries, it seems quantitatively as important as the effect in the opposite direction, through which the parent firms based in the UK and the USA use their FDI abroad as part of a worldwide integrated strategy of technology sourcing. In contrast, the French, German and Japanese firms appear much more inclined to repatriate the technology they capture or accumulate in foreign innovation systems (Lichtenberg and van Pottelsberghe de la Potterie, 1996, p. 21, Table 3). The French (German or Japanese) innovation system is used by FOFs to a much smaller extent as a supplier of technology for their respective cross-border technological network.

The impact on the French innovation system: globally positive, but only in a few selected industries and regions

Such studies do not allow us to draw clear conclusions about the impact of foreign-owned innovation activity on France as a host country. In the case of Lichtenberg and van Pottelsberghe de la Potterie (1996), the main conclusion is that, if any, the international transfer of technology allowed by FDI is generally much more significant in the sense of a repatriation from the host country back to the home country than in the opposite direction, in the form of technological spillovers benefiting the host country. According to the available evidence, as shown by Dyker (1998), it is true that such spillovers are far from guaranteed, although it is widely believed that FDI constitutes a privileged vehicle for international technological transfers in the recipient country.

Sometimes, the engagement of foreign firms in France induces a partly negative impact on the domestic R&D capacity, in particular when it results from mergers and acquisitions. For instance, this is the case with the recent merger between Hoechst and Rhône-Poulenc, insofar as the creation of the new company Aventis will lead to the closure or downsizing of some research sites. In a country such as France, however, the presence of FOFs does not generally harm the domestic innovation system, but it does not necessarily benefit its technological potential greatly either. The nature and intensity of this impact depend to a large extent on the absorptive capacity of the host country or region. As suggested by authors such as Chesnais and Sailleau (2000), Cantwell (1999), Barré (1996) or Dunning (1994), this impact is probably positive and marked when the host country has developed a strong domestic learning capacity in the technological domain concerned, while it is potentially negative or negligible when the recipient country has no sufficient endogenous capacity. Overall, the presence of the FOFs therefore tends to reinforce the specialization of the NIS involved. In the case of France, this analysis probably applies not only for the *national* innovation system, but also for *local* innovation systems. Apart from the Île de France (Paris and its region), there are still only relatively few regional clusters with a sufficient international dimension in the domain of R&D, around cities or regions such as Lyon, Grenoble, Lille, Strasbourg, Toulouse and the Mediterranean coast between Nice and Montpellier (Box 6.2).

5 Conclusion

Authors such as Reich (1990) or Michalet (1999) are right when they explain that the main goal of economic policy for a given country nowadays consists of increasing the competitiveness of its domestic firms, whether or not they are foreign-owned. However, it would be very exaggerated and foolish to draw the conclusion from this that the firms' 'nationality' no longer has any importance, as long as the governments of some of the most influential countries manage to promote the competitiveness of their country's firms, whether at home or overseas: 'In practice, however, governments have structured trade, investment, financial, monetary, and industrial policies to benefit their economies and to create advantages for their firms, both at home and abroad' (US Congress, 1993, p. 7).

   As explained in CGP (1999a) or Mathieu (1998a), the nationality of firms has become fuzzy but remains an important parameter for a series of dimensions such as industrial R&D activities, the location of headquarters, or the geographic orientation of procurement and sales. The above-mentioned evidence makes this clear with regard to foreign trade and to innovation activity in the case of France. The contribution of FOFs to foreign trade and technological change – two key questions in the domain of competitiveness – is therefore different from that of other domestic firms. In France, the presence of these FOFs generally has a positive impact on the domestic economy and employment, particularly through the channels of local procurement and export. However, the impact of these firms on domestic innovation capacity remains unclear, insofar as their R&D activities in France are much more integrated in the corresponding corporate R&D networks than in the French system of innovation. All in all, their contribution can be more or less favourable for the host country, according to the entry mode (greenfield FDI as against M&A) and considering several variables including the industry and host-region, or the home country of the investor. In terms of economic policy and on the scale of a given country or region, pragmatism is of course required, but it seems nonetheless possible to outline a few guiding principles.

1 Intrinsic attractiveness is not a sufficient condition to increase inward FDI in the context of an intense locational competition; as shown in CGP (1992a) and Michalet (1999), appropriate marketing is required.
2 Attractiveness is no goal in itself. It is necessary not only to attract inward FDI but also to retain it and, beyond that, to prevent the domestic firms (be they foreign-owned or not) from relocating elsewhere.
3 In order to obtain not only a long-lasting involvement of FOFs, but also substantial positive spillover effects on the host country's economy, the policy measures should provide enough incentives to persuade these firms to refrain from developing predatory practices and to encourage them to invest in the local human capital and in the domestic innovation system.

Notes

1 Own calculations on the basis of Dreyfus (2000).
2 A similar pattern can also be observed in Germany, where the FOFs represent more than 50 per cent of the total personnel employed in the domain of office and computing machinery (Beise, 1997, pp. 15–16).
3 For a similar perspective, see von Kirchbach (1998, p. 12).
4 Own calculations on the basis of Mathieu and Quélennec (1998, p. 79).
5 For details related to the years 1977, 1990 and 1992, see Chanut and Mathieu (1994, pp. 1–2).
6 This is clearly the case with Toyota's recent greenfield investment in the region Nord-Pas-de-Calais. Concerning the car built there (the Yaris model), imports represent around 50 per cent of the total value added (20 per cent from the rest of Europe and 30 per cent from Japan); see L'Usine Nouvelle, 18 January 2001, p. 51. If Toyota had decided to invest in another country, imports would probably have been much higher (and exports lower).
7 'En fait, un supplément d'un milliard de francs vendu par ces firmes sur le marché intérieur économise approximativement 0.7 milliard d'importation' (Chanut and Mathieu, 1994, p. 4).

8 Pain and Wakelin (1998, pp. 19–21). Note that these authors use export data only for the manufacturing industry, but that their FDI data refer to the whole economy.

9 'Traditional theory could hardly be expected to see a connection that could be formulated as follows: countries tend to develop a comparative advantage in the articles they *import*. This paradox is of course largely a play on words, since "comparative advantage" refers here not to the usual comparison between the actual production processes of various commodities as carried on in different countries but to the choice which a country makes in starting to produce one commodity rather than another' (Hirschman, 1966, p. 122).

10 In 2000, Philips France employed around 12,000 people and exported nearly 60 per cent of its total sales value.

11 For other details concerning the link between the domains of foreign-owned R&D and the country of control, see CGP (1999b, p. 141).

12 On average, the FOFs only show a lower proportion of innovative firms in the case of firms belonging to the aerospace industry and to the pharmaceutical industry. See CGP (1999b, p. 143) and Paul *et al.* (1999, p. 30).

13 The decrease observed between the two years is not significant. According to Paul *et al.* (1999, p. 43), whose study is based on US patent data, this average share increased in France from 22.4 per cent during the period 1991–4 to 25.0 per cent during the period 1995–7. Between these two periods, the corresponding share increased from 20.1 per cent to 21.3 in Germany, and from 38.0 per cent to 45.1 in the UK.

14 In a similar way, Beise (1997, pp. 20 and 23) shows that the relative weight of FOFs in the German manufacturing industry is roughly the same in terms of R&D personnel and in terms of total employment.

15 See Cantwell and Kotecha (1994, p. 129, Table 9). Among the European countries, as shown by Cantwell and Janne (2000, Table 6.5), France ranks third in these terms, with a share of 15.60 per cent in 1991–5 (13.21 per cent in 1969–72), behind Germany (28.87 per cent in 1991–5, 27.03 per cent in 1969–72) and the UK (21.15 per cent in 1991–5, 29.34 per cent in 1969–72).

16 Beise (1997, pp. 32–3) finds similar results for Germany. In this country and among the firms that realize R&D activities, the propensity to source technology from abroad through an intra-firm channel was in 1992 significantly lower on the part of German-owned firms (only 12 per cent of all firms in this category) than on the part of European-owned affiliates (34 per cent), and much lower than on the part of US-owned subsidiaries (86 per cent). Compared with German-owned firms, the FOFs show more intense technological transfers from their respective home country, notably under the form of licence expenditures, R&D contracts and the hiring of qualified personnel. Accordingly and all other things being equal, the FOFs generally source significantly less technical knowledge from German sources.

17 This pattern is also valid for firms with R&D activities located in Germany. Among them, as shown by Beise (1997, p. 33), the proportion of firms that proceed to intra-firm technology outflows to foreign countries was in 1992 significantly lower on the part of German-owned firms (only 24 per cent) than on the part of European-owned firms (43 per cent), and much lower than in the case of US-owned firms (79 per cent).

References

Barré, R. (1996), 'Relationships Between Multinational Firms' Technology Strategies and National Innovation Systems', in OECD, (ed.), *Innovation, Patents and Technological Strategies*, Paris, pp. 201–22.

Barry, F. and J. Bradley (1997), 'FDI and Trade: The Irish host-country experience', *The Economic Journal*, Vol. 107 (November), pp. 1,798–811.

Beise, M. (1997), 'Innovationsaktivitäten ausländischer Unternehmen in Deutschland – Eine Auswertung des Mannheimer Innovationspanel', unpublished paper, Mannheim, ZEW.

Boccara, F. (1997), 'Groupes français, étrangers, entreprises indépendantes: Les contrastes se renforcent', in INSEE *et al.* (eds), *Le commerce extérieur de la France 1980–1996 – Point forts, points faibles, marchés lointains et entreprises* (collection Synthèses), No. 12–13 (November), pp. 143–53.

Bourgeois, P. and L. Estival, (1999), 'Les industries du bois', *Industries*, No. 51 (October), pp. 11–21.

Cambon, P. (1998), 'La France, terre d'accueil des investissements étrangers', *Label France*, ministère des Affaires Etrangères, No. 33, September.

Cantwell, J. (1999), 'Innovation as the principal source of growth in the global economy', in D. Archibugi, *et al.* (eds), *Innovation Policy in a Global Economy*, Cambridge, UK/New York, Cambridge University Press, pp. 225–41.

Cantwell, J. and O. Janne (2000), 'Globalisation of innovatory capacity: the structure of competence accumulation in European home and host countries', in F. Chesnais *et al.* (eds), *European Integration and Global Corporate Strategies*, London/New York, Routledge, pp. 121–77.

Cantwell, J. and U. Kotecha (1994), 'L'internationalisation des activités technologiques: Le cas français en perspective', in F. Sachwald, (ed.), *Les défis de la mondialisation – Innovation et concurrence*, Paris, Masson, pp. 107–52.

CEPII (1998), *Compétitivité des nations*, rapport du CEPII sous la direction de M. Fouquin, Paris, Economica.

CGP (1992), *Investir en France, un espace attractif*, Commissariat Général du Plan, rapport du groupe 'Localisation des investissements transnationaux', présidé par F. Merrien, La Documentation Française (Paris).

CGP (1999a), *La nouvelle nationalité de l'entreprise*, rapport du groupe 'La nouvelle nationalité de l'entreprise dans la mondialisation', présidé par J.-F. Bigay, La Documentation Française (Paris).

CGP (1999b), *Recherche et innovation: La France dans la compétition mondiale*, rapport du groupe présidé par B. Majoie, rapporteur général: B. Rémy, La Documentation Française (Paris).

Chanut, J.-M. and E. Mathieu (1994), *L'investissement étranger dans l'industrie français: effet favorable sur la balance commerciale*, SESSI, Le 4 pages, No. 35 (June), Paris.

Chesnais, F. and A. Sailleau (2000), 'Foreign direct investment and European trade', in F. Chesnais *et al.* (eds), *European Integration and Global Corporate Strategies*, London/New York, Routledge, pp. 25–51.

Davydoff, D. (2000), 'Salaires et capitalisation boursíère', *La Leltre de l' OEE*, December, pp. 28–9.

Dreyfus, A. (2000), 'Stock des investissements directs étrangers en France au 31 décembre 1998', *Bulletin de la Banque de France*, No. 78 (June).

Dunning, J. (1993), *Multinational Enterprises and the Global Economy*, Wokingham, Addison-Wesley.

Dunning, J. (1994), 'Multinational enterprises and the globalization of innovatory capacity', *Research Policy*, Vol. 23, pp. 67–88.

Dupont, M.-J. and J.-P. François (1998), 'L'industrie française fortement pénétrée par les capitaux étrangers', in SESSI (ed.), *Industrie française et mondialisation*, Secrétariat d'Etat à l'Industrie, Paris, pp. 49–61.

Dupont, M.-J. and E. Mathieu (1993), *L'investissement étranger en France–Près de 30 % de la production industrielle*, SESSI, Le 4 pages, No. 21 (June).

Dyker, D. (1998), 'The Role of Foreign Direct Investment in Science in Technology Transformation', in W. Meske, *et al.* (eds), *Transforming Science and Technology System – The Endless Transition*, NATO Science Papers, IOS Press, pp. 49–56.

Favre, F. and E. Mathieu (1998), 'Les échanges technologiques internationaux: internes aux groupes', in SESSI (ed.), *Industrie française et mondialisation*, Secrétariat d'Etat à l'Industrie, Paris, pp. 161–8.

Fontagné, L. (1999), *L'investissement étranger direct et le commerce international: sont-ils complémentaires ou substituables?*, OECD, Document de travail de la DSTI, No. 3 (Paris).

Fontagné, L. and M. Pajot (1997), *How Foreign Direct Investment Affects International Trade and Competitiveness: An Empirical Assessment*, CEPII, document de travail No. 17 (December).

Gerybadze, A. *et al.* (1997), *Globales Management von Forschung und Entwicklung*, Stuttgart, Schäffer-Poeschel.

Gillespie, R. (1972), 'The policies of England, France and Germany as recipients of foreign direct investment', in F. Machlup *et al.* (ed.), *International Mobility and Movement of Capital*, NBER, New York, pp. 397–431.

Grandjean, H. (2000), 'La détention des actions françaises cotées', *Bulletin de la Banque de France*, No. 80 (June), pp. 83–94.

Hamilton, A. (1791), 'Report on Manufactures', in H. Syrett *et al.* (eds) (1961–79), *The Papers of Alexander Hamilton*, 26 vols, New York and London, Columbia University Press.

Hatem, F. (1995), 'La France et l'investissement international', in *Les notes bleues de Bercy*, 67 (16 July), pp. 1–24.

Hannoun, M. and G. Guerrier (1998), 'Les échanges intragroupe des entreprises industrielles – France: un tiers des exportations, un cinquième des importations', in SESSI (ed.), *Industrie française et mondialisation*, Secrétariat d'Etat à l'Industrie, Paris, pp. 121–8.

Hatzichronoglou, T. (1998), 'Les filiales étrangères soutiennent l'emploi dans les pays de l'OCDE', in SESSI (ed.), *Industrie française et mondialisation*, Secrétariat d'Etat à l'Industrie, Paris, pp. 199–212.

Hilferding, R. (1955), *Das Finanzkapital – Eine Studie über die jüngste Entwicklung des Kapitalismus*, Berlin, Dietz Verlag (first edition 1910).

Hirschman, A. O. (1966), *The Strategy of Economic Development*, New Haven, CT, and London, Yale University Press, 10th edn (first published 1958).

Hörning, U. (1998), 'Foreign Direct Investment in France between 1986 and 1996 – Empirical Evidence, Political Framework, Perspectives for the Future', Diploma Thesis, University of Tübingen, February.

Houdebine, M. and A. Topiol-Bensaïd (1999), 'L'investissement direct et les entreprises françaises', *Economie et statistique*, 326–7, 6/7, pp. 113–28.

Hymer, S. (1976), *The International Operations of National Firms: A Study of Foreign Direct Investment*, Cambridge, MA, MIT Press (originally an unpublished PhD in 1960).

Institut der Deutschen Wirtschaft (2000), 'Corporate Governance – Deutschland AG steht noch', *Informationsdienst*, No. 38 (21 September).

Kindleberger, C. (1987), *International Capital Movements*, Cambridge, 1717, Cambridge University Press.

Kirchbach, F. von (1998), *Globalization through trade and FDI – A comparative study of the EU, the USA and Japan based on trade and FDI Data*, Statistical document Theme 6 (External trade) Series D (Studies and research), Luxembourg, Eurostat.

Lallement, R. (2001), 'Foreign Direct Investment and the Diversity of Socio-Economic Systems in Europe: France, Germany and Britain Compared', in M. Maclean and J.-M. Trouille (eds), *France, Germany and Britain: Partners in a Changing World*, London, Palgrave, pp. 85–99.

Lavenir, F. *et al.* (2001), *L'entreprise et l'hexagone*, rapport au ministre de l'Economie, des Finances et de l'Industrie (coll. Etudes), Paris, Les Editions de Bercy.

Le Bris, F. (1998), 'Le rôle des filiales de commerce de gros des groupes étrangers', in SESSI (ed.), *Industrie française et mondialisation*, Secrétariat d'Etat à l'Industrie, Paris, pp. 137–43.

Lichtenberg, F. and B. van Pottelsberghe de la Potterie (1996), *International R&D Spillovers: A Re-Examination*, NBER, Working Paper, No. 5668, July.

Madeuf, B. *et al.* (1992), *Les activités de recherche en France des sociétés étrangères*, rapport pour le ministère de la Recherche et de l'Environnement, December.

Mathieu, E. (1998a), 'Introduction: l'industrie en première ligne', in SESSI (ed.), *Industrie française et mondialisation*, Secrétariat d'Etat à l'Industrie, Paris, pp. 7–22.

Mathieu, E. (1998b), 'La production industrielle française à l'étranger', in SESSI (ed.), *Industrie française et mondialisation*, Secrétariat d'Etat à l'Industrie, Paris, pp. 63–71.

Mathieu, E. (1999), 'Les travaux du SESSI sur l'implantation étrangère en France', in CNIS (2001), *Les investissements directs étrangers en France*, rapport d'un groupe de travail du Conseil national de l'information statistique, présidé par J.-L. Mucchielli, No. 64 (February), pp. 63–75.

Mathieu, E. and Quélennec, M. (1998), 'Production à l'étranger et exportation', in SESSI (ed.), *Industrie française et mondialisation*, Secrétariat d'Etat à l'Industrie, Paris, pp. 73–82.

Mazier, J. (1995), 'Intégration européenne et investissements directs à l'étranger', *Revue du Marché commun et de l'Union européenne*, 385 (February), pp. 112–26.

Michalet, C.-A. (1997), 'France', in J. Dunning (ed.), *Governments, Globalization, and International Business*, Oxford, Oxford University Press, pp. 313–34.

Michalet, C.-A. (1998), *Le capitalisme mondial*, Paris, Presses Universitaires de France (1st edn 1976).

Michalet, C.-A. (1999), *La Séduction des Nations, ou Comment attirer les investissements*, Paris, Economica.

Morin, F. (1998), *Le Modèle français de détention et de gestion du capital – Analyse, prospective et comparaisons internationales*, Rapport au ministre de l'Economie, des Finances et de l'Industrie, (coll. Etudes), Paris, Les Editions de Bercy.

National Science Board (1998), *Science and Engineering Indicators – 1998*, NSB 98–1, Washington, DC, US Government Printing Office.

Nivat, D. (1999), 'Les investissements directs entre la France et l'étranger', *Les Notes Bleues de Bercy*, No. 166 (1 September), pp. 1–8.

OECD (1994), The Performance of Foreign Affiliates in OECD Countries, Paris.

OECD (1999), *Measuring Globalisation: The Role of Multinationals in OECD Economies*, Paris.

OECD (2000), 'Recent Trends in Foreign Direct Investment', *Financial Market Trends*, pp. 23–41.

OMC (1996), *Rapport annuel 1996; Dossier spécial: Le commerce et l'investissement direct étranger*, Vol. 1, Organisation Mondiale du Commerce, Geneva.

OST (2000), *Science et Technologie – Indicateurs 2000*, Rapport de l'Observatoire des Sciences et Techniques, Paris, Economica.

Pain, N. and K. Wakelin (1998), *Export Performance and the Role of Foreign Direct Investment*, NIESR, Discussion Paper, No. 131.

Patel, P. and K. Pavitt (1999), 'Global corporations and national innovation systems: Who dominates whom?', in D. Archibugi *et al.* (eds), *Innovation Policy in a Global Economy*, Cambridge, UK/New York, Cambridge University Press, pp. 94–119.

Paul, M. *et al.* (1999), *Internationalisation de la R&D et de l'innovation: le cas de la France*, rapport au CGP, Paris 12 University, La Varenne Saint Hilaire (December).

Pauly, L. W. and S. Reich (1997), 'National structures and multinational corporate behaviour: enduring differences in the age of globalization', *International Organization*, 51, 1 (Winter), pp. 1–30.

Reich, R. (1990), 'Who is Us?', *Harvard Business Review*, Jan.–Feb., pp. 53–64.

Servan-Schreiber, J.-J. (1967), *Le défi américain*, Paris, Denoël.

SESSI (1989), *13 années d'implantation étrangère dans l'industrie française – Traits fondamentaux du système industriel français*, collection Chiffres et documents, série Industrie, No. 79, Paris.

SESSI (ed.) (1997), *L'implantation étrangère dans l'industrie française*, Paris.

SESSI (ed.) (2000), *L'implantation étrangère dans l'industrie française*, Paris.

Tersen, D. and J.-L. Bricout (1996), *L'investissement international*, Paris, Colin.

Thollon-Pommerol, V. (1999), 'Enterprise Group: the French Methodology and Results', in S. Biffignandi (ed.), *Micro and Macrodata of Firms – Statistical Analysis and International Comparison*, Berlin, Springer, pp. 59–68.

UNCTAD (1999), *World Investment Report 1999–Foreign Direct Investment and the Challenge of Development*, New York/Geneva.

US Congress (1993), *Multinationals and the National Interest: Playing by Different Rules*, Office of Technological Assessment, OTA-ITE-569, US Government Printing Office, Washington, DC (September).

Index